The experience of reading:
Irish historical perspectives

Also published by the Rare Books Group (Library Association of Ireland)

Books beyond the Pale: aspects of the provincial book trade in Ireland before 1850, edited by Gerard Long

Also published by the Economic and Social History Society of Ireland (distributed by Dundalgan Press Ltd, Dundalk, Co. Louth)

Irish emigration, 1801-1921, by David Fitzpatrick
Landlords and tenants in Ireland, 1848-1904, by W.E. Vaughan
Religion and society in nineteenth-century Ireland, by S.J. Connolly
The interwar economy in Ireland, by David Johnson
The modern industrialisation of Ireland, 1940-1988, by Liam Kennedy
The transformation of the Irish economy, 1550-1700, by Raymond Gillespie
Women and work in Ireland, by Mary E. Daly

Irish economic and social history, v.1-, 1974- [published annually]

The experience of reading:
Irish historical perspectives

edited by
Bernadette Cunningham
and
Máire Kennedy

Dublin
Rare Books Group of the Library Association of Ireland
and
Economic and Social History Society of Ireland
1999

First published in 1999 by
Rare Books Group of the Library Association of Ireland
and Economic and Social History Society of Ireland
c/o The Library, Royal Irish Academy,
19 Dawson St., Dublin 2

ISBN 0-947897-33-X

Typeset by Tower Books, Ballincollig, Co. Cork
Printed by Shanway Press, Belfast
Bound by Robinson and Mornin, Belfast

Contents

List of abbreviations

Notes on contributors

Toby BARNARD is fellow and tutor in modern history at Hertford College, Oxford.

Elizabethanne BORAN teaches courses on late medieval and early modern history of ideas in Trinity College, Dublin.

Bernadette CUNNINGHAM is deputy librarian at the Royal Irish Academy, Dublin.

Raymond GILLESPIE is senior lecturer in history at the National University of Ireland, Maynooth.

Máire KENNEDY is senior libarian, Dublin Corporation Public Libraries, The Gilbert Library, Dublin.

John KILLEN is deputy librarian at the Linen Hall Library, Belfast.

Marie-Louise LEGG is honorary teaching fellow in history at Birkbeck College, London.

Rolf LOEBER is Professor of Psychiatry, Psychology and Epidemiology at the University of Pittsburgh (USA), and Professor of Developmental Psychopathology at the Free University, Amsterdam (The Netherlands).

John LOGAN is senior lecturer in history in the Department of Government and Society, University of Limerick.

Magda STOUTHAMER-LOEBER is Associate Professor of Psychiatry and Psychology at the University of Pittsburgh (USA).

Preface

The experience of reading links books with people. This book explores how Irish people in the past accessed and responded to books, newspapers, and other print media. The essays will appeal to educationalists, social, cultural, and religious historians and especially to those interested both in the history of books and in the histories of the people who read books.

Earlier versions of these essays were presented at a joint seminar organised by the Economic and Social History Society of Ireland and the Rare Books Group (Library Association of Ireland). Reading was perceived as a topic of particular interest to both groups, and the joint seminar allowed members to benefit from the overlap of expertise on the subject. The seminar was held in November 1997 at the Dublin Writers' Museum, Parnell Square, Dublin.

We would like to record our thanks for their wholehearted support to the committees of the Economic and Social History Society of Ireland and the Rare Books Group and to the Library Association of Ireland. The British Council gave financial support towards the expenses of speakers coming from Britain, for which we are grateful. The editors would particularly like to express gratitude to their own institutions for moral and practical support: Dublin Corporation Public Libraries, Dublin Diocesan Library and the Royal Irish Academy.

To the contributors we would like to extend special thanks for their co-operation and willingness to be part of the project. We thank Bill Bolger for the cover design and Patricia Daly of Tower Books for help in designing and typesetting the book. Illustrations are reproduced courtesy of the Trustees of the

National Library of Ireland (cover illustration and figure 4), the Bodleian Library, Oxford (figures 1 and 6), and Dublin Corporation Public Libraries (figure 3).

Bernadette Cunningham
Máire Kennedy
27 April 1999

Illustrations

Introduction: the experience of reading

Bernadette Cunningham

BIBLIOGRAPHERS INTERESTED in the history of Irish books have made steady progress in enumerative bibliography.[1] The work of Henry Bradshaw, E. R. McClintock Dix, R. I. Best, R. J. Hayes, Robert Munter and most recently Tony Sweeney has been of fundamental importance in facilitating research into the world of Irish print. Research into the history of the book in Ireland has focused principally on the processes associated with the production of texts. Printing, paper making, typography, book selling and distribution have all been studied in an Irish context, though further work remains to be done.[2] Research into the social and cultural history of print has raised questions about how the 'ordinary people' of Ireland came into contact with the world of books. Questions of literacy, language skills, education and popular culture have given rise to some stimulating publications.[3]

One of the most influential writers on the history of books has proposed that the history of books is about 'how ideas were transmitted through print and how exposure to the printed word affected the thought and behaviour of mankind during the last 500 years'.[4] If we adopt this suggestion, further avenues of research are opened, not least the implications of the experience of reading. If we are to adopt a comprehensive approach to the history of books we need to try to understand what books meant to the people who read them.[5]

Darnton's essay on 'What is the history of books?' discusses the idea of a life cycle of books which begins and ends with readers. Describing what he terms the 'communications circuit' he begins with authors, who are themselves readers,

1

and whose notions of genre, form and style are shaped through reading. Those authors publish texts, relying for production on printers who draw on the resources of suppliers of ink, paper and type. The books are then shipped to various kinds of book-sellers, ranging from wholesalers to peddlars, who distribute the work to readers.[6] The crucial point is that every process in this circuit influences and is influenced by the wider social, economic and political world in which the process takes place. This way of thinking about the history of books is inter-disciplinary to its core. It draws on the expertise of specialists in analytical bibliography, comparative literature, social history and the sociology of knowledge. Robert Darnton argues that research focused on the concept of 'circuits of communi-cation' will illustrate that 'books do not merely recount history, they make it'.[7] Roger Chartier has discussed the ques-tion 'Do books make revolutions?' in the context of the French revolution and concludes that while books may not be revolu-tionary in themselves, transformations in reading practices allow texts to be read in new ways that can have revolutionary consequences.[8] To understand the history of books we must understand the experience of reading in its historical context. Books make history because they are read.

Books come to life when they are read. Each reader, each listener to a text being read, responds to it in the light of his or her own prior knowledge and life experience. Individual responses are socially conditioned by communal norms for reading various kinds of texts, so that a newspaper or popular novel, for example, is not read in the same way as the Bible or a devotional tract. One central idea in current approaches to the history of reading is that texts themselves do not control reader responses. Instead, it is argued that the way readers respond to texts is conditioned by the social, political, economic, cultural and intellectual conditions within which those texts were encountered.[9]

Research has suggested that the experience of reading is influenced by the physical form as well as the intellectual content of the text. Every design feature of a book or other text elicits a response from its readers. The particular form chosen for a text reveals the assumptions of the author or publisher about the capabilities and preferences of the intended audience as well as about the text.[10] But those immediate, even tangible, elements of a text that derive most directly from the work of the author and printer operate within wider physical, social, cultural, and intellectual worlds that form vital elements of the experience of reading.

Social and cultural historians have emphasised the importance of understanding the circumstances of reading – where and when and how people read – as a means of elucidating some of the ways in which the written word is interpreted. The essays in this volume address these questions in an Irish context, examining evidence from the seventeenth to the twentieth centuries. Both personal motivations and communal or societal aspirations – why people read – are central to understanding the meanings readers derive from the texts they encounter. Thus, the history of reading is not only a matter of identifying what people read in the past, though that is an important beginning. It is also necessary to discover why people read particular texts rather than others, and what influences conditioned their responses to the texts they encountered.

Relatively little has been published to date on the experience of reading in an Irish historical context. There is still much scope for further studies of the availability of texts to Irish readers in the past. Both Rolf and Magda Loeber and Marie-Louise Legg emphasise the scarcity of books among the less well off in rural Ireland in the early nineteenth century, and discuss the appropriateness of the texts in circulation to the concerns and interests of readers. In a case study of the availability of English language fiction to tenants and labourers in Ireland before 1850, the Loebers tease out the issue of establishment attitudes to 'popular' literature, and examine a range of strategies that were designed to influence the kind of reading material that was available for popular consumption. The essay combines evidence from late eighteenth-century publishers' lists with documentation on fiction available in schools in the early nineteenth century to provide an overview of the kind of popular texts in circulation. The concerns of some contemporaries regarding the appropriateness of such materials are investigated through an examination of the work of both Protestant and Catholic groups, most notably the Kildare Place Society in

3

overseeing the provision of 'suitable' reading matter for Irish cottagers.

John Logan's essay on how reading was taught and how successfully pupils learned to read in Irish national schools from 1831 to 1900, deals with the practicalities of how readers made sense of the signs on the printed page. He clarifies not just reading abilities but also the social effects of the reading experience of children under the influence of the national school system. He draws attention to the culturally exclusive and intellectually restricted nature of the reading materials available to Irish children following the establishment of the national school system. His findings raise important questions about the capacity of those pupils to construct cultural and political meaning from the texts they encountered.

The essays by John Killen and Marie-Louise Legg, which focus primarily on the emergence of reading societies and reading rooms in late eighteenth- and nineteenth-century Ireland, also consider issues relating to access to reading materials. Such societies helped make books more accessible, but in a controlled way. The control strategies adopted can illuminate for us the perceptions of contemporaries regarding the power of reading. Both essays emphasise the consciousness of contemporaries of the link between reading and moral improvement. Marie-Louise Legg draws attention to the mid-nineteenth-century idea that reading could be harnessed to improve the national character by inculcating an awareness of civic duty. She outlines the link between reading and a succession of national political movements from Daniel O'Connell's movement for repeal of the Act of Union, through the Young Irelanders and the Fenians in mid-century and on to the activities of the Land League in later nineteenth-century Ireland.

Social improvement as well as self improvement had been a core objective in the formation of the Belfast Society for Promoting Knowledge. John Killen's case study, of how and why John Templeton read what he did, depicts a reader whose reading habits appear frequently to have been motivated by a concern for the common good. Toby Barnard's study of the social context of eighteenth-century reading practices notes contemporary concerns for social control and the preservation of the moral order. He argues too that the culture of print could work in contrasting ways. Despite the concerns of those in authority about the possible dangers of uncontrolled reading, a radicalising impact should not necessarily be assumed, reading could equally well reinforce traditional ideas and orthodoxies.

Important utilitarian uses of reading have long been recognised and harnessed. Marie-Louise Legg notes the self-interested motivations of benevolent employers who facilitated factory workers' access to reading materials for training purposes. Landlords who facilitated tenants in a similar way may have had moral rather than utilitarian motives. John Killen's analysis of the objectives of the Belfast Society for Promoting Knowledge stresses the importance attached to the advancement of knowledge, and the consequent emphasis on books of scientific, historical and philosophical interest. Toby Barnard draws attention to the utilitarian nature of many newspaper advertisements disseminating information about new products, thereby linking the diversification of reading matter with increased commercialisation.

Máire Kennedy considers the growing specialisation of targeted readerships in the later eighteenth century. Newspaper advertisements addressing particular target audiences, magazines specifically for women readers, and books designed for children all contain evidence of contemporary assumptions about reading priorities and practices.

Toby Barnard's essay is particularly concerned with how reading has changed over time, as well as the significance of reading for social and cultural change. Thus he considers the impact of the diversification of forms of the written word, including everything from newspapers to lottery tickets in his analysis of the culture of print in the early eighteenth century. The attitudes of contemporaries towards books as objects, the ways in which owners stored and displayed their books are considered in conjunction with the ways in which people read their books. Barnard evaluates the impact of reading in eighteenth-century Irish provincial society by considering the ways in which people shared the contents of what they had read with others through conversation and correspondence as well as through reading aloud. While John Killen shows that books of 'trivial amusement' had no place in the collections of the Belfast Society for Promoting Knowledge, the theme of reading as a pleasure activity for both men and women emerges strongly in the essays by Toby Barnard and Máire Kennedy on eighteenth-century reading practices. In each essay the experience of reading is shown to be strongly influenced by the way society is organised.

That the essays by Raymond Gillespie and Elizabethanne Boran on reading practices in seventeenth-century Ireland should focus particularly on how religious works were read is no mere coincidence. Rather it is a reflection of the category of reading material most readily accessible to contemporaries. Gillespie's analysis of seventeenth-century responses to the Bible, a book known to most Christians whether or not they could read, discusses the available evidence for the technical skill of reading, the availability of Bibles in a variety of languages and editions and the possibilities for non-reader access to the message of the Bible. This is done within an analytical framework that draws on Brian Stock's concept of 'textual communities'.[11] Differences between Catholic and Protestant readings of the Bible are taken as a starting point for an exploration of the various interpretative communities that formed in Ireland around the central text of the Christian faith. The Bible was a complex text that was experienced in a myriad of ways by the inhabitants of seventeenth-century Ireland. In attempting to answer the question of what books meant to people, the case of the Bible is a special one.[12] The analysis of how, where and why it was read sheds much light on the way the inhabitants of early modern Ireland interpreted their world.

Elizabethanne Boran's study of the guided reading of theological texts in seventeenth-century Dublin raises the issue of contemporary views of appropriate lay and clerical reading matter and methods. Like Gillespie she emphasises the importance of the communal or public world within which theology in particular was read. Protestant, no less than Catholic, readings of the Bible she argues, were normally subject to controls designed to guide readers towards orthodox interpretations of the text.

The authors of these essays have drawn on a broad range of source materials and have adopted a variety of approaches to their evaluation of the experience of reading in an Irish historical context. Research into the history of reading involves not just an examination of the texts as issued by the printer but also of annotations and inscriptions in books, commonplace books, private papers containing notes taken from books, subscription lists and publishers' advertisements, library catalogues, historic private library collections, historic public libraries collections, the archives of Societies and educational institutions concerned in any way with the promotion of books and reading. It also encompasses the study of past societies and cultures in all their varied dimensions. The methodologies employed here have implications for custodians of rare books and special collections concerned to facilitate research into the history of books and reading. Máire Kennedy's essay explicitly highlights some of the more immediate issues that require attention if, for instance, the half-hidden world of women's reading experiences in the past is to be recovered.

The examination of personal and communal textual experiences from an Irish historical perspective helps us understand how the intellectual preoccupations of people in the past were shaped. By seeking to understand the cultural implications of people's social and economic circumstances, their educational backgrounds and particularly their expectations, it helps clarify how society worked. If we can understand how people derived meaning from the texts they read we can evaluate why those texts were important to them and to the society in which they lived.[13] If, through the history of reading, we gain insights into how values and attitudes were formed, communicated, nurtured, and interpreted, we can begin to understand the significance of print culture for how history is made.

Bernadette Cunningham

Notes

1. Charles Benson and Mary Pollard, 'The silken purse: bibliography in Ireland', in Peter Davison (ed.), *The book encompassed: studies in twentieth-century bibliography* (Cambridge, 1992), pp 200–205.

2. Important contributions to the history of printing and the book trade in Ireland include M. Pollard, *Dublin's trade in books, 1550–1800* (Oxford, 1989); James W. Phillips, *Printing and bookselling in Dublin, 1670–1800: a bibliographical enquiry* (Dublin, 1998); Niall Ó Ciosáin, *Print and popular culture in Ireland, 1750–1850* (Basingstoke, 1997); Thomas Wall, *The sign of Dr Hay's head: the hazards and fortunes of Catholic printers and publishers from the later penal times to the present day* (Dublin, 1958); Robert Munter, *A dictionary of the print trade in Ireland, 1550–1775* (New York, 1988); Vincent Kinane, *A history of the Dublin University Press, 1734–1976* (Dublin, 1994); Gerard Long (ed.), *Books beyond the Pale: aspects of the provincial book trade in Ireland before 1850* (Dublin, 1996); M. Pollard, 'White paper-making in Ireland in the 1690s', *Proceedings of the Royal Irish Academy*, lxxvii, Sect.C (1977), pp 223–234 and 4 plates.

3. See in particular, J.R.R. Adams, *The printed word and the common man: popular culture in Ulster, 1700–1900* (Belfast, 1987); Mary Daly and David Dickson (eds), *The origins of popular literacy in Ireland: language change and educational development, 1700–1920* (Dublin, 1990); Ó Ciosáin, *Print and popular culture*.

4. Robert Darnton, *The kiss of Lamourette: reflections in cultural history* (New York, 1990), p. 107. [Darnton's essay, 'What is the history of books?' was first published in *Daedalus* (Summer, 1982), pp 65–83.]

5. For a stimulating discussion of the history of books and reading in a north American context see David D. Hall, *Cultures of print: essays in the history of the book* (Amherst, 1996).

6. Darnton, *Kiss of Lamourette*, pp 111–113.

7. Darnton, *Kiss of Lamourette*, p. 135.

8. Roger Chartier, *The cultural origins of the French Revolution* (Durham, NC, 1991), pp 67–91.

9. James Raven, 'New reading histories, print culture and the identification of change: the case of eighteenth-century England', *Social History*, xxiii, no. 3 (1998), pp 268–269; Darnton, *Kiss of*

Lamourette, p. 122; See also James Raven, Helen Small and Naomi Tadmor (eds), *The practice and representation of reading in England* (Cambridge, 1996).

10. D.F. McKenzie, *Bibliography and the sociology of texts* (London, 1985); Roger Chartier, *On the edge of the cliff: history, language and practices* (Baltimore, 1997), pp 81–89.

11. Brian Stock, *The implications of literacy* (Princeton, 1983); Brian Stock, *Listening for the text: on the uses of the past* (Baltimore, 1990).

12. See for instance, David D. Hall, 'The literary practices of dissent', in Kevin Herlihy (ed.), *Propagating the word of Irish dissent, 1650–1800* (Dublin, 1998), pp 11–23.

13. Chartier, *On the edge of the cliff*, pp 81–89; McKenzie, *Bibliography and the sociology of texts*.

Reading the Bible
in seventeenth-century Ireland

Raymond Gillespie

THE STUDY OF THE ACTIVITY of reading poses one of the more difficult, but potentially rewarding, challenges to the early modern historian. The difficulty arises from the diversity of the subject. Reading was not a neutral process. Each person read for a reason and in a specific social context, and hence readings of a text were often emotional and highly subjective. Such readings are difficult to uncover. Sir John Harrington, for instance, reported that in Galway in the 1590s a young lady was so enthusiastic about his newly-published translation of *Orlando Furioso* that she read herself to sleep with it. The reason was 'the verse, I think, so lively figured her fortune', she having been jilted by her lover as one of the characters in the text had been.[1] Again in the late seventeenth century Ezekiel Hopkins, the Church of Ireland bishop of Derry, observed that some in his congregation had stopped reading the Bible since it 'possesseth them with strange fears and fills them with incredible terrors. It raiseth up the dreadful apparition of hell and the wrath of God makes them a terror to themselves.'[2] No two readings of a text could be identical. Harrington recorded that when he read from his translation of *Orlando* for the earl of Tyrone in 1599 'I turned (as it had been by chance) to the beginning of the 45th canto, . . . which he seemed to like so well that he solemnly swore his boys should read all the book over to him.'[3] Tyrone undoubtedly did not understand the forty-fifth canto, which is about rebellious subjects, in the same way as Harrington. As the vitriolic Dublin pamphleteer, Barnaby Rich, put it in 1617 'We are grown so wise and sharp sighted in reading other men's writings that those passages that are but meant and set down in a general manner, they will draw such particular construction as the author himself never so much dreamt on.'[4] The appropriation of texts by individuals makes the history of reading a complex subject.

If this highly fragmented way of reading was the only one, then it would be impossible to reconstruct reading patterns for seventeenth-century Ireland. However, reading was not only an individual activity. People read texts in groups and they managed to agree on common interpretations of certain key texts and shaped their lives around them. Throughout the seventeenth century, Ireland was drawn into a textual culture, both printed and manuscript. By the end of that century texts such as leases, proclamations, letters and pamphlets were all much more common than they had been a century and a half earlier.[5] This was only possible because of the evolution of a number of strategies for dealing with such texts, both by those who were technically literate and those who were not. Those strategies may be loosely grouped together as reading practices, which went far beyond the simple decoding of letters. In this sense the use of the Bible as part of a divination ritual by Ulster presbyterians in the late seventeenth century, its display in the window of a house as a sign that its occupants were of a godly cast of mind, the use of the Bible as a way of swearing an oath or the Catholic practice of tying the opening words of St John's gospel around the neck of a woman supposedly bewitched were all ways of reading or coping with the book.[6] Such examples suggest that the Bible was read in shared ways by different groups of people. As a result such people formed what may be described as textual communities.

I

Of all the books which early modern men and women might come into contact with the most significant was the Bible although some doleful contemporaries lamented that some readers preferred romances and other tales to the biblical text and others complained that it was used as source book of fabulous tales for children.[7] There were many forms in which they might be exposed to the text. For those learning to read for the first time, the Bible was used to teach reading. The young

11

William King noted in his autobiography that after he learned his letters:

> it happened on a certain Lord's day that I was walking about with a woman in the garden and we entered the wood and sat down together; she was reading the Holy Scriptures, and whilst reading sleep stole over her, I took the book falling from her hands and by enumerating the letters, according to my habit I pronounced the words in its beginning and immediately perceived it to contain sense, which I had never before observed. Much captivated with the novelty I earnestly aspired to read and ran through the first three chapters while she was sleeping, sticking fast in a very few places.[8]

Others had a similar experience. The late seventeenth-century biographer of James Ussher, later archbishop of Armagh, recorded piously that the first book the young Ussher read was the Bible. Later Jonathan Swift claimed that by the age of four he 'had learnt to spell and by that time . . . he could read any chapter in the Bible'. The Dublin printer Thomas Gent described in his autobiography how his mother 'Made me to read, betimes, each sacred page.'[9] At a more elementary level basic readers, hornbooks and primers, which flooded into southern Ireland from the late sixteenth century were constructed around the mastery of biblical verses and short texts.[10]

It is impossible to be precise about how many people mastered the technical skill of reading in early modern Ireland although some rather imprecise guesses can be made about the ability to write. Among the 'middling sort of people' evidence from their ability to sign leases suggests that on the earl of Antrim's estate in the 1630s rather over half could write.[11] By the later half of the century the leases of the Herbert estate at Castleisland in county Kerry and the Hill estate in county Down were signed by between 73 and 85 per cent of lessees.[12] There were, however, significant variations which are concealed by such global figures. On the earl of Antrim's estate literacy was significantly higher among those who described themselves in their lease as 'gentlemen' than among 'yeomen' and on the Adair estate in county Antrim in the 1680s urban literacy was much higher than that of the surrounding countryside.[13] In general, however the ability to write seems to have increased among all social groups throughout the century. On the basis of late seventeenth-century Dublin bail books almost 80 per cent, including a large number of the middling and lower social groups, could at least sign their names.[14] However, reading was a skill that was taught before writing, and many did not progress to the more advanced level. Hence many of those who could not write could read. Estimates of signature literacy may have to be inflated by up to 50 per cent to obtain measures of reading ability.[15] Such quantative measures, of course, give no guide to real reading ability which ranged over a wide spectrum. A man who could just recognise his name when written down can hardly be seen in the same class as a sophistcated and regular reader of complex literary works. However given the current scattered nature of the Irish evidence for signature literacy it is impossible to be precise about reading ability, even at a very basic level, save to say that it grew significantly over the seventeenth century and by the end of the century a very substantial portion of the population, both settler and native, had acquired the skill of reading at some level of sophistication.

Once reading had been mastered there was little difficulty in purchasing a Bible. All English language Bibles were privileged books and had to be imported although by 1698 one Dublin merchant, sensing a profitable line, tried to break the London Stationers' monopoly by printing a New Testament in Dublin.[16] In the 1620s a full Bible could be had for 8s. in Dublin and a New Testament for 3s. although there were clearly cheaper editions circulating. In 1614 four Bibles and four psalters imported into Derry were valued at 15s. Such prices were high in relation to those ruling at London and this may have created difficulties for some in acquiring the text. In the 1690s William King, bishop of Derry, did observe that many of the families in his diocese had problems in finding a Bible despite its availability in print and there were complaints in the early eighteenth century about the cost of Bibles in Ireland.[17] Notwithstanding these complaints in the later seventeenth century the Catholic bishop of Ferns, Luke Wadding, could purchase Bibles for between 5s. and 6s. and a New Testament for 1s.[18] Given that real wages rose in Ireland in the later seventeenth century this meant a reduction in the real cost of a Bible in towns, although falling agricultural prices meant that real Bible prices remained high for other groups. For them there was a cheaper second-hand market. It is probably this which was reflected in the 1596 library list of Luke Challoner which noted Bible prices between 6s. and 10s. with Testaments at 6d.[19]

However the market was not the only mechanism for the supply of such books. The Bible was a common and fashionable gift and the earl of Kildare certainly felt it was an appropriate present for the earl of Cork in 1633. By the end of the century this custom was recognised with the Belfast printing of John Taylor's *Verbum sempiternum: the Bible the best new year's gift*.[20] This sort of gift giving extended well beyond fashionable society and some Protestant clergy gave Bibles both to those they confirmed and those too poor to buy their own.[21] Such gift giving extended beyond the grave as contemporaries specifically identified their Bibles in their wills to be left to appropriate persons. The Catholic lawyer Richard Hadsor left his Bible to William Clarke. In Clonmel one gentleman left 10s. to his son to buy a Bible.[22] Some people took advantage of the market and gift giving to acquire Bibles since Bibles and Testaments featured among the goods of several Dubliners who died in the 1630s.[23] Outside Dublin, Bibles were noted in library lists, four copies in one Limerick library in the 1630s and two Bibles and two Greek Testaments in a Munster library later in the century.[24] The presence of such texts in elite households was clearly well known for in 1641 when a soldier in Kilbeggan wished to swear allegiance to the wife of the landlord, Lady Lambert, he knew that her Bible was kept in a cupboard in the main hall of the house.[25] That the text was widespread at a lower social level in provincial Ireland is also suggested by the large number of reports of Bible burnings which occur in the depositions taken after the 1641 rising. In general the Bible was a common text which was well known to many. As Katherine Perceval, from county Cork, wrote to her brother, Sir John, in 1680 she was beginning to learn Latin and wanted Latin copies of familiar texts naming the prayer book and the New Testament.[26]

The distribution of texts was not even across society. As a very broad generalisation Catholics were less likely to have

Bibles than were Protestants. However this was subject to many exceptions. At the upper social levels Catholic access to the biblical text seems to have been common. In his description of Ireland in the 1570s the Catholic Dubliner Richard Stanihurst happily provided biblical references to bolster his case. Among the goods of John Chappell in Dublin in 1617 there was a Latin Testament and a psalter which may have been a Vulgate and certainly others of a higher social level owned a Vulgate text.[27] The alternative translation, the Douai-Rheims translation into English, was also present in Ireland although by the end of the century the Dublin priest Cornelius Nary claimed that these were 'so scarce and dear that the generality of the people neither have nor can procure them for their private use'.[28] Certainly during the seventeenth century the biblical basis of political rhetoric ensured that Catholic gentry were forced to keep their biblical knowledge fresh. Thus when a group of Catholic Old Englishmen, lead by John Bellew of Barmeath, petitioned the Cromwellian regime against their transplantation they felt it worth supporting their case with biblical quotations.[29] There were also Catholics who read their Bibles for spiritual reasons. The Catholic landowner of the Upper Ards, Henry Savage, was described as 'loyal and moderate in his Romish religion and read the Holy Scriptures'.[30] Practical politics and devotion combined to boost demand for copies of the Bible within the Catholic tradition in the early eighteenth century, a demand which the Irish bishops felt was insatiable.[31]

Within the Gaelic Irish tradition there also seems to have been familiarity with the biblical text, at least at an elite level. Native Irish poets had a basic knowledge of the text and featured it in their compositions although the text was often adapted to suit the poetic form.[32] Indeed it was not unusual for one hero of an early seventeenth-century tale to be portrayed as learned in scripture and some poets complained of those who read 'foolish senses' into scripture or 'pulled it to pieces'.[33] Biblical influences through learned texts were also significant. In particular the dominant origin myth of the Irish still prevalent in the early seventeenth century, the *Leabhar Gabhála*, drew heavily on biblical models of chronology and genealogy.[34] While there was no translation of the Catholic text of scripture into Irish in the early modern period two Protestant scholars

15

Raymond Gillespie

William Daniel, archbishop of Tuam, and William Bedell, bishop of Kilmore, did complete a translation and there is a strong possibility that this was read and used by Catholics.[35]

For those who were unable to read in a technical sense the Bible was not necessarily closed to them. There was the possibility of encountering it in other ways: the text could be read for them. Barnaby Rich certainly envisaged that the Irish translation of the New Testament would be used in this way for he claimed it was made for 'the lettered sort that can read their own language and also the unlettered sort that can understand what they hear others read.'[36] This was not restricted to the Catholic community. The Dublin butcher Hugh Leeson recorded in the 1650s how he had been converted by having the Bible read to him by his wife and the late seventeenth-century Presbyterian minister, Robert Craghead, observed 'as for those who cannot read which God giveth a heart for it they take the help of their neighbours who can read.'[37] The various Protestant churches in Ireland also vied with each other as to how much scripture they read to their adherents on a Sunday.[38] However the biblical text came not only in public reading but in other forms also. Both Catholic and Protestant sermons were littered with scriptural allusions and biblical passages. Metrical psalms and, by the end of the seventeenth century, hymns based on scriptural passages also made the text accessible to contemporaries. Through these means the text could be memorised and later recalled. Not all might achieve the heights of the blind aunts of the young James Ussher who had 'such tenacious memories, that whatever they heard read out of the scriptures, or was preached to them, they always retained, and became such proficients that they were able to repeat much of the Bible by heart' but memorisation on a lesser scale was always possible.[39] The Dublin Presbyterian William Cairnes, for instance, on his death bed could repeat large parts of scripture as well as singing psalms while his co-religionist Anne Reading of Rathfarnham could also recite long passages of scripture.[40] Useful as this might be to gain access to a specific part of the text it was clearly less satisfactory than a complete printed volume.

II

For most contemporaries the Bible was not simply a volume or even a disembodied text but a book that was meant to be read. It was, before the end of the century, widely understood to be the inspired word of God and hence it had an importance wider than one sectional interest but was used by the entire body of the faithful as a source for spiritual enlightenment and a way of avoiding damnation. When George Wilde, the bishop of Derry, bequeathed Bibles to his grandchildren in 1665, it was 'for them to use not to look upon.'[41] Indeed one image of George Webb, the bishop of Limerick, preaching in the 1630s depicts him holding a book, presumably the Bible, with his finger marking the place where he had been reading (figure 1). Another image of John Richardson, bishop of Ardagh, shows him as though disturbed in the act of reading his Bible his finger marking his place (figure 2). The impetus to read rather than to gaze was based on the understanding of the Bible as the revealed word of God which had an application to everyday life as well as the world beyond. When in the 1630s the young Richard Boyle, Viscount Dungarvan and seventh son of the earl of Cork, collected together a series of verses which appealed to him, he included one 'on the register of a Bible' which proclaimed:

> And what ye know the hand of God hath writ
> Behold my fingers point to it
> Nor can St Peter with all his keys
> Unlock heavens gate so soon as these.[42]

His sister, Katherine, also owned a Bible in which the English poet and divine Thomas Pestell had written verses which argued that the Bible was a much better mirror of God than the revelations of nature and urged her:

> All books in one, all learning lies in this
> This is your first ABC, the best primer is
> Whence having thoroughly learnt the [Chris]tcross row
> You may with comfort to our Father go
> Who will to you that higher lesson bring
> Which seraphims instruct his saints to sing.[43]

At a rather lower social level another devotional poem copied into the early seventeenth-century commonplace book of the

17

Figure 1: George Webb, bishop of Limerick (1634–42) from George Webb, *The practice of quietness directing a Christian how to live quietly in this troublesome world* (London, 1705). According to the inscription it was 'Drawn first by stranger's hand himself unaware / As he in pulpit did discharge his place.'

Limerick gentleman Edmund Sexten carried the same message:

> One truth there is the scripture saith
> Two Testaments, the old and new
> We must acknowledge to be true.[44]

This view remained unchallenged until the latter half of the seventeenth century when readers, following on a changed intellectual climate, began to notice problems with the biblical text through a changed way of reading it. The Carrickfergus born printer and author, Richard Head, recorded in a semi-autobiographical work how in the 1660s he met a condemned man in Dublin. Refusing the traditional ministrations of the church he did not deny the existence of God but doubted that the Bible was a revelation, desiring Head to:

> quote not from scripture for my conviction is less since they are full of contradictions and contain many things incredible. Neither do I know (since we are forbidden murder) why Abraham should kill his son Isaac and the same person commit adultery with his maid Haggar (which is largely described) yet we are commanded to the contrary . . . In this manner I could cavil ad infinitum and yet this book is the basis of Christianity.[45]

The prisoner ended by recanting on the scaffold which suggests how unrepresentative his views were. However attitudes were changing and perhaps more typical of the late seventeenth-century views of scripture are the comments of William Wright of College Green who felt that the Bible should be read rather more rationally to 'consider what ground we have in the holy scriptures to know and believe [and] what may be expected for the time to come.'[46]

The Bible was therefore a deeply ambiguous text which had to be read carefully and in many different ways. One Munster settler of the early seventeenth century, Robert Marshall, suggested that the Bible had to be read in at least three ways: literally, figurally, which required the drawing of a series of universal types from the biblical text which had universal applications, and consignually, which allowed for the symbolic nature of the text and the interpretation of difficult and

19

Figure 2: John Richardson, bishop of Ardagh (1633–54) from John Richardson, *Observations and explanations upon the Old Testament* (London, 1655).

contentious phrases such as 'This is my body'.[47] These three types of reading are all present in the notes made by the Killileagh Presbyterian merchant James Trail at the beginning of the eighteenth century.[48] Literally, for example he made notes of what the text actually said and tried to place it in its historical context. Thus he commented that 'the book of Genesis which was writ by Moses contains the history of what has happened from the creation of the world to the death of Joseph and comprehends the space of above 2,400 years'. Figuratively he saw in 1 Peter 'superstition is figuratively styled Babylon here and in Rev. 17:18'. His reading of Isaiah as one who 'spoke the most clearly of the coming of Jesus Christ of his suffering, of his kingdom and of the calling of the gentiles' reveals his view of Old Testament figures as types of the New Testament revelation. Chapters nine and ten of the book of Hebrews he saw as consignual or symbolic of the nature of legal ceremonies and the sufficiency of Christ's sacrifice.

This rather sophisticated variety of ways of reading the text, all of which might be in play simultaneously, points to the complexity of the practice of reading the Bible. It is possible to distinguish a number of ways in which an individual might read the text. On the basis of a literal reading the reader might understand the Bible as a chronological narrative. Many read the book in this way and made notes and comments accordingly. In the early part of the seventeenth century, for instance, the Irish judge, Sir Charles Calthorpe, filled his commonplace book with genealogies constructed from the Old Testament on the basis of his reading of the Bible as a narrative. Later in the century the pious James Bonnell, then comptroller general, would attempt to construct a conflated text of the gospels to produce a narrative life of Christ. An early eighteenth-century Irish poet attempted a similar task using the biblical text and a late medieval life of Christ.[49] This sort of reading of the Bible as narrative was especially important where the text was transmitted orally. This was particularly a feature of the Catholic reading of the Bible which tried to dissuade its followers from a verse-by-verse examination and concentrate simply on the biblical text as story. Such an approach did not require a written or printed text. In 1642 Friar Malone on discovering a number of Bibles at Skerries in county Dublin had them burnt explaining to a settler 'it was fitting for every man to have the Bible by rote and not to misinstruct them which should have it by rote.'[50] Indeed the primer composed in the 1680s by the Cavan priest Thomas Fitzsimons suggest that where parts of the biblical text were destined for lay hands it was printed as a narrative without verse divisions.[51] Many Catholic laymen seem to have read the Bible in this way. When the Meath Catholic, John Cusack, composed a commentary on the government of Ireland in 1629 he sprinkled it liberally with his own translation of biblical passages from the Vulgate giving chapter numbers but not verses. When the Limerick doctor Thomas Arthur quoted Job 8:8 from the Vulgate at the beginning of his fee book he did not provide a verse reference.[52] For Irish Catholics the important division in the biblical text was the chapter or narrative rather than the individual verse.

By contrast Protestant readers of the Bible were more orientated to a printed text, read the work much more closely and took advantage of the various divisions into which it was broken down, especially verses which appeared for the first time in 1553. William Sheridan, the bishop of Kilmore and Ardagh, stressed in 1685 'every distinct sentence of holy scripture does command and require our belief as much as the whole or any part of it.'[53] One of the obituary poems composed on the death of Katherine Boyle, Lady Cork, in 1630 by Daniel Spicer of Trinity College, Dublin, claimed:

> That I heard a reverend man profess
> If of the Bible you could but express
> A sentence as't was writ (such was her skill)
> She could denote the chapter and verse.[54]

Others, such as the late sixteenth-century divines Luke Challoner and Ambrose Ussher made detailed verse by verse summaries of parts of books of the Bible to help in the location of verses.[55]

Such close reading of the biblical text sometimes confused as much as it enlightened. The meaning of many biblical texts was not immediately obvious to readers and the Bible often had to be read in conjunction with other works before it could be understood as a meaningful narrative. Sometimes that explanatory context was supplied by the text itself through the sort of notes printed as part of the sixteenth-century Geneva Bible or the Catholic Douai-Rheims translation.[56] Some, such as the late seventeenth-century Dublin doctor, Duncan Cummings, read his Bible daily with the aid of a commentary and others, such as the Limerick Protestant Christopher Sexton had commentaries in their libraries.[57] Commentaries were also available in more popular forms. At least one broadsheet was circulating in Dublin in 1624 which was ruled into five columns which had theological headings such as 'the certainty of our faith and salvation' and 'against merits and righteousness' with corresponding proof texts which could be verified in one's own Bible.[58]

It is difficult to know from large library lists what books individuals actually read and what remained on their shelves but with smaller lists it is more likely that the texts which were owned were read together. Two small early seventeenth-century libraries, that of Lady Anne Hamilton in Dublin in 1639 and the 1628 list of Lady Lettice Digby of Geashill in county Offaly, provide some help here.[59] Anne Hamilton's library of fourteen books included a Greek New Testament and an octavo English Bible suggesting she took her Bible reading seriously. Her other books are a standard fare of godly works including Lewis Bayly's *The practice of piety* (then in its thirty-sixth edition), Nicholas Byfield's, *The marrow of the oracles of God* (in its tenth edition), John Hayward's *The strong helper* and Daniel Featley's *Ancillia pietatis or the handmaid to private devotion* (then in its sixth edition). Together these works were valued at 16s., or two-thirds of the total value of the books. All this suggests a godly concern with the biblical text and a careful reader. Lettice Digby, with a collection of twelve books, was a more conventional figure with a French and Latin Bible, possibly owned as much for their language as their content, and a Book of Common Prayer which suggests a more formal reader with little delving into the biblical text. She did, however, own a Spanish copy of the treatise on prayer by the Spanish Dominican Luis de Granada.

While commentaries were certainly important the more common way of trying to contextualise disparate verses of scripture for those who read the Bible in this way was to make use of a figurative reading of the text and regard it as a series of types which could be applied to their own experience. This could be made to apply in a general way to entire social groups or the nation as a whole.[60] In 1587, for instance, Andrew Trollop saw parallels between the sins described in Ezekiel 16 and those of contemporary Ireland and in 1633 the Cork settler Vincent Gookin paralleled Isaiah 5 and 6 with the state of Ireland. Again in the 1680s the godly comptroller general, James Bonnell, meditated on the image of the beast of Revelation seeing an immediate parallel with the triumph of the Jacobite regime.[61] From a Catholic perspective too this was possible using not verses but narratives. The idea of parallels between the history of Ireland and that of Israel as an elect nation was a commonplace in early seventeenth-century bardic poetry and in the 1640s the events of the Old Testament would be applied to the contemporary world.[62] Again the earliest translator of Geoffrey Keating's history of Ireland into English, Michael Kearney, drew an extended parallel between the Ireland of the 1630s and the world of Canaan in Deuteronomy 8 in his introduction to the translation. The Old English author of 'A light to the blind' saw Naboth's vineyard in 1 Kings 21 as a type of Ireland.[63] Such types might be much simpler and one Dublin man made notes of 'predictions of weather according to sacred scripture' paralleling climatic portents with scriptural verses.[64]

However the types which were sought were usually not so impersonal. The scriptures were more often read for universal solutions to personal dilemmas and many texts had personal associations. The pious Kilkenny Baptist Anne Fowke throughout her life spanning the seventeenth and eighteenth centuries latched on to individual scriptural verses, either read or heard, as a way of finding solutions to problems as they presented themselves to her. Once a verse was read or heard a concordance could be used to locate other texts which would shed light on its meaning.[65] The rather eccentric Walter Gostellow, in Cork during the 1650s, attempted to divine the meaning of one of his dreams by reading his Bible in this way. On 11 March 1655 he opened his Bible at the prophet Haggai, a part he was unfamiliar with, and read a chapter 'directed and overruled (as I then and now believe) by God almighty' which

24

referred to the rebuilding of God's house. This, Gostellow believed, referred to the church at Lismore and he then badgered the earl of Cork until he agreed to rebuild. Dipping further into the text in search of enlightenment he found Psalms 84 and 85 which he believed that God 'who for my further confirmation gave me those psalms of scripture to strengthen me and dispose others to their duty'.[66] In a rather less exalted way one Dublin man on seeing a great fish washed ashore at Dingle in 1673 concluded that it was one of the beasts depicted in Revelation and wrote a detailed account of the biblical parallels of his experience.[67]

The reading of the Bible was therefore a pursuit in which readers actively engaged all their emotions and reason. Reading of pious books, especially the Bible, was, according to Bishop Wetenhall, to be with a heart 'so accommodated and disposed to these employments that the several parts of each office makes suitable impressions on him and naturally drew forth his soul towards God in acts of resignation, humility, faith, hope, joy, love and gratitude.'[68] Such reading of the Bible in small portions and applying it as a series of types to the contemporary world brought forth a myriad of often highly individualistic interpretations of the text. In 1638, for instance the daughter of the Irish lord deputy, Alice Wandesford, then aged twelve, read Luke 2:49 in which Jesus disputed with the doctor in the temple. She later wrote:

> In the reading of which passage . . . I fell into a serious and deep meditation of the thoughts of Christ's majesty, divinity and wisdom, who was able to confound the learned doctors and confute their wisdom who were aged, He being so young himself but then twelve years of age. And then I considered my own folly and childish ignorance that I could scarce understand mean and low things without a great deal of teaching and instruction; and although I daily read the word of God, yet was of a weak capacity to know the way of salvation and therefore in my heart begged my dear saviour to give me knowledge, wisdom and understanding to guide all my days.[69]

In reality this sort of meditative reading of the biblical text had a long tradition stretching back to the medieval *lectio divina*. It certainly seems to have been a feature of Gaelic

25

Ireland and one late sixteenth-century poem by Mathghamhain Ó hUiginn is cast as a long meditation on Matthew 6:4.[70]

III

By the middle of the seventeenth century in the light of the political upheaval of the 1640s such individualistic interpretations posed problems for both church and state. Thus the satirical account of the Reformation by the Catholic bishop of Ferns, Luke Wadding, portrayed 'The cobbler with his great black thumb/ Turning the bible will have it done.'[71] From the religious perspective Timothy Hyatt, a bankrupt and graduate of Trinity College, Dublin, was severely censured for his prophecy that Christ would appear in Dublin on 25 March 1676 a view held later that year to be 'deluded imagination'.[72] From the potentially more dangerous political perspective Roger Boyle, earl of Orrery, writing in the aftermath of the free interpretation of the Bible in the 1640s and 1650s, observed:

> I confess an aversion from the late custom of our age for every private hand as it serves on occasion to draw all stories and expressions of scripture into the consequence for the conduct of our lives and the framing of our opinions. I have observed this to be of mischievous effect and destructive in a great measure to the respect and obedience we owe to civil authority. I revere the scriptures but esteem them given us for other use than to fortify disputes concerning state affairs out of every part of them.[73]

The theological equivalent of these sentiments was articulated by Thomas Haslam, the schoolmaster at Lisburn in the 1630s, who in a sermon condemned those who wrestled with scripture to interpret it since 'the wrestler becomes a new judicier of scripture and takes upon himself the person of God.' In the later part of the century Robert Craghead, the Presbyterian minister at Derry, warned those who 'wrestled with scripture to your own destruction' to desist.[74]

These problems were solved through the formation of interpretative communities around the text of scripture, not all of whose members might be able to read, guided by a professional interpreter. Such a group could take the individualistic understanding of verses and reconstruct them into a narrative which corresponded to the sense of the whole text as that particular community understood it. Within Catholicism great emphasis was placed not so much on reading the Bible early in life as on shaping the elements of belief that would guide any subsequent contact with the text. Emphasis was placed on catechesis and prayers rather than the biblical text. For those children who went to school parents were warned to ensure that the first books their children encountered espoused these principles.[75] From a Church of Ireland perspective Edward Wetenhall, later bishop of Cork, emphasised the importance of the Articles of religion and the catechism in shaping belief but also stressed the importance of Bible reading since:

> it will teach you the same things in different form and besides convince you of their truth and otherwise affect you with them. But when plain persons meet with hard places in their Bibles not relating to these necessaries I would have them pass such difficulties over, and not interpret them on their own heads without a teacher but content themselves commonly to know, to believe, to be affected with and practice these necessary points thus summarily comprised by our church.[76]

The Bible was rarely, if ever, intended to be used as an unmediated text.

In this context public reading of the scriptures and the sermon was vital and provides a good example of the interaction between the text as read privately and the more public oral tradition. The linkages between public and private reading meant that many contemporaries made little distinction between hearing and reading the Bible. Sir Charles Calthorpe, for instance, noted that 'by reading and hearing these godly books and exhortations God speaketh and talketh to us and by preaching and prophesy we speak and talk to God but this reading and hearing must be with sincerity, attendance and imbued with Godly grace, His spirit dres't our understanding with due regard to the matter what we hear or read.' The same sentiments were echoed at the end of the century in the catechism composed by the Presbyterian minister at Larne, Thomas Hall, who regarded the Bible as being read if 'the reading of it whether publicly or privately together with the hearing of the word read, meditating and conferring upon it, making use of it in prayers and singing of psalms.' He duly provided suitable scriptural proofs to support his approach to reading the Bible.[77]

At the simplest level an interpretative community could be built around what was read. In Presbyterian assemblies the practice was to work through a book of the Bible sequentially dealing with all the issues raised by the text.[78] Within the Church of Ireland, however, attention was directed to other passages through the use of the lectionary. As the Church of Ireland divine Henry Dodwell argued in the 1670s:

> I do not think it convenient that the subject to be meditated
> be taken from the scripture allotted for the time unless when
> the place is chosen by special design as in the lessons and
> epistles and gospels for the festivals or feasts of the church
> . . . such portion of scripture must therefore be most apposite
> for our information concerning them.

He held that selecting other passages would look 'more like the exercise of wit than seriousness [and] are not likely to leave such serious impression.'[79]

More important than simply directing attention to appropriate parts of the Bible for reading, the interpretation of those passages in the sermon would provide a guide as to how those passages should be read. The role of the preacher in this context was to reassemble the verses from diverse passages he used into a coherent narrative in which one verse would interpret another. The Dublin Presbyterian minister Joseph Boyse urged that the best way of reading the Bible was by juxtaposing texts with one another while another Dublin minister urged his catechumens to 'be very diligent in comparing one text with another.' In the case of ministers concordances were the key to this activity.[80] Thus at sermons Bible reading was encouraged as an important part of the congregational role. Dissenters in the late seventeenth century were urged to bring their Bibles to public worship. They were advised to turn to the texts of scripture as they were cited by the preacher and to make notes of what was said.[81] The Church of Ireland bishop of Kilmore and Ardagh, William Sheridan, satirised dissenters for going to worship 'carrying a Bible under their arms though they neither understand it nor draw any inferences from it for amendment of their life and practice.'[82] In Church of Ireland churches too, use of the Bible during the sermon was seen as a sign of piety. The vehement Protestant, Robert Ware, claimed that the culprit in the burning of Dublin castle in 1671 was a Catholic who nonetheless 'would walk before the lord lieutenant among the gentry to church with his Bible publicly under his arm to be seen' and 'at church he would seem very zealous turning to the texts of scripture as fast as they were quoted by the preacher.'[83] After the sermon the texts could be read over and the interpretation verified. Elizabeth Chambers, who was a member of John Rogers's Independent Dublin congregation in the 1650s, told that congregation how 'with sighs and tears I took the Bible and looked out for Christ there, and looked out and turned to the proofs that master Rogers mentioned and examined them.'[84] At least some of the elite might get more personal treatment. One judge on the 1627 assize in county Down approached the preacher of the assize sermon, the Presbyterian Robert Blair, with questions about what he had heard. In response Blair noted 'he opened his Bible and I mine. We considered all the points and proofs, turning to the places and reading them over.'[85] This sort of reading was certainly facilitated in the first Dublin printed Bible, that by Aaron Rhames in 1714, by the provision of detailed marginal notes which referred to interconnections between texts of the Old and New Testaments and provided the basic tool for a scriptural paper chase which the reader could follow with pleasure and, possibly, also profit.

The Sunday sermon was not the only way in which the text could be read or given meaning. It could be read and explained in the context of family worship. At the upper social levels where a chaplain was available he could undertake this function. Stephen Jerome, the chaplain to the earl of Cork, for instance reminded the earl's daughters that their days had always begun with prayer and 'in your chambers with scripture, with the best sermons and theological tractates were not read by you or to you' so that the disparate parts of scripture were reunited according to the analogy of the faith as epitomised in the Lord's prayer, the ten commandments and the apostles creed.[86] In another case the Killileagh Presbyterian

29

merchant, James Trail, rose early in the morning to read the Bible and prepare for family worship in an orthodox way.[87] However such sophisticated approaches were unnecessary. At the end of the century the Dublin Presbyterian minister, Joseph Boyse, developed another way of shaping a textual community through hymn singing which was appropriate for family worship. Using the traditional exegetical technique of drawing together a number of verses on a common theme from different parts of scripture he made others familiar with the text and with a way of reading it through singing.[88]

Outside formal worship, both in church and family settings, others encountered the Bible both alone or in smaller groups. The late seventeenth-century Meath landowner Arthur Langford, for instance, read his Bible in private not to obtain 'a system of heavenly doctrine but as a rule of life.' In contrast the late seventeenth-century Dublin doctor, Duncan Cummings, who read the Bible 'to draw instruction from thence for the improvement of his knowledge and salutary rules for the conduct of his life', was prepared to engage in a more communal interpretation. According to his funeral sermon he:

> frequently and freely communicated any difficulties that seemed to him in reading them [the scriptures] in order to gain further light for the resolution of them and he would as freely impart some uncommon and judicious observations of his own upon them.[89]

Such shared readings did not have to be purely devotional. Political meanings of scripture could also be hammered out in shared readings of the text. In 1662 a miller on the Clandeboy estate in county Down, William Fury, revealed to James Phillips of Ballymaconaghy his interpretation of Micah 5:5-6 and Jeremiah 4:20 and 6:23. This involved a Spanish invasion of Ireland and the Scottish army which had recently been in Ulster under General Monro together with some rather elliptical statements about the king. The Dublin government clamped down firmly on Fury who clearly had a fright for:

> being demanded whether he thought he himself a prophet or had the interpretation of the scriptures or if what he said were by a revelation or inspiration or by his own imagination

and conception of the text, he sayeth only by his own imaginations and conceptions of the text and that he both believes
his interpretation of them to be true but if this be past by in
silence he will never interpret again.[90]

There is little doubt but that Fury was only the tip of a large
interpretative iceberg.

IV

Reading the Bible in the seventeenth century, even for the
humblest practitioners of the art, was not a simple task. It
required the blending of a number of different ways of
approaching a complex and sometimes contradictory text
which was part of everyday life. It involved reading on a
number of levels, both as narrative and in much more fragmented ways, utilising different types of guidance to reveal the
complexities of the text. While there were as many readings as
there were individuals these were also bound together by broad
social and cultural agreements shared within the textual
communities who met around the book. Perhaps the most basic
insight into Bible reading in seventeenth-century Ireland was
that of the Dublin Presbyterian minister, Robert Chambers,
who observed in his manuscript catechism that it was a book
that 'influences our affections and conversations very much.'[91]

Notes

1. N. McClure, *The letters and epigrams of Sir John Harrington* (Philadelphia, 1930), p. 74.

2. *The works of the Rev and learned Ezekiel Hopkins, lord bishop of Londonderry* (London, 1710), p. 710.

3. McClure, *Letters and epigrams*, p. 77.

4. Barnaby Rich, *The Irish hubbub or the English hue and cry* (London, 1617), sig. A3–A3v.

5. Raymond Gillespie, 'The circulation of print in seventeenth-century Ireland' in *Studia Hibernica*, no. 29 (1995–7), pp 31–58.

6. Presbyterian Historical Society, Belfast, Carnmoney session book, 1 Aug 1703; Union Theological College, Belfast, MS. Robert Chambers, 'Explanation of the Shorter Catechism', pp 270–271; G.T. Stokes (ed.), *The memoirs of mistress Anne Fowke nee Geale* (Dublin, 1892), p. 21; St John D. Seymour, *Irish witchcraft and demonology* (Dublin, 1913), p. 216; Raymond Gillespie, *Devoted people: belief and religion in early modern Ireland* (Manchester, 1997), p. 34.

7. P.R.O., London, SP63/256/9i; Barnaby Rich, *A true and kind excuse written in defence of that book entitled a new description of Ireland* (London, 1612), p. 4; Samuel Foley, *An exhortation to the inhabitants of Down and Connor concerning the education of their children* (Dublin, 1695), pp 19–20.

8. C.S. King (ed.), *A great archbishop of Dublin* (London, 1908), p. 3.

9. Richard Parr, *The life of the most reverend father in God James Ussher* (London, 1686), p. 3; T.C.D., MS. 1050, p. 14; *The life of Mr Thomas Gent, printer, of York written by himself* (London, 1832), p. 23.

10. Raymond Gillespie, 'The book trade in southern Ireland, 1590–1640' in Gerard Long (ed.), *Books beyond the pale* (Dublin, 1996), pp 4, 13. For illustration of these, Margaret Spufford, *The world of rural dissent, 1520–1725* (Cambridge, 1995), pp 69–76. The only surviving Irish language primer was William Bedell, *The ABC or the institutes of a Christian* (Dublin 1631) which used a number of scriptural passages described as 'The sum of the gospel' to teach reading. Others clearly existed since one book entitled *The ABC with the church catechism* was on sale in Dublin in 1695, list of books for sale by Richard Wild, bookseller, in William Sherlock, *A sermon preached at the Temple Church, December 30 1694* (Dublin, 1695).

11. Raymond Gillespie, *Colonial Ulster* (Cork, 1985), p. 230.

12. Gillespie, 'Circulation of print', pp 32–33.

13. Raymond Gillespie, 'Church, state and education in early modern Ireland' in Maurice O'Connell (ed.), *O'Connell: education, church and state* (Dublin, 1992), pp 50–51.

14. Toby Barnard, 'Learning, the learned and literacy in Ireland, c.1660–1760' in Toby Barnard, Dáibhí Ó Cróinín, Katharine Simms (eds), *'A miracle of learning': studies in manuscripts and Irish learning* (Aldershot, 1998), pp 220–221.

15. R.S. Schofield, 'The measurement of literacy in pre-industrial England' in Jack Goody (ed.), *Literacy in traditional societies* (Cambridge, 1968), pp 323–324.

16. M. Pollard, *Dublin's trade in books* (Oxford, 1989), pp 9–10.

17. Raymond Gillespie, 'Irish printing in the early seventeenth century' in *Irish economic and social history* xv (1988), p. 88; Leeds City Library, Temple Newsham MSS, Irish customs records I(4)a, Derry port book 1614, f. 3; William King, *A discourse concerning the inventions of men in the worship of God* (Dublin, 1694), pp 89–90; Scott Mandelbrote, 'John Baskett, the Dublin booksellers, and the printing of the Bible' in A. Hunt, G. Mandelbrote, A. Shell (eds), *The book trade and its customers* (Winchester, 1997), p. 117. For London prices of Bibles, A.S. Herbert, *Historical catalogue of printed editions of the English Bible* (London, 1968), pp 182–185.

18. P.J. Corish (ed.) 'Bishop Wadding's notebook' in *Archivium Hibernicum*, xxix (1970), pp 63, 64, 69, 72. For even lower prices, George Benn, *A history of the town of Belfast* (London, 1877), p. 316.

19. T.C.D., MS. 357, f. 4; MS. 287, f. 194v. Luxury editions could be imported specially. One quarto Bible imported into Drogheda from Liverpool in 1683 was valued at 15s. and in 1670 the Dublin parish of St Catherine ordered a pulpit Bible specially from England, Representative Church Body Library, Dublin, MS. P117/5/1, p. 189; J.T. Dolan (ed.), 'Drogheda trade and customs, 1683' in *County Louth Archaeological Journal*, iii (1912–15), pp 96–97.

20. A.B. Grossart (ed.), *Lismore papers* (10 vols, London, 1886–8), 1st ser., iv, p. 5; Wesley Mc Cann, 'An unrecorded edition of John Taylor's *Verbum Sepiterum*' in *Linen Hall Review*, vi, no 2 (1989), pp 14–15. A work entitled *The best new year's gift or an epitome of the Bible dedicated to King William and Queen Mary* was being sold by Richard Wild in 1695, Sherlock, *A sermon preached*.

21. T.C.D., MS. 562, f. 41; Robert Craghead, *An answer to a late book entitled a discourse concerning the inventions of men in the worship of God* (Edinburgh, 1694), p. 86.

22. John Ainsworth, 'Abstracts of seventeenth century Irish wills in the prerogative court of Canterbury' in *Journal of the Royal Society of Antiquaries of Ireland*, lxxviii (1948), p. 24. Marsh's Library, Dublin, MS. Z3.2.6, no. 58; W.P. Burke, *History of Clonmel* (Waterford, 1907), p. 327.

23. Dublin City Archives, MS. C1/J/2/4, pp 228, 216, 200.

24. B.L., Add MS. 19865, ff 74–4v; 'A seventeenth-century Anglo-Irish library' in *Irish Book lover*, xxx (1946–8), p. 31. The early sixteenth-century library list of the earl of Kildare contained French and Latin translations of the Bible, Gearóid Mac Niocaill (ed.), *Crown surveys of lands, 1540–1* (Dublin, 1992), pp 312, 313, 355.

25. T.C.D., MS. 817, f. 38.

26. B.L., Add. MS. 46957, f. 36.

27. Liam Miller, Eileen Power (eds), *Holinshed's Irish chronicle* (Dublin, 1979), pp 25–27, 28, 30, 33, 36–37; Stanihurst's verse translations of the first four psalms are in his *The first four books of Virgil his Aeneid* (Antwerp, 1582), pp 86 ff; Dublin City Archives, MS. C1/J/2/1, p. 78.

28. C[ornelius] N[ary], *The New Testament of our Lord and Saviour Jesus Christ* ([Dublin], 1718), sig. a2v.

29. N.L.I., MS. 31996. I am grateful to Harold O'Sullivan for this reference.

30. George Hill (ed.), *The Montgomery manuscripts* (Belfast, 1869), p. 328.

31. Patrick Fagan, *Dublin's turbulent priest: Cornelius Nary* (Dublin, 1991), pp 83–84.

32. Lambert Mc Kenna (ed.), *Dán Dé* (Dublin, n.d), pp x–xi; Lambert Mc Kenna (ed.), *Aithdíogluim dána* (2 vols, Dublin, 1939–40), i, p 280, stanzas 10 and 15 using John 8:4–5 and Matthew 26:52–3. It is more likely that Tadhg Dall Ó hUigínn's account of Noah and the Flood was done from memory judging by the new elements he introduces. Eleanor Knott (ed), *The bardic poetry of Tadhg Dall Ó hUigínn* (2 vols, London, 1922–6), i, pp 16, 46–47.

33. Caoimhín Breatnach, *Patronage, politics and prose* (Maynooth, 1996), pp 18, 45; Lambert McKenna (ed.), *Iomarbhágh na bhfileadh* (2 vols, London, 1918) i, pp 54–57.

34. For example, Cecile O'Rahilly (ed.), *Five seventeenth century political poems* (Dublin, 1952), pp 59–60 and most famously in Geoffrey Keating's, *Foras feasa ar Éirinn*. For a more generalised biblical chronology being used by a poet, O'Rahilly (ed.), *Five seventeenth century political poems*, p. 43. For a similar tracing of the inhabitants of Ireland to Adam using biblical materials R.I.A., MS. I iv 1, pp 1–3.

35. Nicholas Williams, *Í bprionta í leabhar: na Protastúin agus prós na Gaeilge, 1567–1724* (Dublin 1986), pp 131–133 argues this case on the basis of similarities of texts in Gaelic Irish devotional works and the Protestant translation of the Bible.

36. Barnaby Rich, *A new description of Ireland* (London, 1610), p. 34.

37. John Rogers, *Ohel or Beth Shemesh* (London, 1653), p. 412(10); Craghead, *An answer to the late book*, p. 86; Edward Wetenhall, *A practical and plain discourse of the form of godliness visible in the present age* (Dublin, 1683), p. 158.

38. King, *A discourse concerning the inventions of men*, pp 55–73.

39. Parr, *Life of . . . Ussher*, p. 2.

40. *The works of the Rev and learned Joseph Boyse* (2 vols, London, 1728) i, p. 440; J[oseph] B[oyse], *Sermons preached on several subjects* (2 vols, Dublin, 1708), ii, pp 583–584.

41. P.R.O.N.I., T808/14615.

42. Folger Library, Washington D.C., MS. V.a.125, f. 7v.

43. Hannah Buchan (ed.), *The poems of Thomas Pestell* (Oxford, 1940), pp 2–3, 105.

44. N.L.I., MS. 16085, p. 136.

45. Richard Head, *The English rogue described* (London, 1666), p. 81.

46. William Wright, *A chronological account on the age of the world* (Dublin, 1700), sig. A1v.

47. B.L., Royal MS. 17 A xviii, f. 3v. While Marshall's theology is undoubtedly Protestant he also owned a number of Catholic devotional objects which he used, Brian Donovan, David Edwards (eds), *British sources for Irish history, 1485–1641* (Dublin, 1998), p. 43. For other examples of this trait see Raymond Gillespie, *Devoted people*, pp 9–10 and the notebook of Sir Charles Calthorpe (T.C.D., MS. 676) which has a dramatic image of the crucifixion pasted into the inside cover.

48. These are contained in his autobiography in P.R.O.N.I., D1460/1.

49. T.C.D., MS. 676, pp 323–329; William Hamilton, *The life and character of James Bonnell* (Dublin, 1703), p. xiii. For an Irish case Áine Ní Chróinín (ed.), *Beatha Chríost* (Dublin, n.d.).

50. T.C.D., MS. 834, f. 63v.

51. Thomas Fitzsimons, *The primer more ample and in a new order* (Rouen, 1684), sigs c3v–d6, pp 390–420.

52. Folger Library, Washington D.C., MS. G.a.10, B.L., Add. MS. 31885, f. 14.

53. William Sheridan, *St Paul's confession of faith or a brief account of his religion* (Dublin, 1685), p. 18.

54. *Musarum lacryamyra* (Dublin, 1630), sig D3v.

55. T.C.D., MS. 287, ff 200–4, 229, 275v–6; MS. 357, ff 25–9.

56. The chronology of the replacement of the Geneva Bible with the King James version is unclear for Ireland but some Geneva versions clearly had long lives. In the 1690s the Geneva Bible was still in use in the Church of Ireland at Greyabbey in county Down and it was also circulating in county Tyrone in the middle of the eighteenth century (Hill, *Montgomery manuscripts*, p. 124; N.L.I., MS. G730, pp 79–105). It may be that some of those Bibles imported from Holland in the late seventeenth century, as for example that imported by the Belfast merchant David Buttle in 1698 (P.R.O.N.I., D1449/13/1, p. 53), were Geneva Bibles or they may have been pirated authorised versions. One Bible which acted as the family Bible of Nathaniel Trumble (probably a brother of George Trumball the Irish accountant general in the 1680s) contained a King James text with the notes of the Geneva Bible (N.L.I., MS. 5187). For the importance of determining the versions read see Harry S. Stout, 'Word and order in colonial new England' in N.A. Hatch, Mark Noll (eds), *The Bible in America: essays in cultural history* (New York, 1982), pp 19–38.

57. *The works of . . . Joseph Boyse*, i, p. 316; B.L., Add. MS. 19865, f. 74.

58. Society of Antiquaries, London, Broadsides, no. 30.

59. Dublin City Archives, MS. C1/J/2/4, p. 228; B.L., Add. Charter 13340, m.4d.

60. For other ways in which the Bible defined national identity, Scott Mandelbrote, 'The Bible and national identity in the British Isles, c.1650–c.1750' in Tony Claydon and Ian McBride (eds), *Protestantism and national identity: Britain and Ireland, c. 1650–c.1850* (Cambridge, 1998), pp 157–181.

61. *Calendar of State Papers, Ireland, 1586–8*, p. 424; *Calendar of State Papers, Ireland, 1647–60*, p. 182; Hamilton, *Life of Bonnell*, p. 47.

62. J.T. Gilbert (ed.), *A contemporary history of affairs in Ireland* (3 vols, Dublin, 1879), i, pp 174, 210, 214; ii, p. 126; iii, pp 123–124; Marc Caball, 'Providence and exile in seventeenth-century Ireland' in *Irish Historical Studies*, xxix, no. 114 (Nov. 1994), pp 175–188.

63. R.I.A., MS. 24 G 16 'To the reader'. The manuscript refers to Deuteronomy 18 but this seems to be a transcription error. J.T. Gilbert (ed.), *A Jacobite narrative of the war in Ireland, 1688–91* (Dublin, 1892), pp 20, 187.

64. Dublin City Libraries, Gilbert Library, Pearse Street, Dublin, Bound volume of pamphlets, 183/1/7F.

65. Stokes (ed.), *Anne Fowke*, pp 42–43, 44, 48, 53.

66. Walter Gostellow, *Charls Stuart and Oliver Cromwell united* (London, 1654), pp 17–22, 34–35, 45.

67. Letter bound with pamphlet in N.L.I., Thorpe p. 11.

68. Wetenhall, *A practical and plain discourse*, p. 58.

69. Charles Jackson (ed.), *The autobiography of Mrs Alice Thornton* (Durham, 1875), p. 13.

70. Mc Kenna (ed.), *Aithdioglaim dána*, i, pp 287–289.

71. [Luke Wadding], *A small garland of pious and godly songs* (Ghent, 1684), p. 51.

72. Bodl., Rawlinson MS. D843, ff 111–2.

73. Roger Boyle, earl of Orrery, *The Irish colours displayed* ([London, 1662]), p. 16.

74. P.R.O.N.I., Mic 1/5; Craghead, *An answer to the late book*, p. 88.

75. Cainneach Ó Maonaigh (ed.), *Seanmónta chúige Uladh* (Dublin, 1965), pp 39–40; Cuthbert Mhag Craith (ed.), *Dán na mBráthar Mionúr* (2 vols, Dublin, 1967–80), i, pp 45–47.

76. Edward Wetenhall, *Collyrium: a sense of destructive ignorance and saving knowledge preached in Christ Church Dublin, August 4, 1672* (London, 1672), pp 17–18.

77. T.C.D., MS. 676, p. 493; Thomas Hall, *A plain and easy explication of the Assembly's shorter catechism* (Edinburgh, 1697), p. 203.

78. Joseph Boyse, *A vindication of the remarks of the bishop of Derry's discourse* (Dublin, 1695), pp 7, 8.

79. Francis de Sales, *An introduction to the devout life* ed. Henry Dodwell (Dublin, 1673) sig. A6.

80. Joseph Boyse, *Remarks on a late discourse of William, lord bishop of Derry* (Dublin, 1694), pp 93, 95; Union Theological

College, Belfast, MS. Robert Chambers, 'An explanation of the Shorter Catechism', p. 28.

81. Joseph Eyres, *The church sleeper awakened* (London, 1659), pp 48–9, 52; Boyse, *Remarks on a late discourse*, pp 98, 145.

82. Sheridan, *St Paul's religion*, p. 11.

83. [Robert Ware], *The second part of foxes and firebrands* (Dublin, 1683), p. 112.

84. Rogers, *Ohel*, p. 407.

85. Thomas McCrie (ed.), *The life of Mr Robert Blair* (Edinburgh, 1848), p. 79.

86. S[tephen] J[erome], *The souls centinel ringing an alarm against impiety and impenitencie* (Dublin, 1631), sig A3v, p.7.

87. P.R.O.N.I., D1460/1.

88. Raymond Gillespie, '"A good and godly exercise": singing the Word in Irish dissent, 1660–1701' in Kevin Herlihy (ed.), *Propagating the word of Irish dissent, 1650–1800* (Dublin, 1998), pp 24–45.

89. *The works of . . . Joseph Boyse* i, pp 309, 316.

90. Bodl., Carte MS. 32, ff 216–6v, 276.

91. Union Theological College, Belfast, MS. Robert Chambers, 'An explanation of the Shorter Catechism', p. 479.

Reading theology within the community of believers: James Ussher's 'Directions'

Elizabethanne Boran

Wouldst thou as all God's children would, conceive and understand
What thou dost read in holy Writ, as God doth thee command?
Wouldst thou attain true sense of words, and matters in them hid,
What meaning each word doth contain, from error to be rid?[1]

THE 'DIRECTIONS FOR READING Theology', compiled
by James Ussher, the seventeenth-century archbishop of
Armagh, sets out his thoughts on the thorny issue of
reading and interpretation of theology within the community of
believers.[2] As such it forms part of a whole body of literature
developed in the seventeenth century, which sought, like
Thomas Wilson's *Christian dictionary* from whence the quota-
tion derives, to inculcate among the reading public a correct
methodology for reading Scripture. Ussher's list of works
'approved' and authors 'disliked' not only offers us valuable
evidence for the types of books which a young clergyman
'newly enter'd into Holy Orders' might read but also, and
perhaps more importantly, *how* they should be read and transmitted to the public.[3] The 'Directions', drawn up to instruct
young ministers as to how they should communicate the fruits
of their university training in a practical situation, is therefore
of immense interest as it gives us a glimpse of methods of
reading in the 'high culture milieu' of the universities, and how
these methodologies could be transposed beyond the university.

The bibliographical information that Ussher affords us is
slight, and the document is difficult to date precisely from
internal evidence. Though Ussher cites many authors he rarely
gives us titles and when they are mentioned, they are invari-
ably shortened in such a way as to make a positive

identification well nigh impossible. However, the presence of 'William Ames on ye psalms' can only mean that our list must be at least as late as 1635, the date of the first edition of this work. This date – or a date in the late 1630s – would seem most likely as many of the works were published in the early 1630s.

Having stipulated that a knowledge of biblical languages is an all important requirement Ussher naturally begins with the Bible:

> Read the Bible with 2 Readings. 1. Daily 3 or 4 chapters to have gone over all the Canonical Scriptures within the year: then begin again, though you miss one day, make amends the next. This, though it seem but a superficial kind of reading, yet it will benefit much. Use [it] to give a prick at such a place as toucheth you. Read the doctrinal books thrice over for the historical once, for, they are harder to be remembered. 2. Read it with expositions, & here you need not be so tied to your daily task, but read as you have leisure.[4]

The emphasis on repetition here mirrors sixteenth-century Reformers' attitudes to reading and learning, as we can see in John Fox's celebrated (if somewhat polemical) account of the reading habits of the citizens of Hadleigh in Suffolk, during Henry VIII's reign:

> A great number of that parish became exceeding well learned in the holy Scriptures, as well women as men, so that a man might have found among them many, that had often read the whole Bible through, and that could have said a great sort of St. Paul's epistles by heart, and very well and readily have given a godly learned sentence in any matter of controversy. . . . the whole town seemed rather a university of the learned, than a town of cloth making or labouring people.[5]

This emphasis on repetition is also echoed in the later 'Directions for Study' compiled by Richard Holdsworth who declared that:

> There are two ways to get without book, either conning it as boys do, or frequent reading over the same thing for certain days together, which is easier, & will be as effectual to all ends, & purposes, as the former.[6]

The similarities between Ussher's approaches and Holdsworth's suggestions for reading material, coupled with Holdsworth's emphasis on the reading of three chapters a day, demonstrates that Ussher was not concocting a new system of reading but rather was utilising an already established method of reading and learning.[7]

The methodology was necessarily influenced by modes of instruction in the universities. It has sometimes been suggested that the arts training of later clergymen was somehow at odds with their calling, even a distraction.[8] The clergymen themselves would not have agreed.[9] Their training in the humanist disciplines of grammar, rhetoric and logic taught them above all how to read books and understand them. Humanist methodologies of interpretation offered them at times conflicting ways of understanding/reading a text. They could, for example, take Buonaccorso Massari's approach and limit the text to a particular time and place or, on the other hand, they could take the view of Lorenzo Guidetti and read the text as a document which has something to tell them about how one should live – this latter approach was in accordance with attitudes to the Bible as a normative document.[10] That humanist learning effectively prescribed the form of scriptural and hence theological knowledge can be seen in the famous Grashop diagram in the Geneva Bible.[11] This diagram, which outlines 'How to take profit by reading of the holy Scriptures', was heavily influenced by Ramist theories of arrangement of knowledge.[12]

A more obvious use of 'learned' methodologies being transposed beyond the confines of the universities may be seen in Ussher's advocation of the use of commonplace books. The importance of commonplace books and how they functioned was later expressed by Holdsworth in the following terms:

> Get some handsome paperbooks of a portable size in octavo, & rule them so with ink or black lead that there may be a space left on the side of a margin & at the top for a title. Into them collect all the remarkable things which you meet with, in your historians, orators, & poets.

> Ever as you find them promiscuously, especially if out of the same book, in the little space set down the name of the author with the book, or c[h]ap[ter] & after every collection, the number of the page, or section whence it is taken, that so you may speedily recourse to the author him self upon occasion.[13]

41

That this was a common practice may be deduced from the habits of Arthur Hildersham, one of the authors recommended by Ussher, who we are told 'read constantly a chapter, whence he gathered some observation, and wrote them in a book, with the reference to some common-place in the margin, which he referred to his commonplace book by numbers.'[14]

A slightly less elaborate version could also be used in the parish setting by those parishioners whose literate ability was of a high standard. Byfield, in another treatise in the same genre, his *Directions for the private reading of the Scriptures*, instructed readers to:

> First make thee a little paper book of a sheet or two of paper, as may be most portable. Then write upon the top of every leaf the title for that thou wouldest observe in reading. Choose out only six or eight titles out of the whole number of such as for the present thou hast most need to observe: or only so many as thou art sure thy memory will easily carry to thy reading, whether more or fewer. In reading observe only such places as stare thee in the face, that are so evident, thy heart cannot look off them. Trouble not thy self with that objection, that there are many things which thou canst not discern, take thou only such as thou canst not pass over, they are so clear and evident. In noting the places set down under each title only the book, chapter, and verse, and not the words, for that will tire thee in the end.[15]

Ussher tells preachers to 'Add notes of your own observation, as you meet them, that so your common place may be full and furnished, & so your matter will be ready all but for dressing when you are to come to any auditory.'[16] The chief advantage in using commonplace books in which to record key passages in reading was that the action of compartmentalising ideas corresponded to the actual process taking place in the brain – at least if you agreed with the model of Rudolph Agricola in his *De formando studio* of 1484. As Holdsworth pointed out, the very act of note-taking ensured a greater understanding of the text :

> And besides though this noting were of no use to the memory, yet it hath another advantage which alone would make it worthy in the mean while & that is it helps you to the fuller & clearer understanding of what you read, while you endeavour to abbreviate and contract the sense &

makes you take notice of many things which otherwise you
would have passed over.[17]

Ultimately, though, Ussher was not writing with the university
setting in mind. He tells us that 'a divine cannot be complete
without much reading but 'tis the country makes a preacher.
He must be able in controversies against the Papists, especially
if he live among such.'[18] Ussher's summary of the books necessary for theological reading is not meant to be taken as a guide
to reading theology in the university but rather at the coal face
– in the parish pulpit. He was very aware that the two audiences – the elite of the universities and the 'mixed' of the
parish might respond differently to both hearing and exposi-
tion of a printed text or, if some were literate, reading the text
themselves. His biographer Richard Parr notes that Ussher was
always sensitive to the effect on his audience :

> He never cared to tire his auditory with the length of his
> sermon, knowing well, that as the satisfaction in hearing
> decreases, so does the attention also, and people, instead of
> minding what is said, only listen when there is like to be an
> end.[19]

Likewise, Ussher told the preacher to use simple language so
that he might be understood 'by the meanest of your
auditors.'[20] To facilitate true understanding he deemed it:

> necessary to back all practical Precepts, and Doctrines, with
> apt proofs from the Holy Scriptures; avoiding all exotic
> phrases, scholastic terms, unnecessary quotations of authors,
> and forced rhetorical figures, since it is not difficult to make
> easy things hard, but to render hard things easy is the
> hardest part of a good orator, as well as preacher.[21]

Ussher's recognition of these differing audiences may be seen
in his demarkation of subjects, some of which were the
preserve of the scholar cleric:

> Nor did he advise students in Divinity to spend more time
> than was necessary, in the subtilities of the school-men, only
> so far as might serve for the understanding and answering the
> controversies between those of the Church of Rome and us;
> saying, that they were good to puzzle mens heads with
> unnecessary doubts, but bunglers in resolving them, and that

their writings had done more mischief to the Church, than
brought advantage either to learning, or religion. That they
might serve for controversial disputes in the schools, but
were very improper in the pulpit, and altogether useless for
the functions of a civil life.[22]

His advice to 'a learned man' who wished to extend his
knowledge and reading differed subtly from his suggestions for
ministers in the parish setting:

He said it might be thus performed.
1. By learned notes, and illustrations on the Bible.
2. By censuring, and inquiring into the ancient Councils, and
   the works of the Fathers.
3. By the orderly writing and digesting of ecclesiastical
   history.
4. By gathering whatsoever may concern the state of the
   Jews, from the destruction of Jerusalem to this present age.
5. By collecting of all the Greek and Roman histories, and
   digesting them into a body.
And to effect all this, he proposed, that the most ingenious
and studious men of both universities, being preferred to
prebends in cathedral churches should be enjoyned, and
amply encouraged to prosecute this design, for the advancement of this most profitable learning. And how much the lord
primate desired the performance of these so useful works
appears by what he had long since recommended to the
University of Oxford, touching the revising the works of the
ancient Fathers of the Church.[23]

The emphasis in the pastoral milieu is above all on practical
divinity rather than the more contentious areas of controversy.
The reason for this is that Ussher is primarily concerned with
the *effects* of reading – both the reading of the preacher as he
interprets it to the faithful, but also, implicitly, the reading of
the faithful as directed by the preacher. The minister has to
beware firstly of misinterpreting doctrines and secondly of
propagating heresy:

In the pulpit always beware of –
1. Heresies, never tell what they were or who were the
   Authors: for many had never knowne Arianism nor what
   Arrius was; had not the minister told them.

2. Controversies, state you but make not any objections, for many take such hold of that coming first that the answer does not satisfy them.[24]

The minister is advised to 'Read no Jesuits at all, for they are nothing but ostentation and never understood the Scriptures.'[25] This particular advice demonstrates that the audience Ussher is addressing is definitely not an academic one, where reading controversial works had a key role to play.[26] The advice here is directed to the minister in his pastoral role, and, through him, at the members of his parish.

This distrust of the ability of parishioners to correctly interpret the meaning of Scripture in their reading was not solely the result of a certain humanist distain for the 'vulgar' but rather had its roots in a fundamental problem of the Reformation. As Annabel Patterson has suggested, the reader, by the very act of reading, was involved in an act of interpretation.[27] Herein lay pitfalls which opened up into veritable chasms when it came to biblical interpretation. There was, for example, more than one way of interpreting scripture and, as Tyndale admitted in the preface to his English translation of the New Testament, 'the kingdom of heaven, which is the scripture and word of God, may be so locked up, that he which readeth or heareth it, cannot understand.'[28] In addition, to truly interpret the correct meaning involved not solely a mental process but also a spiritual experience. According to William Perkins, one of Ussher's favourite authors, 'One of the greatest helps and best means to understand the scripture was to keep a good conscience, living according to that we know out of the word, being joined with continual and fervent prayer.'[29]

The divine authorship of the Bible inevitably necessitated a different approach to reading Scriptures. Readers of the Geneva Bible, the edition of the Bible recommended by Ussher, (1599 edition) were told that 'who so ever mindeth to take profit by reading scriptures' must (among other things):

1. Earnestly and usually pray unto God that he will vouchsafe to . . . give understanding.
2. Diligently keep such order of reading the scriptures and prayer as may stand with his calling and state of life, So that . . . superstition be avoided . . . .
6. Mark and consider the . . . coherence of the text, how it hangeth together.[30]

Elizabethanne Boran

The sixth point referred to the belief that essentially the Scriptures, both Old and New Testament, formed a harmonious whole, a belief graphically illustrated in the 1630s by the inhabitants of Little Gidding, Huntingdonshire, when they built a concordance room where they chopped up bits of scripture and pasted them onto placards which were then hung around the room.[31] The belief in the harmony of the Bible made this possible. It also gave rise to the hermeneutic principle that difficult parts of scripture might be explained by reference to other easier places of holy writ. Thomas Wilson, the author of the *Theological rules, to guide us in the understanding and practice of holy Scripture,* was adamant on this point: 'The surest means of interpretation of scripture, is by scripture, which is the best commentary of itself, when the phrase is marked, and matter, and scope, and place compared with place, hard with easy.'[32]

Yet another factor in reading Scripture was identified by William Whitaker, another favourite author of Ussher's:

> We determine that the supreme right, authority, and judgement of interpreting the Scriptures, is lodged with the Holy Ghost and the Scripture itself . . . we say that the Holy Spirit is the supreme interpreter of Scripture, because we must be illuminated by the Holy Spirit to be certainly persuaded of the true sense of Scripture.[33]

The implications of this statement for the reading public were immense, whose interpretation of scripture was now, theoretically at least, on a par with their clerical brethren. Whitaker was continuing the traditional optimistic view of the lay reader expressed by the author of the 1547 homily entitled 'A fruitful exhortation to the reading of Holy Scripture':

> And if you be afraid to fall into error by reading of Holy Scripture, I shall show you how you may read it without danger of error. Read it humbly, with a meek and a lowly heart, to the intent you may glorify God, and not your self, with the knowledge of it. And read it not without daily praying to God that he would direct your reading to good effect, and take upon you to expound it no further then you can plainly understand it . . . the humble man may search any truth boldly in the Scripture without any danger of error. And if he

be ignorant, he ought the more to read and to search Holy
Scripture to bring him out of ignorance.[34]

A century earlier the playwright Jörg Wickram had identified this new reader 'the learned peasant' in his play *Derr irr
reintende Pilger*, of 1556. He describes the reformed peasant
as follows :

> Holding the Bible, he drew near
> To the good pilgrim, saying, 'hear
> How I find my greatest pleasure
> And spend my evening hours of leisure.
> My labour done in field and stable,
> I place the Bible on my table
> And study it two hours or three.
> On holidays, when I am free
> Of work, I spend the day
> Reading the Scriptures, for my way
> To church is far, two hours to reach
> My parish to hear the pastor preach.'

When the pilgrim asks the peasant how he can be sure that he is
interpreting the text correctly he is given the following answer :

> The peasant answered, 'here by my side
> I have some other books, to wit
> Explanations of Holy Writ,
> And these I use to teach myself.'
> He showed the pilgrim a tall shelf
> Filled with bound volumes: history,
> Chronicles and theology,
> All German titles, well selected,
> Which this simple person had collected.[35]

Subsequent historians continue to argue that the chief difference between Catholic and Protestant readings of scripture
was that Protestants could read it freely, whereas Catholics
were subject to the authority of the tradition of the Church.[36]
This is true in theory but in practice it represents an over-
simplification. The somewhat polemical picture that Wickram
draws here is of the ultimate success of the Reformation but it
held inherent dangers. What if the peasant – lay reader –
misinterpreted the Bible? How could the minister be sure that
the commentaries that the laity used were the right ones?

That this was something very much on the minds of ministers can be seen from James Calfhill's rumination of 1565 :

> If every man shall have authority to give his verdict upon a controversy which shall seem and say that he hath the spirit, no certain thing shall be decreed; every man shall have his own way; no stable opinion and judgement to be rested on.[37]

Calfhill was not alone in his belief that open access to the scriptures could prove dangerous. Thomas Wilson explained his decision to compile the *Christian dictionary* in the following terms:

> Again, the right distinguishing of things, the one from the other, when the Nature & due bounds of every word is declared, would prove some preservative against errors and heresy, which commonly arise upon the ignorance of things, while they are shuffled confusedly together, one thing being taken for another; or some thing being taken to be that it is not . . . .[38]

Martin Luther himself had foreseen difficulties in widespread lay access to the Scriptures, a policy he had initially welcomed. His experiences of the wilful misinterpretation by the peasants of some of his key concepts during the 1525 revolt in Germany, caused him to be less enthusiastic about lay reading of the Bible: 'Nowadays everyone thinks he is a master of Scripture and every Tom, Dick and Harry imagines he understands the Bible and knows it inside out.'[39] Instead he developed catechisms as suitable forms of theological instruction for the laity: 'The catechism is the layman's Bible. It contains the whole of what every Christian must know of Christian doctrine.'[40] Likewise in the Lutheran *Schulordnungen* of the 1530s a growing tendency towards catechetics rather than admonitions to Bible reading may be seen.[41]

Conversely, an illiterate community might easily turn to heterodoxy as the examples of several well-known radicals demonstrated.[42] The answer was not to keep the people illiterate but rather to direct their studies and reading of scripture. Hence one finds the enhancement of the role of the minister as the instructor of the people, a theme that is reiterated again and again in treatises about the ministry in the early seventeenth century. Emphasis on the education of ministers was a result of this function of the clergy. In order to properly instruct their parishioners, so that they might read scripture *correctly*, the minister had to be sufficiently educated. This was one of the spurs to the increased numbers of clergymen going to university, as gradually a university degree became a basic requirement if one wished for a ministerial position.

Patrick Collinson has pointed to the prophesying movement in the sixteenth century and the prevalent combination lectures of the seventeenth century, when ministers would gather and effectively train their less educated brethren in preaching and pastoral techniques as an essential step in the 'professionalisation of the ministry.'[43] Once instructed, the ministers could then go out and bring their training to bear on the pastoral situation. Ministers were well aware that not all parishes were alike, just as not all parishioners were equally skilled in reading and writing. Richard Bernard, a correspondent of Ussher's and the author of the famous treatise *The faithfull shepherd*, a guide to preaching and ministry, identified at least six possible congregation types: first, the 'ignorant and undocible'; secondly, the 'ignorant but willing to be taught'; thirdly, the 'taught but unsanctified, who know much but practice little'; fourthly, 'people having knowledge, and shewing forth the fruits of sanctification' (no doubt a minority!); fifthly, the 'declining, or already fallen back'; and finally, the 'mixed company', who made up the greater part of any congregation.[44]

It is difficult to determine the extent of the lay reading community in early seventeenth-century Ireland – it very much depended on a host of factors, not least actual geographical location.[45] Not all those who could read would be able to write and there were differing levels of fluency.[46] Those who could read were not limited to their own book collections but could augment their supply by borrowing from other lay members and above all from the minister.[47] We need to think in terms of communal libraries and a community of readers. Reading could be a public act – one that was undertaken in a communal setting. This is especially true of reading theology.

Jörg Wickram's lone reader might have been less common than he suggested but there was always the problem that lay members of the church might, in their reading, misinterpret the scriptures and fall into heresy. To counteract this danger strategies were adopted by ministers to deal with possible problems. We must read Ussher's suggestions about avoidance of controversial matters in this context. Ussher was very aware that the ability of members of the laity to read inevitably changed the way they reacted to theology. As Jack Goody has stated in another context: 'literacy encouraged criticism and commentary on the one hand and the orthodoxy of the book on the other.'[48] Direction of reading and interpretation by the minister was essential as was selection of texts that the laity might read. Holdsworth also recognised the importance for the 'amateur' of selection if sense was to be made of the findings while careful choosing of texts might lead the laity away from 'unwary passages' which they might well misinterpret and on to the 'True light of the Gospel.'[49] Ussher certainly approved selection of texts and, indeed, a form of censorship in some cases. His stipulations to Luke Challoner on the need to curtail access to the English popish books in the library of Trinity College, Dublin, by the younger students is symptomatic of this paternalistic trend. Writing in 1612 to Challoner he stated that:

> I would wish those English popish books were kept more privately, as the books of discipline are, in a place by themselves: for it would be somewhat dangerous to have them remain in the public library, and being conveyed thence, they will not so easily be gotten again,[50]

a sentiment he reiterated in 1613.[51] Likewise, his reaction in 1635 to a book by Shelford which had caused an uproar in Ireland illustrates his protective approach to the reading public: 'I pray God this sin be not deeply laid to their charge, who give an occasion to our blind thus to stumble.'[52]

Selection might prove difficult, though, with the proliferation of texts, and so the real emphasis was placed on the minister's role as director and interpreter of reading among the laity. This is why there was such an emphasis on preaching, particularly, of course, among puritan ministers. No less an authority than the Geneva Bible stipulated that in order to truly read Scripture one should: 'Take opportunity to 1. Read interpreters, if he be able; 2. Confer with such as can open the Scriptures; 3. Hear preaching and to prove by the Scripture which is taught.'[53] The last injunction perhaps suggests not only a lay desire to test their minister but also a clerical desire to encourage communal, *directed*, reading of the scriptures. It certainly contrasts with the prohibition in 1579 on reading *private* devotions in church during the sermon.[54]

But not all the community were able to read. John Dod, yet another author approved by Ussher, was highly praised by Clarke because he normally 'took great care to speak to the meanest capacity, and to feed the lambs, saying, he must stoop to the lowest capacity, and if he could reach them, others might help themselves.'[55] His method was to take 'some portion of Scripture in order before him, opening a verse or two, or more at a time, first clearing the drift and connection, then giving the sense and interpretation briefly, but very plainly, not leaving the text until he had made it plain to the meanest capacity.'[56] Preaching was all very well but the most important agent of instruction was the catechism, a fact identified by Melanchthon in his popular *Loci Communes*: 'Rightly oriented teachers are needed . . . to clarify and preserve the proper meaning of the words of the prophets and apostles . . . This should be the purpose of a catechism.'[57] Perhaps the emphasis on catechisms related to their continuity with oral forms and methods of transmitting knowledge. Again and again we find emphasis being laid on the memorisation of either catechism or Bible, though memorisation of the Bible might not be limited to the lower strata of society.[58]

Richard Greenham, one of Ussher's approved authors, delineated the difference between preaching and the use of catechisms:

> Preaching is the dilating of one member of religion into a just treatise: catechising is the contracting of the whole into a sum. Preaching is to all sorts: catechising to the younger and rude. Preaching is not exacted to be repeated: catechising is exacted.[59]

In order to ensure that the laity attended catechetical meetings, meetings above all designed to ensure their orthodoxy, it was declared that a sound catechism meeting was a prerequisite for reception of the sacraments.[60] Catechism, because of its focus on the faith of the individual, was felt to be favourable to sermons for 'at sermons, and prayers, men may sleep and wander; but when one is asked a question, he must discover what he is. This practice exceeds even sermons in teaching . . .'.[61] Ian Green has pointed to the fact that between 1549 and 1646 there were at least 280 different catechetical forms. Catechisms proved to be the great theological best sellers.[62] That Ussher agreed with Richard Bernard's declaration that 'preaching doth little good without catechising' may be deduced from the fact that he too produced a catechism.[63]

Preaching and the catechism were useful aids in directing the reading and interpretations of the laity but it was also necessary for the minister to hold communal meetings in order to ensure orthodoxy. An exemplary communal interpretation that was typical of biblical study within many other parish communities was that of Nicholas Ferrar's at Little Gidding, who taught 'not only the young people, but by the elder sort, and he would even hire the poorer sort, parents as well as children, to this task.'[64] Communal meetings also could be seen by the non-literate members of the community as a continuation of forms of communication with which they were familiar, as oral culture depended on 'a long chain of interlocking conversations between members of the group'.[65] A somewhat ideal situation of communal reading was outlined by Richard Bernard to Ussher in a letter of 26 May 1619:

> I have a very gentlemanlike assembly, and a rich people, and yet, blessed be God, very tractable, sanctifying the Sabbath with reverence. Between morning and evening prayer many come to my house to have the sermon repeated, which divers write, and having their notes corrected, do repeat them after publicly before the congregation, by way of question and answer. I asking the date and ground, then the proofs, with reasons, and after the uses, with motives, and they answer accordingly, which they do very willingly. Besides the catechism questions, and sometimes questions out of a chapter, and all before the second service in the afternoon; and yet for all this variety I avoid tediousness, which keepeth the people constant, who have greatly increased their knowledge beyond that which I am willing to speak.[66]

Ussher was well aware that this task might prove difficult as not all parishioners would be tractable and he suggested that:

> To avoid giving the persons intended to be wrought upon, an alarm before-hand, that their faults, or errors were designed to be attacked; for then the persons concerned, look upon the preacher as an enemy, and set themselves upon their guard. On such occasions he rather recommended the choosing of a text, that stood only upon the borders of the difficult subject; and if it might be, seemed more to favour it; that so the obnoxious hearers, may be rather surprised, and undermined, than stormed, and fought with: And so the preacher, as St Paul expresses it, being crafty, may take them with guile.[67]

Directed communal reading of the scriptures was at the heart of practical divinity. In effect, practical divinity was the implementation in the parish setting of the theoretical knowledge developed in the universities. Much has been made of the minister's social role within the community and the debate on the 'professionalisation' of the ministry tends to focus on the minister's disciplinary role in society, coupled with an analysis of the increasing tendency towards acquisition of a university degree. Eamon Duffy's declaration that 'there might be very much more to catechism than *mere* instruction', is symptomatic of a trend which tends to disregard the function of the minister as instructor. However, this is to ignore the chief function of the ministry as perceived by ministers *themselves* – and the implications of it for the original Lutheran concept of the 'priesthood of all believers', an idea already undermined by Calvin's theory of ministry.[68] Emphasis on leading a Christian life was directly linked to the minister's reputation as a 'godly preacher'. As Ussher said, ministers should 'get your heart sincerely affected with the things you persuade others to embrace, that so you may preach experimentally, and your hearers perceive that you are in good earnest, and press nothing upon them but what may tend to their advantage, and which your self would venture your Salvation on.'[69]

George Downame was certainly not alone in his decision to place the instruction of the ignorant and the reduction of the erroneous at the head of his list of the principal duties of the minister.[70] The chief method of accomplishing this was by preaching and so we find Richard Bernard devoting most of his treatise to the preaching role of the minister. As Patrick Collinson has pointed out, puritan ministers often attempted to suggest that it was the 'sermon' and not solely the reading of scripture, which actually had the power to save.[71] Samuel Hieron, yet another author cited on Ussher's list, went so far as to say that 'it is strongly thought by many, that it were no danger to men's souls, though there were no minister at all to instruct them . . . [yet] ordinarily there is no hope of man's salvation without an able and industrious minister, than there is that the fish of the sea will of itself come ashore.'[72] Anglican ministers were equally anxious to ensure that their parishioners would accept that 'the word is the light, but the Church is the lantern.'[73] The inevitable result of this stance was a perception of a two-tier system, startlingly identified by John Dury in the following terms: 'The ecclesiastical conditions are distinguished also into superiors and inferiors or rather into the pastoral estate, and that of the sheep.'[74]

To conclude, by carefully chanelling the reading patterns among the laity, the minister might just about manage to avoid ruling over a nest of heretics and, in the process, augment the status of his own religious function! In a way we see here another transplantation of the modes of university models of discourse to the parish setting. The minister's sermon acted as the *lectio* – the reading and interpretation of the text – for after all *legere* meant both to read and lecture. However, because of the increased literacy rates the inculcation of doctrine in the community could not stop there – now the minister also had to function as moderator in an abbreviated form of the academic *disputatio* – in an attempt to maintain the cohesive structure of the church. In a sense, the minister could be said to be a mediator between the text and the congregation. In the words of George Downame, another author favoured by Ussher and a member of his friendship circle, the minister was to be 'the mouth of God to his people, and the mouth of the people unto God.'[75] Literacy and ways of reading might enhance the spread both of civility and reformation but it was a two edged sword, which, unless fully understood could eventually prove detrimental to the institutional Reformation.

Notes

1. Thomas Wilson, *A Christian dictionary opening the signification of the chiefe words dispersed generally through holy Scriptures of the Old and New Testament, tending to increase Christian knowledge* (London, 1611), preface.

2. Queen's College, Oxford, MS. 217 ff 41v–42v. This is a copy of Ussher's 'Directions', another version of which may be found in Richard Parr, *The life of the Most Reverend Father in God, James Ussher, late Arch-Bishop of Armagh, Primate and Metropolitan of all Ireland* (London, 1686), pp 87–90.

3. Parr, *Life of Ussher*, p. 87.

4. Queen's College, Oxford, MS. 217, f. 41v.

5. Patrick Collinson, '"The coherence of the text, how it hangeth together", the Bible in Reformation England' in W.P. Stephens (ed.), *The Bible, the Reformation and the Church* (Sheffield, 1995), p. 88.

6. H.F. Fletcher, *The intellectual development of John Milton* (2 vols, Urbana, 1956–61), ii, Appendix 2 contains the 'Directions', p. 639. On the authorship of this document see John A. Trentman, 'The authorship of "Directions for a student in the universitie"' in *Transactions of the Cambridge Bibliographical Society*, vii (1978), pp 171–183.

7. See Holdsworth on theological reading, Fletcher, *Intellectual development*, ii, p. 640.

8. See, for example, Neal Ennsle, 'Patterns of Godly life: the ideal minister in sixteenth and seventeenth century English thought' in *Sixteenth Century Journal*, xxviii, no. 1 (1997), p. 15.

9. Richard Bernard, *The faithfull shepherd: wholly in a manner transposed, and made anew, and very much inlarged both with precepts and examples, to further young Divines in the studie of Divinitie* (London, 1621). Chapter 3 is on the learning necessary for a minister.

10. Anthony Grafton, *Defenders of the text: the traditions of scholarship in an age of science, 1450 – 1800* (Harvard, 1991), p. 25.

11. For an illustration of this see Rivkah Zim, 'The Reformation: the trial of God's Word' in Stephen Prickett (ed.), *Reading the text: biblical criticism and literary theory* (Oxford, 1991), p. 72.

12. On Ramist theories of methodology see W.J. Ong, *Ramus, method and the decay of dialogue* (Harvard, 1983) and Neal W. Gilbert, *Renaissance concepts of method* (New York, 1960).

13. Fletcher, *Milton*, p. 651.

14. Samuel Clarke, *The lives of thirty-two English divines* (London, 1677), pp 121–122.

15. Nicholas Byfield, *Directions for the private reading of the Scriptures* (London, 1626) preface. Interestingly, this work was dedicated to Sir Horace and Lady Mary Vere, who were members of Ussher's friendship circle – see Elizabethanne Boran, 'An early friendship network of James Ussher, archbishop of Armagh' in Helga Robinson-Hammerstein (ed.), *European universities in the age of Reformation and Counter Reformation* (Dublin, 1998), pp 128–129.

16. Queen's College, Oxford, MS. 217, f. 41v.

17. Fletcher, *Milton*, p. 650.

18. Queen's College, Oxford, MS. 217, f. 41v.

19. Parr, *Life of Ussher*, p. 86.

20. Parr, *Life of Ussher*, p. 87.

21. Parr, *Life of Ussher*, p. 88.

22. Parr, *Life of Ussher*, p. 98.

23. Parr, *Life of Ussher*, p. 96.

24. Queen's College, Oxford, MS. 217, f. 42r.

25. Queen's College, Oxford, MS. 217, f. 42v.

26. See Elizabethanne Boran, Libraries and learning: the early history of Trinity College, Dublin from 1592–1641, Ph.D. thesis, T.C.D., 1995.

27. Annabel M. Patterson, *Censorship and interpretation: the conditions of writing and reading in early modern England* (Wisconsin, 1984), p. 7.

28. Stephen Prickett, 'Introduction' in Prickett (ed.) *Reading the text*, p. 1.

29. Zim, 'The Reformation', p. 73.

30. Zim, 'The Reformation', p. 72.

31. Collinson, 'Coherence', p. 105.

32. Zim, 'The Reformation', p. 68.

33. Zim, 'The Reformation', p. 71.

34. Ronald B. Bond (ed.), *'Certain sermons or homilies' (1547) and 'A homily against disobedience and wilful rebellion' (1570)* (Toronto, 1987), p. 65.

35. Gerald Strauss, 'Techniques of indoctrination: the German Reformation' in Harvey. J. Graff (ed.), *Literacy and social*

development in the West: a reader (Cambridge, 1981), pp 321–322.

36. See, for example, Gerald Bray, *Biblical interpretation, past and present* (Leicester, 1996), p. 192.

37. Zim, 'The Reformation', p. 71.

38. Thomas Wilson, *Dictionary*, preface.

39. Cited in Richard Gawthrop and Gerald Strauss, 'Protestantism and literacy in early modern Germany' in *Past and Present*, no. 104 (1984), p. 35.

40. Gawthrop and Strauss, 'Protestantism', p. 35.

41. Gawthrop and Strauss, 'Protestantism', p. 38.

42. Keith Thomas, 'The meaning of literacy in early modern England' in Gerd Baumann (ed.), *The written word: literacy in transition* (Oxford, 1986), p. 105.

43. Patrick Collinson, 'Lectures by combination: structures and characteristics of church life in seventeenth-century England' in Patrick Collinson (ed.), *Godly people: essays on English Protestantism and Puritanism* (London, 1983), pp 467–498. On the broader issue of the professionalisation of the ministry see Rosemary O'Day, *The English clergy: the emergence and consolidation of a profession, 1558 – 1642* (Leicester, 1979) and Michael Hawkins, 'Ambiguity and contradiction in the "rise of professionalism": the English clergy, 1570–1730' in A.L. Beier (ed.), *The first modern society* (Cambridge, 1989), pp 241–270.

44. Bernard, *Faithfull Shepherd*, p. 99.

45. See Raymond Gillespie, 'The book trade in southern Ireland, 1590–1640' in Gerard Long (ed.), *Books beyond the Pale: aspects of the provincial book trade in Ireland before 1850* (Dublin, 1996), pp 1–18.

46. Margaret Spufford, 'First steps in literacy: the reading and writing experiences of the humblest seventeenth-century spiritual autobiographers' in *Social History*, iv, no. 3 (1979), pp 407–435.

47. For a discussion of book-borrowing habits see Elizabethanne Boran, 'The libraries of Luke Challoner and James Ussher, 1595–1608' in Robinson-Hammerstein (ed.), *European universities*, pp 109–115.

48. Jack Goody, *The domestication of the savage mind* (Cambridge, 1977), p. 37.

49. Fletcher, *Milton*, p. 649.

50. C.R. Elrington (ed.), *The whole works of the most Reverend James Ussher D.D.* (17 vols, Dublin, 1864), xvi, p. 319.

51. Ussher, *Works*, xv, p. 74.

52. Ussher, *Works*, xvi, p. 9.

53. Zim, 'The Reformation', p. 72.

54. Patrick Collinson, 'Shepherds, sheepdogs, and hirelings: the pastoral ministry in post-Reformation England' in W.J. Sheils, and Diane Wood (eds), *The ministry, clerical and lay: studies in church history, xxvi* (Oxford, 1989), p. 193.

55. Clarke, *Lives*, p. 176.

56. Clarke, *Lives*, p. 176.

57. Gawthrop and Strauss, 'Literacy', p. 43.

58. Collinson, 'Coherence', p. 91.

59. Enssle, 'Pattern of Godly life', p. 22.

60. Enssle, 'Pattern of Godly life', p. 23.

61. Enssle, 'Pattern of Godly life', p. 24.

62. Ian Green, '"For children in yeeres and children in understanding": the emergence of the English catechism under Elizabeth I and the early Stuarts' in *Journal of Ecclesiastical History*, xxxvii (1986), p. 400.

63. Collinson, 'Shepherds', p. 201.

64. Collinson, 'Coherence', p. 91.

65. Jack Goody and Ian Watt, 'The consequences of literacy' in *Comparative Studies in Society and History*, v (1962–63), p. 306.

66. Ussher, *Works*, xvi, p. 360.

67. Parr, *Life of Ussher*, p. 89.

68. Eamon Duffy, 'The long Reformation : Catholicism, Protestantism and the multitude' in Nicholas Tyacke (ed.), *England's long Reformation, 1500–1800* (London, 1998), p. 44 (my italics). For a similar reaction see Ennsle, 'Patterns of Godly life', p. 18, who defines the primary function of the minister as leading the congregation in prayer, though his sources appear to contradict his view. For an alternative view see Ian Green, 'Reformed Pastor and Bon Curés: the changing role of the parish clergy in early modern Europe' in Sheils and Wood (eds), *The ministry*, pp 249–286. He is, however, rather tentative about the role of the ministry as a mediator between the Bible and the laity – see page 284. For a discussion of Calvin's ideas about ministry see George Yule, 'Calvin's view of the ministry of the church' in Sheils and Wood (eds.), *The ministry*, pp 167–177.

69. Parr, *Life of Ussher*, p. 88.
70. Ennsle, 'Pattern of Godly life', p. 3.
71. Collinson, 'Coherence', p. 107.
72. Samuel Hieron, *Spirituall fishing* (London, 1618), p. 17.
73. Zim, 'The Reformation', p. 71.
74. T.C.D., MS. 294, f. 91r.
75. George Downame, *Two sermons; the one commending the ministrie in general : the other defending the office of bishop in particular* (London, 1608), pp 15–16.

Reading in eighteenth-century Ireland: public and private pleasures

Toby Barnard

EARLY IN 1735 A COUPLE WERE sitting on either side of their chimney-piece in their elegant Dublin house. While their children played around them, a servant fiddled with the window curtains. The parents were reading. In the absence of painted conversation pieces throughout much of eighteenth-century Ireland this word picture, conveyed in a letter, offers a rare glimpse into a domestic interior. It is a scene in which we learn incidentally that reading is taking place.[1] Unfortunately, as so often with evidence, it conceals as much as it tells. Is the husband reading aloud to his wife; or *vice versa*? Is each reading separately and silently? Or is it only the man who is thus engaged, as befitted a professional – a bishop – whose calling depended on mastery of sacred writings? His wife may conform to a gender stereotype, listening while about another task, such as embroidery or sewing. We do not know, and our ignorance reminds of problems which crowd around the subjects of print and literacy.

Thanks to the heroic researches of pioneers like Ronnie Adams, Paul Pollard and Hugh Fenning, much is now known about books in eighteenth-century Ireland: how many were printed first in Dublin and then in provincial towns; how many were imported; and who owned what.[2] But these welcome increases in knowledge darken the shadows which envelop the daily practices of reading. Often, in default of testimony from Ireland itself, there has been an understandable tendency to transpose to Irish conditions findings and hypotheses from elsewhere. One quandary is over the extent to which eighteenth-century Irish book owners and readers slavishly reproduced or deviated strongly from patterns which have been reconstructed in Britain, North America or continental Europe. The arguments have relied less on empirical data, which is sparse, than on prior assumptions about the nature of Ireland's societies. Some regard the chief characteristic of Ireland as its remoteness, so that, like other distant provinces, it lagged behind but happily imitated fashionable metropolises. Others insist on Ireland's status as a colony, with the attendant cultural and economic subjection. On balance, researches into the uses of print in Anglophone Ireland place it most plausibly among provincial societies.[3]

One type of evidence can rescue any enquiry into the prevalence and functions of reading from aimless impressionism. Educational opportunities expanded. Thanks to corporate, philanthropic and private schemes, schooling became more generally available in the towns of early eighteenth-century Ireland.[4] Little if any of it was truly free. Access remained restricted, albeit less restricted than it had been a century earlier. This more abundant schooling connects with another variety of evidence: that for functional literacy. The hazards of counting signatures and deducing from them proportions of the literate are now notorious, as once the counting of manors entranced economic historians. Yet, the dangers notwithstanding, Irish findings allow some trends to be discerned. Dangerously small samples from Dublin in the 1690s and the city of Waterford in the following century reveal high literacy among the middling sort – petty functionaries, skilled craft-workers and modest traders and their sons.[5] A picture emerges, disconcertingly hazy in many details, which corresponds with what investigations into other European groups might lead us to expect: a widening gap between the *menu peuple* in the larger towns and their equivalents in the countryside. Among the civic elite of the Cavan borough of Belturbet in the early 1680s, almost half could not sign their names. Still in the 1750s, among some who served as churchwardens in a county Meath parish, this basic attribute was wanting. If literacy was indeed permeating the modestly circumstanced in the towns, then the growth of locally produced print becomes more comprehensible. It links with the new success of printed newspapers, first in Dublin, but soon in the provinces.[6] It can also be detected in the subscription lists for productions such as Laurence Whyte's *Poems* of 1740 or William Starrat's treatise on ballistics of 1733.[7] Whyte's *Poems* appealed, as the subscribers reveal, not just to the endangered Catholic gentry of the Pale. Fully a third of the subscribers whose occupational designations are disclosed were drawn from the professionals, merchants and skilled of the towns, particularly Dublin. Moreover, writers, including Whyte, catered to tastes other than those of the landed elites.[8]

Evidence of this kind implies the existence of numerous readers in the bigger Irish towns. The consequences of such a readership could be large. They may, for example, make it plausible to apply, to later eighteenth-century Ireland, the hypothesis of Habermas.[9] The increase in a powerful and literate bourgeoisie cherished a distinctive culture of print, which in turn opposed and subverted the state, first by criticising and then replacing it. Traces of such developments have already been unearthed. David Dickson's model analysis of the many editions of Paine's *Rights of Man* between 1791 and 1798 showed how widely this critique circulated.[10] More generally, J. S. Donnelly and Kevin Whelan have argued for the role of print in the processes of political mobilisation and radicalisation in George III's reign, assisting in the creation of the vibrant 'republic in the village'.[11] Just how new these movements were would be worth pondering. A bookish culture certainly existed in the Dublin of the 1720s and 1740s, perhaps even in the 1670s and 1690s.[12] Without it, the pamphlet controversies would hardly have erupted. Locals contributed as authors, printers, publishers and readers. Views critical of the English state in Ireland were stridently voiced. Also, the inventiveness of the satires and invectives entertained. In 1749, the Speaker of the Irish house of commons conceded of the current demagogue, Charles Lucas, 'sure it is that he is a very devil of a fellow, and writes well'.[13] Others sought the latest additions to the debate. Pamphleteers, Lucas among them, borrowed heavily, in terms and techniques, from contemporary England. If the impact of the squibs owed much to the artifices of their authors, it depended too on the presence of an alert audience. Titles multiplied. Often, as Speaker Boyle's response showed, they diverted. Too frequently, perhaps, it is the energising and even revolutionary effect of print which is emphasised. It could also sedate by spreading traditional ideas further through the provinces.[14]

Another type of evidence has long exerted a seductive fascination: subscription and library lists. It is well known that simply because a particular book was subscribed for or is listed on the shelves of an Anglesey, Ormonde or Orrery, it was not necessarily read.[15] It is always tempting to trace ideas back to a specific text. Thus, during the 1650s when the future earl of Orrery was striving to construct a Cromwellian monarchy, he demanded from Munster his copy of Machiavelli.[16] Those who analyse the theory rather than the practice of English colonisation and government in Ireland are frequently persuaded to attribute innovations in official policy to individual authors.[17] The difficulty is that past readers seldom tell in any helpful detail how they responded to their books. When comments have more than a telegraphic brevity, they follow conventions now hard to penetrate. Even those who digested their reading into commonplace books rarely spell out their reasonings. The Kennedys, presbyterian ministers in county Tyrone in the late seventeenth and early eighteenth centuries, abstracted an impressive assortment of works on history, medicine, theology and science. How much they selected from Robert Boyle, Isaac Newton, William King or Richard Cox (and many others), and what they misunderstood or reinterpreted will be clarified only after a minute analysis of their extensive notes.[18]

More casual reactions, dashed off in letters, are constrained by the formulae of letter-writing. The polite and polished learnt from their masters and mistresses or from manuals how to express themselves. The personal was as a result inevitably subordinated to a standardised approach. In addition, the vocabulary of evaluation was terse. It hardly permitted many nuances in individual opinions. Popular texts, in any case, were to be understood in approved ways. Not only did novices have to be taught how to read; they had also to be instructed as to how to receive the proper message from what they so laboriously deciphered. The pedagogic tyranny which could attach to reading is well illustrated in the letters of Bishop Synge of Elphin to his daughter. Time and again she is required to elaborate and explain her views on fictional characters. First her orthography, punctuation and grammar are corrected; but then too the moral conclusions which she draws from her reading have to be amended.[19]

Reading instilled more than a useful skill. Properly employed it possessed a moral value. Since right principles and perceptions of creation were conveyed through books, they had to be regulated and restricted. At the most extreme, they might be censored. The clergy, Protestant no less than Catholic, were chary about giving an ignorant laity unfettered access to holy writ. In this spirit, the Synod of Ulster in 1747 advised 'unlearned men not to read erroneous books'. Instead they must confine their attention to the 'sacred scriptures, and such practical sound writings as by divine blessing may be of use to fill their hearts with grace and not their heads with vain disputes or dangerous errors'. Faced with the spread of what were regarded as heretical notions, the custodians of ortho-doxy concluded that 'putting erroneous books into the hands of unlearned men' was tantamount to 'putting swords into the hands of children, who know not how to use them'.[20] Some-thing of the same discrimination between what the learned and unlearned might safely read is found in the dynasty of the Presbyterian Kennedys. The men of the family, doctors and divines, ranged freely across available print. Not only did they read new publications which publicised discoveries in and speculations about the natural world, they paraphrased what Arians and deists were writing. But to their own servants, they supplied only Bibles.[21]

The worries revealed by the devout should caution against assuming too blindly that the seventeenth- and eighteenth-century emphases on improvement through education meant that written and printed tools were to be given to all. Contrary testimony is supplied by the admittedly wayward Charles Vallancey. Early in the nineteenth century he bemoaned the inaccessibility of texts through which the puzzles about ancient Ireland might be solved. They were, he alleged, 'imprisoned for ever . . . in the manuscript closet of Trinity College'. There, he feared, they would never be perused.[22] No doubt Vallancey had hit on an extreme case. Even so, it illus-trated how enthusiasm for unrestricted reading might be tempered. In eighteenth-century Ireland, many materials were controversial and potentially inflammatory. Even maps which recorded the old and supplanted owners were felt to sustain the grievances of the dispossessed and could, in time, assist them to restoration. Trinity College since the 1740s housed the bound volumes of depositions relating to the 1641 uprising and supposed massacres.[23] At least in purpose-built libraries, documents could be restricted to approved readers.[24] Despite the craze in the late seventeenth and eighteenth centuries for the establishment of 'public' libraries, which spread into Ireland, these were mainly created and endowed by the clergy for the edification of their fellow clerics. Access among the laity was carefully supervised. Furthermore, the contents of the collections were vetted. In practice, however, all donations seem to have been received gratefully. As a result, collections formed serendipitously took whatever was offered, even when it might undermine orthodoxy. [25]

The guardians of literate mysteries turned print and reading to their own ends. In the church, law and medicine, the adepts and initiates alone could fully expound the principal texts.[26] Many of them were still locked in strange tongues and bizarre scripts, such as the court hand of numerous legal instruments. The professions were powerful in Protestant Ireland, as they had been in Gaelic and Old English society. Their power elicited contradictory responses. Professional services were needed. Moreover, the professions offered livelihoods to the prolific cadets of the new landed order. But the professionals were firm in upholding their monopolies. Their ability to do so depended on their unique command of the hermetic texts. Each of these callings was angrily denounced by those who had to buy the services of professionals.[27] The latter contended that they alone had the skill to interpret and read correctly. But not the least of the reasons why their pretensions were being questioned was the way in which print brought technical knowledge to those outside the learned professions. The laity were to be provided not only with cheap Bibles, but devotional tracts which would lead the unskilled through the scriptural maze. Many of these manuals were penned by clergymen, whose wish to maintain their power as sole expositors was modified by the belief that the means of salvation should be available to all.[28] Similarly, digests and *vade-mecums* offered to turn each owner into his own lawyer. As early as the seventeenth century, the ubiquitous almanacs printed information which helped the purchaser to act as attorney, apothecary, surveyor or farrier. Since almanacs varied in price from 3*d.* to 2*s.*1*d.*, they differed both in bulk and in the sorts of information which they furnished.[29] Comparable differences separated handy compilations from bulky disquisitions which told of the law as it related to the offices of justice of the peace and sheriff or in relation to tenants and servants. Learning acquired from such books seldom altogether cut out the costly specialist. Conscientious squires when entering into the magistracy or shrievalty might buy the relevant publications.[30] However, they continued to be directed towards their judgements by the assize judges or the legally qualified clerks of the crown and peace who sat in court with them. In the same manner, landowners feed their own lawyers and surveyors. The availability of the printed tracts – theological, medical or legal – allowed amateurs to discern how they were being gulled. Antipathy towards the incompetent, dishonest or negligent worsened, but few could dispense with the costly services of the professionals.

Such informed critiques arose from the purchase and study of costly publications, and so remained the preserve of the elites. But in other ways, print and number percolated through everyday life, especially in the towns. Houses came to be numbered, streets named and directions or mileages signposted. Also, fees and charges were tabulated and displayed in offices. Posters advertised lands for sale and lodgings to rent. Lottery tickets were numbered and printed; so too were bills and receipts. In 1757, a 'publication posted on the church door at Ballynaboy' announced a campaign to withhold tithes.[31] These uses, even for sedition, gave the literate an advantage. Yet, as has so often been stressed, it required only one reader within a household or neighbourhood to tell the message on the placards. In such a situation, the skill might be misused, and even impostures attempted. Power reposed both in the evidences themselves and in the ability to decipher them. Little, wonder, then, that the Dublin gentleman, Benjamin Parry, possessed of property in the city and in distant Armagh, specified the fate of all the papers and manuscripts which related to his estate, 'which I desire may be kept safe for the use of such as may in time have occasion for them'.[32] Canny landowners, from the first earl of Cork in the early seventeenth century to the Galway lawyer, Patrick French of Monivea, during the 1730s scooped up parchments offered to them by locals, since they could then employ experts to interpret the documents.[33] Just how they might back land claims and intimidate rivals was shown by an early seventeenth-century settler in county Roscommon, Anthony Brabazon. He gained control of writings which an adversary had supposed to be in safe custody. Brabazon then took advantage of an Irish rival, who, it was said, 'was simple and illiterate and well stricken in years'. For Brabazon possessing the evidences and then having them decoded enhanced his standing as 'a powerful and potent man in the said province'.[34] Later, during a land dispute in county Limerick in the 1730s, Standish O'Grady overawed the occupiers by entering their cabins and there reading from papers. 'The poor people being frightened could not give any account of what it was.'[35] This powerlessness may speak simply of the illiteracy of the cabin-dwellers or of the legal mumbo-jumbo which was spouted at them. Here, as elsewhere, reading aloud refined or redefined relationships. Some were equal, as pleasure and information were shared for their own sakes: others unequal, when husbands read to wives and children, mistresses to servants, clergy to congregations or agents to tenants. On occasion the haltingly literate would confess their inadequacies. In 1753, for example, an Irishman in France wrote to a Kerry notable with apologies for his ignorance of the English tongue and its orthography.[36]

If those who read aloud to others wielded a valuable power, they also helped to dissolve any rigid demarcation between 'modern' literate culture and customary oral traditions. They also raise questions about whether reading was typically a private or public activity. Reading aloud occurred in many settings, including the house. The lack of painted and posed conversation pieces denies us the images in which the casual recourse to books might be captured.[37] Sometimes portraits of prelates place them in front of books on shelves, much like the props in early photographers' studios. Here too is a formula. The manner in which the tomes are arranged, the gold-stamped spines towards the viewer, accurately represents how these collections were organised.[38] This seemingly trivial matter of storage and display may recover altering attitudes to the book both as object and as source of pleasure and enlightenment. Few, even in eighteenth-century Ireland, had rooms designated as libraries. The most precocious seems to have been that of Bishop Thomas Rundle of Derry in his house on St Stephen's Green in Dublin in the later 1730s. Rundle was soon followed by the Delanys at Delville. These were spaces dedicated as much to society and conversation as to silent study.[39] The books catered to conviviality. Owners whose livelihoods were bound up with print, notably lawyers and clergy, kept their working collections more commonly in closets. How much they opened their shelves to others varied. Some, indeed, distinguished between the arcane reserved for their own instruction and those which might be left in communal spaces. On the one hand, Bishop Robert Howard in his mansion at Elphin provided volumes from which visitors, including country parsons, could profit. In contrast, a county Down squire, Samuel Waring, absent in Dublin in the 1720s, was outraged to hear the neighbours had been making free with the contents of his book closet which he had supposed was locked.[40]

Most book owners numbered their collections in tens rather than hundreds, many of them flimsy and ephemeral. For most, plain shelves sufficed. Sometimes they were located in bed-chambers, so implying a solitary recreation.[41] But caution is needed before deducing too much. In the cramped houses of the seventeenth and eighteenth centuries, bed chambers were often shared or doubled for diurnal functions. Even books kept in this sanctum might nevertheless be read aloud. More usual was the placing of the shelves in rooms where all members of the family and their guests mingled. The probability of shared access is increased by the nature of requests for loans. Visitors remembered what they had spotted when with their acquaintances. In 1721, a letter-writer asked a correspondent if he might borrow a copy of a history of the Council of Trent which he had seen in the latter's house. The volume was sought as a means of whiling away the long winter west of the Shannon.[42] A clergyman at Hillsborough in the 1720s entreated a brother in London to supply books. The cleric's tastes were catholic: the *History of*

Ireland by Anthony Raymond, 'the art of contentment' by Allestree or 'travels and sea journeys into the remoter parts of the world' would please. Alternatively, the gift of a London watch would give equal satisfaction.[43] Particularly for those facing long periods alone or in uncongenial company, reading was a boon. A garrison officer quartered in the west in 1739-40 set himself an intensive course of reading rather than join in the customary military pastimes of drinking and brawling.[44]

At the same time, in county Limerick, an agent on the fringes of the local gentry noted the many days which he passed at home in reading. Sometimes it was varied by walking as well. This reader, Nicholas Peacock, still a bachelor, maintained a modest establishment in which his servants or 'family' were probably confessionally, ethnically and maybe linguistically distinct from him. Tantalisingly only once does he name what he was reading: a Spanish romance, presumably in translation.[45] His recorded purchases, such as three books for 1s. 9d. from the auction of the effects of a former employer, an almanac for 3d., the 'news' for 1d., or parcels from the nearby Limerick printer, are untitled.[46] It is tempting to deduce from the greater frequency with which he mentioned reading in 1744 and 1745 signs of heightened apprehensions about possible foreign invasion or domestic insurrection. Peacock was buying newspapers in Limerick city, presumably to keep abreast of distant events.[47] Later in the decade, now married and with children, he referred to his reading less frequently. However, it did not vanish from his life. But once again we are left to puzzle whether it entailed a reversion to the solitude of his bachelor years or now meant reading aloud to his wife and children. The size and disposition of his house hardly permitted privacy. Peacock belonged to a circuit on which he regularly met squires, gentlemen, petty functionaries, farmers and tradespeople. Through these encounters, the news that he had read would be constantly updated and modified. More rumours and reports were picked up from the quays, taverns and shops of Limerick city.

For those anxious for topical information or simple diversion, letters often sufficed. The isolated pleaded with friends for regular correspondence. Some took the unwillingness of acquaintances to keep up epistolary contact as a slight. From

Dingle in 1715 came a request for this kind of entertainment: 'your pen would be as diverting to me as a novel and the weekly packet equal in a manner to a history'.[48] A similarly circumstanced inhabitant of county Kerry in 1737 appealed to a former neighbour now on his travels for the favour of even occasional letters. Thus he confided, 'I employ myself, I may rather say divert myself, with reading, and be assured there is nothing I can read would relish more agreeably than a line which comes from a friend I love.'[49] Expectations like this created their own conventions among correspondents, so strengthening the belief that letter-writing was an art which had carefully to be studied. The personal missive continued to be valued. The busy man, close to a centre of power yet willing to take time to write to country connections, conferred a particular boon. Such a letter was appreciated as much as evidence of esteem as for its news.[50]

By the early eighteenth century, an alternative supplemented but did not completely supplant the more personal communication. Newspapers featured in the purchases, and so presumably in the reading, of Peacock in the 1740s. These publications even when printed in Ireland notoriously were bulked out with foreign and British tidings. Other than advertisements they contained little specific to Ireland. Something more solid than heresay and rumour was easily sought. During the reign of Charles II, at least two Munster boroughs paid to have the news sent regularly. Probably it arrived in the shape of manuscript 'separates' produced in Dublin as multiples. Just how these 'publications' were then circulated remains unclear. Maybe they were kept in central and public locations, such as a tavern or council room.[51] By the early eighteenth century, the desire for regular news is attested by the subscriptions paid to stationers or printers in Dublin who undertook to furnish named journals, English as well as Irish.[52] The demand now sustained the continuous production of several titles, first in Dublin and then in provincial towns. Access to newspapers enabled their subscribers to lord it over neighbours. Being first with the news helped to put a distinctive imprint on it. The well-connected reported what they had read, whether in the public prints or their private correspondence. In time, back-numbers were handed on to subordinates, as Archbishop King's butler did to the librarian, Bouhéreau. This favour created fresh obligations. At Lismore in the early eighteenth century, the agents of the absent earls of Cork and Burlington valued the editions of London papers provided by a considerate employer. When, in 1706, Lady Burlington, bent on one of the footling economies favoured by the very rich, proposed to cancel the subscriptions, the protests of the agents persuaded her to relent. Thanks to the annual expenditure of three guineas these functionaries, important already in their own rights as squires and by virtue of their positions, had their power as mediators with 'the gentlemen of Lismore' enlarged.[53] Through first conning the newspapers from England, they argued that they could then shape opinion and reactions in the county Waterford borough. In arguing thus, they no doubt exaggerated. Others in the vicinity had the same or alternative sources of information. Rival versions of events could therefore take hold.

The popularity of newspapers, together with their survival, owed much to the lengthening columns of advertisements which they printed. Already specialists have scanned them to document the greater range of services and commodities in Hanoverian Ireland.[54] Novelties in diet, utensils and furnishings when read about were desired, especially if puffed outrageously as the latest from England, France or more exotic spots. In order to cope with this bewildering world of goods a fresh and complicated vocabulary had to be learnt. Shopping was added to the favours expected by country cousins of kinsfolk, acquaintances and neighbours when in Dublin or England. It caused embarrassments and misunderstandings as the novice struggled for the right words to denote what was wanted. Whether it was an equipage with which to brew the still unfamiliar tea, a desirable wig, hat or shoes or a variety of cloth, requests had to be verbalised. The advertisements which were read in the newspapers simultaneously engendered desire to possess the goods and words in which they could be described. However, what was learnt from the press made less impact than what was seen in the houses of others or was spoken of by visitors who had themselves encountered the commodities.[55] So, once more, the silent act of reading merged into reading aloud, conversation and the concrete world of objects.[56] Even so, those who paid to advertise houses, lands, horses or desirable imports would hardly have done so had they not expected the notices to be read by would-be customers. Since print itself, including the regular newspapers, belonged to the quickening pattern of consumption, subscribers to diurnals could be expected to rise to the baits of the advertisement. However, some notices inserted into the papers looked to a different readership. In 1744, recruits were sought for a regiment by means of advertisements in Belfast and Dublin journals. Farriers and smiths were among those needed.[57] Appeals of this type again collapse any rigid barrier between orality and literacy. As with the handbills posted in public places, so these newspaper displays were likely to be brought to the attention of the interested as much by word of mouth as by reading for oneself. Whether at home, in tavern or coffee-house, the printed contents of the papers would be shared. So much could be safely assumed by the authorities who went to the expense of placing such advertisements. Substantial sections of the middling and lower orders either could read themselves or were in touch with those who could do so.

Notes

1. R. Howard to H. Howard, 23 Jan. 1735, N.L.I., PC 227.

2. J.R.R. Adams, *The printed word and the common man: popular culture in Ulster, 1700–1900* (Belfast, 1987); Hugh Fenning, 'Cork imprints of Catholic interest, 1723–84: a provisional checklist' in *Journal of the Cork Historical and Archaeological Society*, c (1995), pp 129–148; Hugh Fenning, 'The Catholic press in Munster in the eighteenth century' in Gerard Long (ed.), *Books beyond the Pale: aspects of the provincial book trade in Ireland before 1850* (Dublin, 1996), pp 19–32; M. Pollard, *Dublin's trade in books, 1550–1800* (Oxford, 1989). A wide-ranging recent survey is Raymond Gillespie, 'The circulation of print in seventeenth-century Ireland' in *Studia Hibernica*, xxix (1995–7), pp 31–58.

3. The most accessible introduction to the situation elsewhere in Europe remains R.A. Houston, *Literacy in early modern Europe: culture and education, 1500–1800* (London, 1988). For Ireland, the most sophisticated analysis is now, Niall Ó Ciosáin, *Print and popular culture in Ireland, 1750–1850* (Basingstoke, 1997).

4. T.C. Barnard, 'Protestants and the Irish language, c. 1675–1725' in *Journal of Ecclesiastical History*, xliv (1993), pp 243–272; D. W. Hayton, 'Did Protestantism fail in early eighteenth-century Ireland? Charity schools and the enterprise of religious and social reformation, c. 1690–1730' in Alan Ford, James McGuire and Kenneth Milne (eds), *As by law established: the Church of Ireland since the Reformation* (Dublin, 1995), pp 166–186; Kenneth Milne, *The Irish Charter schools, 1730–1830* (Dublin, 1997).

5. These findings are summarised in Toby Barnard, 'Learning, the learned and literacy in Ireland, c. 1660–1760, in Toby Barnard, Dáibhí Ó Cróinín, and Katharine Simms (eds), *'A miracle of learning'; studies in manuscripts and Irish learning* (Aldershot, 1998), pp 219–221.

6. Robert Munter, *The history of the Irish newspaper, 1685–1760* (Cambridge, 1967).

7. William Starrat, *The doctrine of projectiles* (Dublin, 1733); Laurence Whyte, *Poems on various subjects, serious and diverting* (Dublin, 1740).

8. T.C. Barnard, 'The gentrification of eighteenth-century Ireland' in *Eighteenth-century Ireland*, xii (1997), pp 137–155; cf. Kevin Whelan 'An underground gentry' in Kevin Whelan, *The tree of liberty* (Cork, 1996), pp 19–20.

9. J. Habermas, *The structural transformation of the public sphere*, tr. T. Burger (Cambridge, 1989); C. Calhoun (ed.), *Habermas and the public sphere* (Cambridge, Mass, 1992).

10. David Dickson, 'Paine and Ireland' in David Dickson, Dáire Keogh and Kevin Whelan (eds), *The United Irishmen* (Dublin, 1993), pp 135–150.

11. J.S. Donnelly, 'Irish agrarian rebellion: the Whiteboys of 1769–1776' in *Proceedings of the Royal Irish Academy*, sect. C, lxxxiii (1983), pp 293–331; Kevin Whelan, 'The republic of the village' in Whelan, *The tree of liberty*, pp 59–98. Another version of Whelan's essay is published in Long (ed.), *Books beyond the Pale*, pp 101–140.

12. On the eighteenth-century controversies see J.G. McCoy, Local political culture in the Hanoverian empire: the case of Ireland, 1714–1760, unpublished D. Phil. dissertation, Oxford, 1994; Patrick McNally, *Parties, patriots and undertakers: parliamentary politics in early Hanoverian Ireland* (Dublin, 1997). For earlier manifestations see T.C. Barnard, 'Conclusion: settling and unsettling Ireland: the Cromwellian and Williamite revolutions' in J.H. Ohlmeyer (ed.), *Ireland from independence to occupation, 1641–1660* (Cambridge, 1995), pp 272–277. P.H. Kelly, 'The Irish woollen export prohibition act of 1699: Kearney revisited' in *Irish Economic and Social History*, vii (1980), pp 22–44.

13. H. Boyle to M. Crosbie, 23 March 1749, N.L.I., Talbot-Crosbie MSS, folder 46.

14. Niall Ó Ciosáin, 'Printing in Irish and Ó Súilleabháin's *Pious Miscellany*', in Long (ed.), *Books beyond the Pale*, pp 87–99.

15. Anglesey's library: *Bibliotheca Anglesiana* (London, 1686); Ormonde's: P.R.O., FEC.1/877; Historical Mss. Commission, *Ormonde Mss*, new ser., vii, pp 513–527; Orrery's: Petworth House, West Sussex, Orrery MSS, general series, 14.

16. T.C. Barnard, 'The Protestant Interest, 1641–1660' in Ohlmeyer (ed.), *Ireland: from independence to occupation*, p. 235.

17. Brendan Bradshaw, 'Sword, word and strategy in the Reformation in Ireland' in *Historical Journal*, xxi (1978), pp 475–502; Ciaran Brady, *The chief governors: the rise and fall of reform government in Tudor Ireland, 1536–1588* (Cambridge, 1994), p. 297.

18. Three notebooks in Presbyterian Historical Society Library, Belfast, tin box, labelled 'PA 48'.

19. Marie-Louise Legg (ed.), *The Synge letters: Bishop Edward Synge to his daughter, Alicia, Roscommon to Dublin, 1746–52* (Dublin, 1996).

20. *Records of the General Synod of Ulster* (3 vols, Belfast, 1897), ii, p. 330.

21. J. Kennedy notebooks, Presbyterian Historical Society, PA 48.

22. Charles Vallancey, *An account of the ancient stone amphitheatre lately discovered in the county of Kerry* (Dublin, 1812), pp 25–29.

23. William O'Sullivan, 'The eighteenth-century rebinding of the manuscripts' in *Long Room*, i (1970), pp 21, 28; Aidan Clarke, 'The 1641 depositions' in Peter Fox (ed.), *Treasures of the library, Trinity College Dublin* (Dublin, 1986), p. 112.

24. Loans book, library, T.C.D., MS. 2089.

25. See, for example, the contents of the library of the Green Coat School in Cork, recorded in [H. Maule], *Pietas Corcagiensis* (Cork, 1721), and the marks of ownership in the surviving books from the vestry of St Luke's Cork, now in Boole Library, N.U.I. Cork.

26. This theme is explored in Penelope Corfield, *Power and the professions in Britain, 1700–1850* (London, 1995).

27. Alexander the Coppersmith, *Remarks upon the religion, trade, government, police, customs, manners and maladys of the city of Corke* (Cork, 1737), pp 34–49.

28. T.C. Barnard, 'Reforming Irish manners: the religious societies in Dublin during the 1690s' in *Historical Journal*, xxxv (1992), pp 805–838; Barnard, 'Protestants and the Irish language', pp 243–272; Scott Mandelbrote, 'John Baskett, the Dublin booksellers and the printing of the Bible, 1710–1724', in A. Hunt, G. Mandelbrote and A. Shell (eds), *The book trade and its customers* (Winchester, 1997), pp 115–131.

29. Accounts of Richard Edgeworth, 14 Feb. 1735, 14 Dec. 1741, 9 Aug. 1744, 18 Dec. 1745, N.L.I. MSS, 1511, 1515, 1516; Journal of Nicholas Peacock, 28 Dec. 1743, 2 Jan. 1747, 12 Feb. 1749, 21 Dec. 1750, N.L.I., MS. 16901.

30. Robert Southwell to T. Southwell, 13 Dec. 1662, Boole Library, N.U.I. Cork, Kinsale manorial papers, 1662–65; accounts of R. Edgeworth, 3. Dec. 1737, N.L.I., MS. 1512.

31. Barnard, 'Learning, the learned and literacy', pp 217–219.

32. Will of Benjamin Parry, 6 Sep. 1734, National Library of Wales, Puleston deeds.

33. R. Cox to R. Southwell, 20 Oct. 1688, B. L., Additional MS. 38153, f. 5; T.C. Barnard, 'The worlds of a Galway squire: Robert French of Monivea' in Gerard Moran (ed.), *Galway: history and society* (Dublin, 1996), pp 273–274.

34. Salvaged chancery bills, N.A.I., CP.F, p. 6.

35. Powell to Lord CastleDurrow, 2 June 1732, N.L.I., MS. 11479.

36. C. O Scanlan to M. Crosbie, 19 May 1753, N.L.I., Talbot-Crosbie, MSS, folder 40.

37. Anne Crookshank, 'The conversation piece in Irish painting in the eighteenth century' in Agnes Bernelle (ed.), *Decantations: a tribute to Maurice Craig* (Dublin, 1992), pp 16–20.

38. Portraits of this type are reproduced in Legg (ed.), *The Synge letters*, p. 94 (of Archbishop Synge of Tuam); in C. Saumarez Smith, *Eighteenth-century decoration: design and the domestic interior in England* (London, 1993), plate 66 (erroneously said to be the Irish philosopher, Francis Hutcheson); and in Anne Crookshank and D.A. Webb, *Paintings and sculptures in Trinity College Dublin* (Dublin, 1990), p. 79. For the genre, J. Ingamells, *The English episcopal portrait, 1559–1835* ([London], c. 1981).

39. Barnard, 'Learning, the learned and literacy', pp 215–217.

40. Note by Samuel Waring on letter of E. Fitzsimmons to him, 21 June 1729, Private collection, county Down; Barnard, 'Learning, the learned and literacy', pp 209–210.

41. Effects of Sir. P. Perceval, 3. Nov. 1680, B.L., Add. MS. 47037, f. 20v.

42. M. Keon to A. Vesey, 5. Oct. 1721, N.A.I., Sarsfield-Vesey MSS, letter 152.

43. J. Leathes to W. Leathes, 3 Dec. 1726, 18 Mar. 1727, Suffolk County Record Office, Ipswich, de Mussenden MSS, HA 403/1/6/49,52.

44. Autobiography of J.A. Oughton, National Army Museum, London, MS. 8808.36.1, p. 43.

45. Journal of N. Peacock, 6 July 1740, 27 July 1740, 24 Aug. 1740, 14 Sep. 1740, 12 Oct.1740, 9 Nov. 1740, 21 Dec. 1740, 16 Sep. 1741, N.L.I., MS. 16091. The work was the second part of 'Gusmand', i.e. M. Aleman, *The Spanish rogue, or the life of Guzman de Alfarache*.

46. N.L.I., MS. 16091, 28 Dec. 1743, 25 Apr. 1744, 18 May 1744, 7 Aug. 1744.

47. N.L.I., MS. 16091, 17 July 1745, 23 Oct. 1745, 26 Oct. 1745.

48. M. Fitzgerald to M. Crosbie, 1 Nov. 1715, T.C.D. MS. 3821/163.

49. J. Scoles to W. Crosbie, 13 Oct. 1737, N.L.I., Talbot Crosbie MSS, folder 58.

50. R. Edwards to F. Price, 8 Oct. 1744, 16 Feb. 1745, 9 Apr. 1747, 7 Jan. 1748, National Library of Wales, MS. 3577E.

51. Barnard, 'Learning, the learned and literacy', pp 218–219.

52. T. Fitzgerald to T. Vesey, 10 Jan. 1699, 31 Oct. 1704, De Vesci MSS, J2, formerly in Damer House, Roscrea, now in N.L.I.; journal of Elie Bouhéreau, 15 June 1705, 9 May 1706, 7 July 1711, Marsh's Library, Dublin, MS. Z.2.2.2.

53. A. Spurrett to Smith, 18 July 1704, Chatsworth House, Derbyshire, Spurrett letter book, 1703–4; J. Waite to R. Musgrave, 25 Feb. 1707, Chatsworth House, Waite letter book 1706–9; accounts of 1 July 1730, 13 Aug. 1731, 2 Sep. 1732, Chatsworth House, Andrew Crotty account book 1726–32, pp 81, 100, 114.

54. S. Foster, 'Buying Irish: consumer nationalism in eighteenth-century Dublin', in *History Today*, xlvii (1997), pp.44–51; Foster, 'Going shopping in Georgian Dublin: luxury goods and the negotiation of national identity', unpublished M.A. dissertation, Royal College of Art / Victoria and Albert Museum, 1995; Desmond Fitzgerald, Knight of Glin, *A directory of the Dublin furniture trade, 1752–1800* (Dublin, 1993); J. Greene and E McCrum, '"Small clothes"; the evolution of men's nether garments as evidenced in The *Belfast Newsletter* index, 1737–1800', in *Eighteenth-Century Ireland*, v (1990), pp 153–172.

55. T.C. Barnard, 'Integration or separation? hospitality and display in Protestant Ireland, 1660–1800', in. L.W.B. Brockliss and D.S. Eastwood (eds), *A union of multiple identities: the British Isles, c. 1750–1850* (Manchester, 1997), pp 127–146.

56. Suggestive on this topic is Roger Chartier, 'Leisure and sociability: reading aloud in early modern Europe' in S. Zimmerman and R.F.E. Weissman (eds), *Urban life in the Renaissance* (Newark & London, 1989), pp 103–120.

57. Account of Holt Waring with Sir J. Ligonier, 13 Mar. 1744, Private collection, county Down.

Women and reading in eighteenth-century Ireland

Máire Kennedy

WHEN CONSIDERING QUESTIONS of readership in eighteenth-century Ireland the researcher is faced with a dearth of contemporary sources. Reliable statistical data are not forthcoming and even evidence for book ownership is unreliable and weighted in favour of specific groups in society. The question of female readership is problematical, especially outside the more favoured social circles. Yet, a certain amount of progress can be made. Books, as surviving material objects, contain internal evidence of ownership and sometimes even of readership. Because, by its nature, reading was a pursuit of the literate and educated, accounts of reading can be found in contemporary documents: in published biographies or travel accounts, and in published or unpublished letters and diaries. Contemporary paintings, illustrating the world of the privileged classes, portray books and reading as standard motifs. These images, however, can be misleading, and cannot be taken as evidence without more concrete supporting material.

Up to now evidence for women's reading has come largely from contemporary accounts and letters. Thus we are aware of the reading tastes of the Duchess of Leinster and her family, Mrs Mary Delany, Maria Edgeworth, and most recently Alicia Synge, the young daughter of Bishop Edward Synge of Elphin.[1] These documents are very valuable and give an immense insight into contemporary reading habits at a certain social level. In this essay I would like to consider other, less well known sources, and what they can tell us of women's reading further down the social scale.

That women of a certain social standing could and did read is undisputed, but how many of them read, what did they read, where and in what manner? To what extent was reading confined to women in privileged circumstances? A distinction must be made between the ability to read on the part of women and the practice of reading. Research based on the history of the book in Ireland has made most progress in revealing what books were owned, and by whom, or concentrating on the social or political aspects of reading, rather than being able to provide figures for literacy levels. Niall Ó Ciosáin, using the 1841 census figures and projecting back to the late eighteenth century, has calculated that by the 1770s reading ability among women was established at about 50 per cent.[2]

A further distinction can be made between utilitarian and literary reading. Evidence relating to the higher social levels tends to favour literary reading, or reading as a cultural activity. However, women who became teachers, governesses, 'upper servants', or who practised a trade needed to read to earn their living in these capacities. At this level women's reading was functional, rather than a leisure pursuit. Reading in French as well as in English was a necessary skill for governesses to teach their pupils, or for ladies' companions to serve their mistresses. Evidence for reading in this manner can be gleaned from newspaper advertisements which pointed to the skills in demand for these careers.

Women in the book trade displayed a high level of reading ability as a necessary pre-condition to the practice of their trade. During the eighteenth century there are several instances of women who ran successful printing houses and newspaper offices.[3] They usually stepped into the role on the death of a father or husband, and often only carried on business until a son came of age, or until they remarried. In other cases, however, they became the driving forces behind an expanding enterprise. Catharine Finn of Kilkenny is one such success story. Widowed in 1777 with seven small children, she took over her husband's bookshop and printing office and continued publication of *Finn's Leinster Journal*, until at least 1800.[4] In this period she expanded circulation of the *Journal*, sending it via the Post Office network all over Ireland, and to London and Bath, as well as running the bookshop and lottery office, importing books from Dublin and London and doing some local printing.

The frequency with which women were able to take over printing houses suggests that they already carried out some of the functions before the demise of husband or father. Reliance on a journeyman printer or senior apprentice was necessary in such cases, and this working partnership was often formalised by marriage. Proofreading, typesetting, tending the shop, and keeping accounts were the likely tasks carried out by women, although typesetting may have been a male preserve at this time, as it was later. One woman whose role went beyond this was Constantia Grierson (d. 1733), the wife of George Grierson, King's printer in Dublin. She was regarded as one of the most advanced scholars of her day, as well as being a poet she was learned in Hebrew, Greek, Latin, French and mathematics.[5] She took an active part in the production of Latin works published by her husband and edited a three volume set of *The works of Tacitus* in 1730, which was highly acclaimed. Scholarly involvement at this level was rare, but the more mundane tasks of proofreading and selling could have been carried out by literate women.

Evidence of women's reading is less forthcoming further down the social scale. Eighteenth-century newspapers suggest a female readership among the middle classes. Reports describing the latest fashions in clothes and hair from Paris and London, and accounts of fashionable balls and masquerades clearly had a dedicated readership. Advertisements were placed for products of interest to women, such as patent medicines and toiletries, millinery, clothing and lace, hair dressing, musical instruments, art materials, books and stationery. Notices of theatrical performances were addressed to both 'ladies and gentlemen'. Publications aimed at women were advertised regularly, for example in 1778 *Finn's Leinster Journal* headed an advertisement 'To the Ladies' and it described *The lady's assistant . . . being a complete system of cookery* by Mrs Charlotte Mason, which could be purchased for 3s.3d. and was aimed at young married ladies.[6] The *Freeman's Journal*'s advertisements under the same heading, 'To the Ladies', advertised *The lady's tablet or, town and country pocket journal and select memorandum book* for 1776 and

1777. These annual publications could be purchased in a range of bindings, costing from 1*s*.7½*d*. for plain to 6*s*.6*d*. for the most elegant.[7] Other advertised works geared especially to the female market included *The ladies' almanack, The ladies' own memorandum book* (annual publications), *The experienced English housekeeper* by Elizabeth Raffald, confectioner at Manchester, *The housekeeper's daily journal*, and *The young lady's pocket library*.[8]

Newspapers which had a 'poet's corner' or literary section attracted women contributors. William Flyn, bookseller in Cork, offered his newspaper, *The Hibernian Chronicle*, as a 'rendezvous for volunteer Authors of both sexes'.[9] Advertised products and entertainments were geared towards women with a comfortable standard of living, and in the case of books and stationery, were obviously intended for literate customers. We know of one group of women whose members may not all have been literate; they had the *Freeman's Journal* read to them in 1766: 'several Housekeepers of St. Anne's Parish meet at a friendly Club, and have the Freeman's Journal constantly read to them, in order to make observations, and if necessary to make them public for the Good of their Fellow-citizens.'[10]

Monthly magazines, reprinted from English originals, such as *The Gentleman's Magazine* and *The London Magazine*, had a readership in Ireland from the 1730s. They were distributed throughout the countryside by the newspaper carriers or by the Post Office. Magazines for women made their appearance in the second half of the century. *The Lady's Magazine* was the most prominent.[11] Published in London from 1770 at 6*d*. per issue, it was advertised regularly in the Irish newspapers.[12] It was imported from London by James Williams of Dublin and supplied by him to the provincial booksellers; in November 1772 Edmund Finn in Kilkenny advertised the September issue, as well as volumes of the first two years bound.[13] A French language periodical, the *Magazin à la mode*, had as its subtitle 'dedié aux femmes'. It was produced in Dublin by a teacher of French, Charles Praval, in 1777 and 1778, and was sold by subscription or in individual monthly issues (at one British shilling per issue) in bookshops around the country.[14]

More general literary periodicals, such as the *Hibernian Magazine*, also envisaged a female readership. They carried

81

fashion reports with engraved plates and patterns for elegant accessories, engraved music, selections of poetry and extracts from novels. Readership figures for these periodicals are not known, but the list of provincial suppliers is impressive and suggests a widespread availability of this type of reading matter. At a cost of 6*d*. to 1*s*. per month and containing a variety of articles, music and gossip, they may have been an attractive choice for many less well-off female readers.

In the second half of the eighteenth century newspaper advertisements for books were aimed at 'good little Masters and Misses', suggesting a readership among children that was worth targeting. Books for children's pleasure were especially advertised at Christmas, New Year and Easter. In April 1772 William Flyn of Cork advertised Newbery's books as an Easter gift for children, listing twenty-six titles selling at 2*d*. to 8*d*. each.[15] At the same period Thomas White of Cork advertised 'Hymns for the amusement of Children, with cuts.'[16] The cheap price of the Newbery books 'elegantly gilt and adorned with handsome cuts' put them within the reach of middle class parents. Amusing books with woodcut illustrations, aimed at children, were an important progression from schoolbooks, and suggest a literate market at this level.

Contemporary literature points to the extensive use of circulating libraries by women, most notably in Sheridan's *The rivals*.[17] Many Irish booksellers in the last quarter of the eighteenth century ran circulating libraries. They prided themselves on stocking the very latest and most fashionable reading matter, especially novels, plays and poetry. For a modest sum, equal to the charges made at Bath (6½*d*. per week, 5*s*.5*d*. per quarter, or 16*s*.3*d*. per year in the 1780s and 1790s) books could be borrowed, read and returned, leaving no evidence at all of their readers.[18] In 1794 some women proprietors proposed to establish a circulating library in Cork. They required 200 subscribers, each paying 11*s*.4½*d*. per annum to make the venture possible.[19] They intended to stock only the most approved writers, those who 'may safely be committed to the inspection of Young Persons.' As they wished particularly to attract women to the library, they arranged that the books could be browsed, 'which, it is presumed, will be more pleasing than the usual method of sending Servants.' It is not known, however, if the plan became a reality.

Subscription libraries, or library societies, established in several major Irish cities at the end of the eighteenth and early nineteenth centuries, seemed much less attractive to women readers. They were set up in a more formal manner than the circulating libraries, with the emphasis on the quality of the holdings. Expensive works of scholarship in the sciences, history and literature were collected; novels, plays and political tracts were normally excluded. The stock was meant to endure as a lasting resource for its members, therefore catalogues were published of their holdings. Surviving membership lists and rules of societies show that women played a very small role in them: in some they were not allowed membership, in others they had no deciding powers.

Women had a very low profile as book collectors, as people whose taste formed libraries. Book sale catalogues frequently refer to the judicious care with which a library was assembled, the specialist knowledge, or distinguished taste with which the collection was created. Of nearly 200 book auction catalogues of private named owners from the eighteenth and the first half of the nineteenth centuries only three women are named as consignors: Mrs Walcott (1800); Lady Anne Fitzgerald (1809) and Mrs Grace Digges La Touche (1843).[20]

In the case of the Edgeworth family library, the tastes of many readers were represented. A surviving portion of the hand-written catalogue of the library notes the initials of each book's owner, thus we know some of the books owned by Maria, for example *Democracy in America* by de Tocqueville, Fénelon's *Education des filles*, *Mémoires de Madame de Genlis*, Rousseau's *Inégalité des hommes*, Montesquieu's *Lettres persanes* and *De l'esprit des loix*, and we also know which books were easily accessible to her in the family library.[21] It is very unusual for individual ownership to be documented in this way; at least sixteen members of the family are represented in the library. Book sale catalogues and library listings normally present a monolithic aspect, often with only the more prestigious titles appearing, with pamphlets, plays, magazines, newspapers, school books and ephemeral items completely absent. Women's reading matter and ownership of books can be submerged in these sources.

What can books tell us about their readers, and how reliable is the information which they present? The most unequivocal evidence comes from annotations and comments in books, which can be shown to be in the hand-writing of the owner. Thus, in the sale catalogue of Swift's library in 1745, the books which contained annotations in the Dean's writing were marked with an asterisk.[22] This strategem was clearly aimed at increasing the value of the books at auction. Daniel O'Connell, too, was an annotator, as evidenced by his books. Only certain types of books, however, were likely to attract marginal notes. Works of scholarship, school books, Greek and Latin authors, and history books most often contained the comments of their owners, while novels, poetry and religious works were more likely to be unmarked.

In the United States 'reader response criticism' is coming into vogue as the study of just such material evidence for the readership of books. A recent exhibition held at the Beinecke Library in Yale, entitled 'Renaissance Readers', displayed 160 volumes from the fifteenth and sixteenth centuries which had extensive manuscript annotations by their readers. The books mostly fell into the categories of textbooks in medicine, astronomy and law, and as such, demonstrated an exclusively male readership.[23]

In most cases, the only evidence of the owner's identity is a bookplate, or a name written on the title page or flyleaf, sometimes with a date. The use of a bookplate signified the book's place in a library of some standing, the design depicting the coat of arms of a family, and therefore not pointing to the taste of an individual. Of more interest in the context of individual reading are the young men and women who inscribed their names on school books, almanacs and similar texts. In surviving copies of these books glimpses can be caught of otherwise unknown female readers, and the ordinary reading public who were not renowned for fine libraries or for literary or scholarly endeavour. As an example, a copy of the 1768 Dublin edition of Chambaud's *Fables choisies* held in Cambridge has the manuscript name 'Anne Mahon Annaduff', the copy of the 1771 edition held in the National Library of Ireland bears the names of Lydia Jacob and Susanna Grubbs, with the date 1791, suggesting that they were not the book's first owners, while another copy of the 1771 edition in the British Library has the name of Miss Power.[24]

Similarly the National Library copy of Praval's *The idioms of the French language* (1783) has the inscription: 'Margaret Stronge her Book Febry 16th', the copy held in Cambridge was owned by Miss Millicent Montgomery and the British Library's belonged to Elizabeth Putland. The later edition of 1794 in the British Library was Miss Graham's and that of 1803, also in the British Library, was Sarah Hamilton's.[25] *The young lady's pocket library, or parental monitor* was widely advertised by its publisher, John Archer, as a Christmas and New Year gift in 1790 and 1791. There are two copies in the National Library, one has the signature of Sarah Hamilton, and the other belonged to Anne Louise Henrart, dated May 1791. The Gilbert Library copy was owned by Catharine Wilson in 1796.[26] (figure 3) The National Library copy of Mary Wells' *Triumph of faith over the world*, a religious work published by subscription in Mullingar in 1796, was the gift of John Woods junior to his mother Susana Woods.[27]

One book which was read by its owner, also tells us something about her. *La liturgie*, a new edition of the Anglican rite in French, with *Les pseaumes de David*, published in Dublin in 1777, was the property of Araminta Louisa Monck.[28] It was a luxury edition in red morocco binding with a gilt flower motif. The flyleaf has the inscription: 'Araminta Louisa Monck the gift of Emily Sophia Monck July the 28th 1790', and on the blank pages at the back the owner has transcribed some prayers and signed it: 'Araminta Louisa Hume January 23d 1795 Dieu la benisse!' Araminta Louisa had married the Revd Gustavus Hume in February 1794.[29] By an examination of book provenance we discover a great many female book owners who had a proprietorial interest in their books, who used the school books and who are likely to have read the novels, poems and other books bearing their names.

Only a handful of female readers have been known to us by name, and what information there is has emerged because of letters or diaries written by women of some standing. Surviving copies of eighteenth-century books, as we have seen, reveal

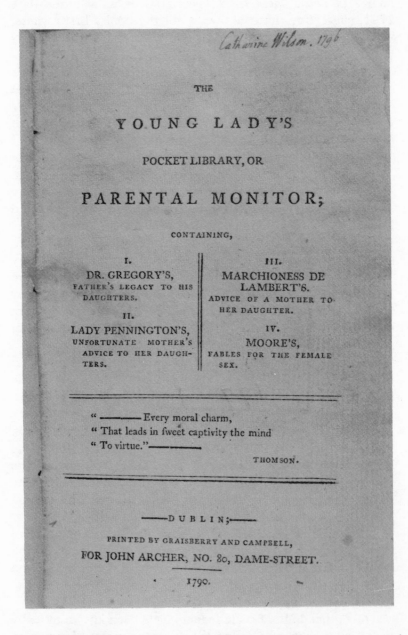

Figure 3: Title page of *The young lady's pocket library, or parental monitor* (Dublin, 1790), bearing the name Catharine Wilson who owned the book in 1796.

scores of otherwise unknown female book owners, many from well-known Irish families, Putland, Jacob or Grubb, many more unidentifiable. Until recent years there has been no sustained policy in many libraries for gathering information on the provenance of books in their collections, and therefore the names of these female owners/readers has remained obscure and the evidence untapped. Wesley McCann in 1984 has stated the case for the importance of recording provenance in library collections.[30]

The Early Printed Books Department at Trinity College Dublin has been among the first to create and maintain a provenance record here in Ireland. Now that their catalogue is computerised it is very easy to search for the names of former owners. As more libraries with early printed book collections become computerised it is hoped that the recording of provenance will take its rightful place as a searchable field in their catalogues. In this way it will be possible to build up some picture, however piecemeal, of ordinary book owners and readers. One very interesting pilot project based on the Early Science and Philosophy Collection at the University of Bristol has recently become available on the internet, entitled 'An electronic pictorial index for provenance research in book history', with over 400 images scanned into the database.[31] These initiatives will permit a great deal of future research into individual ownership.

Book subscription lists are also worth considering as indicators of women's reading. Books were published by subscription to help finance the publication, to gain an idea of the size of the interested market, and, in some cases, to discourage unauthorised reprints. Subscription lists indicate support and patronage for the author rather than readership, yet possession of a book, especially one by an author whom the subscriber wished to support, suggests that it would have been read.

A typical book published by subscription in Ireland was a religious work, or a collection of poems, in small format, duodecimo or octavo, and printed for the author. Provincial printers often produced the works of local authors by subscription. In general 200 subscriptions were required to make a venture viable, but sometimes lists containing 100 names or less are found. The usual range of commitment was from 200 to 500 names, some subscribing for multiple copies. Women's names appear less in subscription lists than men's, on average amounting to less than one-third of subscribers.

What works attracted the greatest proportion of women subscribers? Did women support the writings of other women to a greater degree? Was there a specific effort made to attract women readers for certain publications? I carried out two sample surveys in an attempt to address these questions. In the first a cross-section of books published by subscription in Ireland at five points in the century were examined. A total of thirty-nine books from the periods 1738, 1756–7, 1770, 1786–7 and 1796 yielded an average of just 14.2 per cent of women subscribers. Larger percentages are evident for certain kinds of books: poetry and religion in particular (see Table 1). One work geared towards the 'Entertainment and Instruction of Younger Minds', *Allegories and visions* (1770), with a running title 'Allegories for Young Ladies', achieved 57.3 per cent of female subscriptions.[32] Perhaps predictably scientific and economic works attracted less than 2 per cent of women subscribers, for instance Rutty's *Essay on mineral waters* (1757) with 1.6 per cent and Archdall's *Monasticon Hibernicum* (1786) at 0.8 per cent.[33] Covey's *Scheme for building a bridge over the river Suire* (1770), Steuart's *Inquiry into political oeconomy* (1770) and Irwin's *Treatise on gunnery* (1787) had no women subscribers, with the exception of the publisher of Covey's book, Mrs Esther Crawley of Waterford; and Mrs Elizabeth Lynch, bookseller, for six copies of Steuart's *Inquiry.*[34]

In the second survey nineteen books with women authors or translators, published by subscription in Ireland, or with a sizable proportion of Irish subscribers, between 1734 and 1797, were chosen (see Table 2). The subscription lists reveal a higher level of interest among female purchasers, with an average of 30 per cent. The largest percentage was for Charlotte Brooke's *School for christians* (1791) at 61.1 per cent. Elizabeth Carter's *All the works of Epictetus* was the lowest with only 6 per cent of women subscribing.[35] The list for Charlotte Brooke's book is rather unusual in that it has a total of thirty-six subscribers taking 483 copies of the work. Only one is a bookseller, taking fifty copies (Mr White). The book has as its subtitle 'for the use of children', therefore it is

TABLE 1

BOOKS PUBLISHED IN IRELAND BY SUBSCRIPTION

Year	Author	Title	Subs	Wn	%
1738	David Bindon	*A political essay upon commerce*	535	9	1.7
1738	[Mary Broggin]	*The pettycoat*	193	53	27.5
1738	Joseph Harrison	*A scriptural exposition*	1250	215	17.2
1738	Comtesse D'Aulnoy	*Ingenious and diverting letters*	116	11	9.5
1738	John Locke	*Epistles of St Paul*	71	1	1.4
1738	John Ozell	*Works of Rabelais*	128	2	1.6
1756	W.R. Chetwood	*Memoirs of Ben. Jonson*	309	52	16.9
1756	John Campbell	*The rational amusement*	150	19	12.7
1756	John Rocque	*Survey of Dublin*	334	5	1.5
1757	A Gentleman	*Twelve designs of country houses*	288	22	7.7
1757	Dudley Bradstreet	*Bradstreet's lives*	683	6	0.9
1757	[Robert Manning]	*A single combat*	212	7	3.3
1757	John Rutty	*Essay on mineral waters*	377	6	1.6
1770	Anon.	*Allegories and visions*	152	87	57.3
1770	Thomas Covey	*Scheme for building a bridge*	191	–	0.0
1770	James de la Cour	*Prospect of poetry*	338	23	6.8
1770	James Dodd	*Essays and poems*	255	24	9.4
1770	Robert Kirk	*Memoirs and adventures*	123	7	5.7
1770	Laurence Nihell	*Rational self love*	199	21	10.6
1770	Glocester Ridley	*Sermons*	393	82	20.9
1770	[Josiah Sheppard]	*The christian's companion*	153	49	32.0
1770	James Steuart	*Political oeconomy*	203	–	0.0
1786	Mervyn Archdall	*Monasticon Hibernicum*	128	1	0.8
1786	[William Wilson]	*Postchaise companion*	651	12	1.9
1787	Abraham Bosquet	*Howth: a descriptive poem*	98	14	14.3
1787	George Cheyne	*Treatise on health and long life*	95	9	9.5
1787	William Digby	*21 lectures on divinity*	785	201	25.6
1787	Anna M. Edwards	*Poems*	414	160	38.7
1787	John Ferrar	*History of Limerick*	436	27	6.2
1787	James Irwin	*A treatise on gunnery*	145	–	0.0
1787	Abraham Rees	*Chambers' cyclopaedia*	439	12	2.8
1787	Sigaud de la Fond	*School for happiness*	349	140	40.1
1796	M. de Cervantes	*Don Quixote*	339	11	3.3
1796	Mrs Creech	*Mary*	179	61	34.1
1796	John Ferrar	*A view of Dublin*	296	37	12.5
1796	Jane E. Moore	*Poems*	315	91	28.9
1796	Joseph Morony	*Sermons*	217	26	12.0
1796	Mary Wells	*The triumph of faith*	124	26	21.0
1796	[Thomas Wilson]	*Sacra privata*	256	37	14.5
TOTAL:			11004	1566	14.2

TABLE 2
BOOKS BY WOMEN AUTHORS/TRANSLATORS
PUBLISHED BY SUBSCRIPTION

Year	Author/Translator	Title	Subs	Wn	%
1734	Mary Barber	*Poems*	918	360	39.2
1738	[Mary Broggin]	*The pettycoat*	193	53	27.5
1738	Comtesse D'Aulnoy	*Ingenious and diverting letters*	116	11	9.5
1746	Eliza Haywood	*The female spectator*	357	136	38.1
1759	Elizabeth Carter	*All the works of Epictetus*	135	8	6.0
1760	E. & R. Griffith	*A series of genuine letters*	244	32	13.1
1768	Comtesse D'Aulnoy	*History of Hypolitus*	292	44	15.1
1775	Lady Guion	*Exemplary life of Lady Guion*	126	25	19.9
1782	Margaret Davidson	*Extraordinary life of M. Davidson*	102	49	48.0
1787	Anna M. Edwards	*Poems*	414	160	38.7
1789	Charlotte Brooke	*Reliques of Irish poetry*	288	82	28.5
1791	Henrietta Battier	*Protected Fugitives* (Irish subs)	302	46	15.2
1791	Charlotte Brooke	*School for christians*	36	22	61.1
1793	Anna Millikin	*Corfe castle*	139	32	23.0
1795	Anna Millikin	*Eva: an old Irish story*	171	59	34.5
1796	Mrs Creech	*Mary*	179	61	34.1
1796	Jane E. Moore	*Poems*	315	91	28.9
1796	Mary Wells	*The triumph of faith*	124	26	21.0
1797	[Sophia Briscoe]	*History of Julia and Cecilia*	281	123	43.8
TOTAL:			4732	1420	30.0

probable that copies were taken for distribution to schools or charitable institutions.

Subscription lists are determined by many factors, some of which will not be known to a modern researcher. Subscriptions gathered by influential persons will result in a large list, composed of the wealthy or celebrated figures of the time. Lists with a strong regional bias are found. Richard Houghton's *Part of the spiritual works of Fenelon* (1771) was supported by the translator's colleagues in the medical profession, while Samuel Whyte's *The shamrock* (1772) was purchased by the pupils from his school.[36] Anna Millikin thanks the subscription gatherers for her novel *Eva* (1795): 'her most grateful acknowledgments to those friends, who have so kindly exerted themselves in her favour, as to enable her to produce the following List, without having recourse to the public Prints.'[37]

The process of subscription collection at the highest level is revealed in Jonathan Swift's letters recommending Mrs Mary

Barber's *Poems on several occasions* to his many highly placed friends and acquaintances. Mrs Barber, 'a woollen-draper's wife, declined in the world' was recommended to Swift by Dr Patrick Delany.[38] Swift took up her cause with enthusiasm, and with the organised system of one who perfectly understood the process of subscription gathering. He sought support for the venture in Ireland and in England. The subscription price was one guinea and Swift advised Mrs Barber to collect it in 'ready money' only; he was of the opinion that 'twenty Collectors of both sexes would suffice.'[39] He undertook to write to several influential persons and gain their support for the venture, nominating a number of collectors and ensuring their coopera-tion. He pointed to her genius as a poet and to her worthiness as a person: 'She is by far the best Poet of her Sex in England, and is a virtuous modest Gentlewoman, with a great deal of good sense, and a true poetical Genius.'[40]

The book, published in London in 1734, in quarto format, had a large subscription list, over 900 persons subscribing to over 1,000 copies of the book.[41] The list of English and Irish subscribers is overwhelmingly composed of members of the gentry and aristocracy, 39.2 per cent of the subscribers were women. The subscription campaign was not geared in particu-lar to women's tastes, the quality and quantity of names on the list seemed to be the objective, and in this the author was particularly fortunate. The subscription list to Mrs Barber's *Poems*, however, is not typical for books printed in Ireland, written either by men or women. Only books with a universal or countrywide appeal would have attracted such a large number of subscribers.[42]

The female spectator, published in four volumes, duodecimo format, in 1746, was aimed very much at a female audience.[43] (figure 4) Each volume was dedicated to a patron: the Duchesses of Leeds, Bedford, Queensbury and Dover, and the Duchess Dowager of Manchester respectively. The set attracted 357 subscribers, 136 (or 38.1 per cent) of whom were women. However, twenty-two of those on the list were booksellers, subscribing to 281 sets. These sets were all destined for the retail market in Dublin, Belfast, Cork, Limerick and Waterford. A number of other individuals, listed as merchants, may have intended the set for resale. This list reveals a hidden layer of

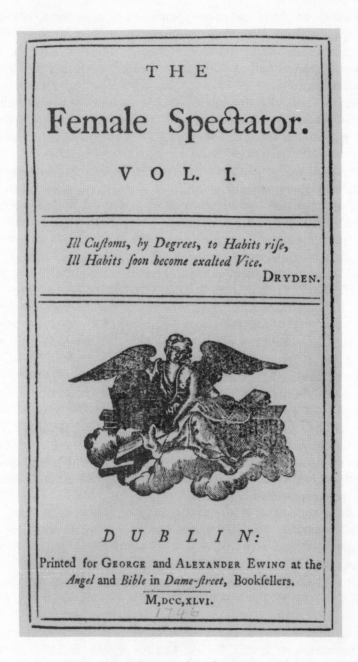

Figure 4: Title page of the first volume of
The female spectator (Dublin, 1746).

purchasers and readers, potentially the most interesting segment of the market: the purchasers in the major Irish towns.

In the 1790s a number of novels by women were published by subscription in Cork, all with an interested female public, ranging from 23 per cent for Anna Millikin's *Corfe castle* (1793), to 43.8 per cent for the *History of Julia and Cecilia de Valmont* (1797).[44] In each case the lists show a strong local support in the Munster region. Anna Millikin, from Castlemartyr, was supported by many of the important local families: Lord Boyle, Countess Shannon, Lady Harriet Bernard of Bandon, members of the Freke family, as well as her neighbours in Castlemartyr, Youghal, Killeagh, Ardmore and across the harbour in Passage West. The National Library's copy of the *History of Julia and Cecilia* has the inscription: 'Elizabeth Sayers, Bridges Square, Limerick, 22 May 1798.'[45] Miss Sayers appears in the subscription list, as do seven other subscribers with an address at The Square in Limerick.

These novels, published within a five year period expected a large general readership, with booksellers subscribing to substantial quantities. Anna Millikin's *Eva* appealed to the trade as a certain bestseller. John Connor, bookseller and proprietor of the circulating library in Cork, the publisher of the work, subscribed to 100 copies, as did Patrick Wogan, bookseller in Dublin. John Millikin in Dublin, who may have been a relative, took fifty copies while James Johnson in Youghal and Thomas White in Cork took twelve each. In this case the copies of the book ordered by booksellers greatly outnumbered those pledged to subscribers.[46]

As noted at the beginning contemporary sources are inadequate to the task of compiling statistics for reading, or even literacy, for eighteenth-century Ireland. Anecdotal evidence from letters and diaries is perhaps the best known and the most persuasive evidence, but it is very much confined to the social and literary elites. The limited evidence has been used time and again and has very little new to say on women's reading tastes.

Inevitably several questions remain unanswered. In this paper the emphasis has been placed on the who and the what, more than on the how, the why and the where. While not being able to obtain quantitative data for reading levels among eighteenth-century women, we can piece together a certain amount of information from the objects of reading themselves: newspapers and books. Newspapers and periodicals reveal that women were among their target audience of readers. From advertisements we know that reading was a skill required for employment in many areas. Women were encouraged to contribute to literary matters in the press.

Books are the most fruitful sources of information, individual books often revealing their owners and readers, and subscription lists show a segment of the book-buying market. Flawed as they are, these sources can give us valuable information on women readers and on reading tastes in general. However, a great deal of ground-work needs to be done in recording book provenances and compiling master subscription lists before meaningful conclusions can be attempted. In Britain the work of assembling and computerising master subscription lists has been ongoing for many decades, chiefly at Newcastle-upon-Tyne.[47] This work needs to be done here but it is a slow process. However, I suggest that it is well worth doing, and the benefits will be many for future analysis and synthesis.

Notes

1. Emily Duchess of Leinster, *Correspondence of Emily, Duchess of Leinster (1731–1814)*, ed. Brian Fitzgerald, 3 vols (Dublin, 1949–1957); Mary Delany, *Letters from Georgian Ireland: the correspondence of Mary Delany, 1731–1768*, ed. Angélique Day (Belfast, 1991); Maria Edgeworth, *The life and letters of Maria Edgeworth*, ed. Augustus J.C. Hare (London, 1894); Maria Edgeworth, *Maria Edgeworth: chosen letters*, ed. F.V. Barry (London, 1931); Marie-Louise Legg (ed.), *The Synge letters: Bishop Synge to his daughter Alicia, Roscommon to Dublin 1746–1752* (Dublin, 1996).

2. Niall Ó Ciosáin, *Print and popular culture in Ireland, 1750–1850* (Basingstoke, 1997), p. 33.

3. Vincent Kinane, 'A galley of pie: women in the Irish book trades', in *Linen Hall Review*, 8, no. 4 (Dec. 1991), pp 10–13.

4. *Walker's Hibernian Magazine* (April 1777), p. 296; Máire Kennedy, 'Eighteenth-century newspaper publishing in Munster and South Leinster', *Journal of the Cork Historical and Archaeological Society*, 103 (1998), pp 67–88.

5. John T. Gilbert, *A history of the city of Dublin* (Shannon, 1972 with introd. by F.E. Dixon, of orig. ed., 3 vols, Dublin, 1854–9) ii, pp 155–160.

6. *Finn's Leinster Journal*, 25–28 Nov. 1778.

7. *Freeman's Journal*, 18–21 Nov. 1775; 14–16 Jan. 1777.

8. *Hibernian Chronicle*, 6 Jan. 1772; 17 Sept. 1772; 24 Dec. 1772; *Dublin Chronicle*, 27 Nov. 1790; 22 Dec. 1791.

9. *Hibernian Chronicle*, 2 Jan. 1772.

10. *Freeman's Journal*, 23–27 Sept. 1766.

11. *The Lady's Magazine: or, entertaining companion for the fair sex* (London, vols I–L, 1770–1819).

12. *Waterford Chronicle*, 7–11 June 1771; *Hibernian Chronicle*, 6 Jan. 1772; *Finn's Leinster Journal*, 1–4 July 1772.

13. *Finn's Leinster Journal*, 4–7 Nov. 1772.

14. Máire Kennedy, 'The distribution of a locally produced French periodical in provincial Ireland: the *Magazin à la mode*, 1777–1778', *Eighteenth-century Ireland*, ix, (1994), pp 83–98.

15. John Newbery, (1713–67) and his successors, Francis Newbery and Elizabeth Newbery, London booksellers who specialised in children's books, produced hundreds of titles in the second half of the eighteenth century. John Newbery's *A little pretty pocket*

book (1744) is credited with being one of the first books for the amusement of children. Elizabeth Newbery, the widow of John's nephew Francis, produced over 300 titles between 1780 and 1801.

16. *Hibernian Chronicle*, 20 Aug. 1770; 2 Jan. 1772; 16 Apr. 1772; 20 Apr. 1772; 24 Dec. 1772.

17. Richard Brinsley Sheridan, *The rivals* (Dublin, 1775), act I, scene II.

18. The circulating library at Essex Gate advertised at this rate in 1783, claiming that the charges equalled the 'very moderate Terms at Bath'. *Volunteer's Journal*, 15 Dec. 1783. Vincent Dowling's Apollo library in Suffolk Street also lent at this rate in 1792. *Freeman's Journal*, 6–8 Sept. 1792.

19. *Cork Gazette*, 8 Feb. 1794.

20. *Catalogue of the books and manuscripts of the late Mrs Walcott* (Dublin, 17 July 1800). *Catalogue of a capital collection of miscellaneous books, books of prints, mathematical instruments &c., being the library of Lady Anne Fitzgerald* (Dublin, 7 Dec. 1809). *Catalogue of a choice collection of books including the library of the late Mrs Digges La Touche of 35 Stephen's Green North* (Dublin, 5 July 1843).

21. Manuscript catalogue of the Edgeworth family library, Longford 1830–39, N.L.I. microfilm p.7655. In alphabetical order, contains letters A–P only.

22. *A catalogue of books, the library of the late Revd. Dr Swift, Dean of St Patrick's, Dublin* (Dublin, 1745). Some of the annotations amounted to no more than Swift's signature.

23. Beinecke Library, Yale, Exhibition from 20 January to 28 March 1997.

24. Lewis Chambaud, *Fables choisies* (Dublin, 1768), [Cambridge Hib.7.768.58]; (Dublin, 1771), [N.L.I. I 6551 Dubl 1771]; [B.L. 1607/5845].

25. Charles Praval, *The idioms of the French language* (Dublin, 1783), [N.L.I., I 6551 Dubl 1783]; [Cambridge, Hib.7.783.37]; [B.L., 1568/3940]; (Dublin, 1794), [B.L., 1509/3157]; (Dublin, 1803), [B.L., 1607/2215].

26. *Dublin Chronicle* (27 Nov. 1790; 22 Dec. 1791). *The young lady's pocket library, or parental monitor* (Dublin, 1790), [N.L.I., I 6551 Dubl 1790; Ir 6551 y1]; [Gilbert Library].

27. [Mary Wells] *The triumph of faith over the world, the flesh, and the devil* (Mullingar, 1796), [N.L.I., I 6551 Mullingar 1796 (1)].

28. *La liturgie, ou formulaire des prières publiques selon l'usage de l'eglise anglicane* (Dublin, 1777), [B.L., 3408.bbb.36].

29. *Appendix to the 26th report of the Deputy Keeper of the Public Records and Keeper of the State Papers in Ireland* (Dublin, 1895), marriage licence 1794, p. 440; *Walker's Hibernian Magazine* Feb. 1794, p. 288; *Ennis Chronicle*, 11 Sept. 1794.

30. Wesley McCann, 'The study of provenance in older printed books: some examples from the Henry Davis collection', in *An Leabharlann*, new ser., 1, no. 3 (1984), pp 73–85.

31. Erle Randall, 'An electronic pictorial index for provenance research in book history' (http://www.bris.ac.uk/Septs/ContEd/ E.Randall). I am very grateful to Dr Sarah Preston for giving me this reference.

32. *Allegories and visions for the entertainment and instruction of younger minds* (Dublin, 1770).

33. John Rutty, *An essay towards a natural, experimental and medicinal history of the mineral waters of Ireland* (Dublin, 1757); Mervyn Archdall, *Monasticon Hibernicum* (Dublin, 1786).

34. Thomas Covey, *A scheme for building a bridge over the river Suire at the city of Waterford* (Waterford, 1770); Sir James Steuart Bart., *An inquiry into the principles of political oeconomy* (Dublin, 1770); James Irwin, *A treatise on gunnery in theory and practice* (Limerick, 1787).

35. Charlotte Brooke, *The school for christians* (Dublin, 1791); Elizabeth Carter, *All the works of Epictetus* (Dublin, 1759).

36. Richard Houghton, *Part of the spiritual works of . . . Fenelon* (Dublin, 1771); Samuel Whyte, *The shamrock; or, Hibernian cresses* (Dublin, 1772).

37. Anna Millikin, *Eva: an old Irish story* (Cork, 1795), advertisement.

38. Harold Williams (ed.), *The correspondence of Jonathan Swift* (Oxford, 1965), 5 vols. Swift to Alexander Pope, iii, 479.

39. Swift, *Correspondence*, Swift to Mrs Barber, iii, 440.

40. Swift, *Correspondence*, Swift to the earl of Oxford, iv, 187.

41. [Mary Barber], *Poems on several occasions* (London, 1734).

42. For example Taylor and Skinner's *Maps of the roads of Ireland*, of interest to landowners in every county, was supported by 1,552 subscribers in 1778, John Donovan's *Sublime friendship delineated*, printed in Cork in 1789, with a strong local interest, had 607 subscribers taking 1,584 copies of the book, while Bond's *A digest of foreign exchanges*, a necessary working

document for all merchants and traders, attracted 1,764 names in 1795. George Taylor and Andrew Skinner, *Maps of the roads of Ireland* (London and Dublin, 1778); John Donovan, *Sublime friendship delineated* (Cork, 1789); Sir Thomas Bond, *A digest of foreign exchanges* (Dublin, 1795).

43. [Eliza Haywood], *The female spectator* (Dublin, 1746).

44. Anna Millikin, *Corfe castle; or, historic tracts* (Cork, 1793); Millikin, *Eva*; Mrs Creech, *Mary; or, the uses of adversity* (Cork, 1796); [Sophia Briscoe], *History of Julia and Cecilia de Valmont,* (Cork, 1797).

45. [Briscoe], *History of Julia and Cecilia.*

46. Millikin, *Eva*, 171 subscribers for 464 copies of the book.

47. F.J.G. Robinson and P.J. Wallis, *Book subscription lists, a revised guide* (Newcastle upon Tyne, 1975); R.C. Alston, F.J.G. Robinson and C. Waldham, *A check-list of eighteenth-century books containing lists of subscribers* (Newcastle upon Tyne, 1983); P.J. and R.V. Wallis, *Eighteenth-century medics*, 2nd ed. (Newcastle upon Tyne, 1988).

The reading habits of a Georgian gentleman, John Templeton, and the book collections of the Belfast Society for Promoting Knowledge

John Killen

O N 13 MAY 1788, EIGHT MEN in the town of Belfast in the North of Ireland, banded together to form the Belfast Reading Society, a local instance of a widespread British, European and North American movement towards self-improvement through the establishment of libraries, museums, debating societies and schools. These men were not of the middle or merchant class in the growing mercantile town: rather they were skilled artisans.

Martha McTier, that inveterate letter writer and sister of Dr William Drennan, described them as: 'Worthy plebians who would do honour to any town, [of whom there was] not among them one of higher rank than McCormick the gunsmith, or Osborne the baker'.[1] Roger Mulholland, builder and architect, was the society's first president, and Robert Carey, house-painter, its first librarian.

Quite early in its history, the society's growing collection of books came to the attention of the leaders of Belfast society. In 1791, and throughout 1792, membership of the Belfast Reading Society expanded, with young and energetic men and women joining. These new members were recruited by Dr James McDonnell and others. On 1 September 1792, John Templeton was admitted a member of the society.

John Templeton was born in 1766, the son of James Templeton, 'a merchant of good rank and connections', and Mary Eleanor Legg, daughter of Mr Benjamin Legg of Belfast and Malone. As a child he suffered ill health and spent a lot of his time reading, especially books of natural history. His health was restored to him by long walks in the countryside where his love of nature was given practical and intellectual scope. A man of independent means, he devoted his life to examining and recording the flora and fauna of his native place.

At that meeting of the Belfast Reading Society on 1 September 1792, when Templeton was accepted as a member, it was resolved that the name of the society be changed, and that the committee consider a proper appellation for the society and make their report at the next monthly meeting. This proposed name change was undoubtedly prompted by the need to define (or re-define) the aims of the society in the light of its changing membership. Self improvement and the improvement of society in general were the motivating impulses of the newcomers. On 11 September 1792 at a general meeting of the society, the following resolution was passed: '[That] this Society adopt the . . . appellation – The Belfast Society for Promoting Knowledge'. In October of the same year, the presidency of the society was offered to Dr Alexander Halliday.

Halliday had an extensive medical practice in Belfast and the surrounding countryside. With his professional background, his ready wit and his literary tastes, he was one of the most influential figures in the growing town. Dr Drennan had this to say of him:

> On every public occasion when Belfast wished to place itself in the most respectable point of view to visitors, distinguished by rank, station or talent, Dr Halliday, at the head of the table, was in his appropriate place, and his guests, however eminent, never failed to find in the physician of a country town, an urbanity of manners, a variety of information, a happy and opportune wit, a just tone or timing in whatever he said, which set him, at the least, on a level with those who possessed patents of dignity, or high official situation.[2]

Drennan's sister, Mrs McTier, possibly understood the motivations of the library's committee better in electing him president when she wrote: 'I think they had an eye to his books more than himself when they paid him the compliment.'[3]

And it was for the collecting of books, and for their reading, that the society had been founded. But what sort of books? The library of the Belfast Society for Promoting Knowledge was based on the Library Company of Philadelphia founded by

Benjamin Franklin. The *Belfast Newsletter* for 18-22 October
1793 drew the comparison when it described the state of literary pursuits in Philadelphia in the early part of the eighteenth
century:

> The promotion of literature had been little attended to in
> Philadelphia. Most of the inhabitants were too immersed in
> business to think of scientific pursuits . . . in such circum-
> stances, the establishment of a public library was an
> important event. This was set on foot by Franklin, about the
> year 1731. Fifty persons subscribed forty shillings each, and
> agreed to pay ten shillings annually . . . The library . . . now
> contains about eight thousand volumes on all subjects, a
> philosophical apparatus, and a good beginning towards a
> collection of natural history and artificial curiosities.[4]

Certainly the books in the first – 1793 – catalogue of its
Belfast imitator reflect the worthy aims of Franklin's library.
Early in that year the Revd James Bryson, minister of the
second Presbyterian congregation, and John Templeton were
asked to prepare a catalogue of the books in the Belfast
Society's library. Some 140 volumes were listed in this catalogue, with an additional fifty-four books which were on order.
By November 1794, however, the need was expressed for an
updated, alphabetical catalogue of the books, and the society's
second librarian, Thomas Russell, was asked to prepare it. It is
almost certain that Templeton did most of the work on this
second – 1795 – catalogue.

Russell – one of the most attractive characters associated
with the library – was an interesting choice for librarian; and
really was offered the job by his political friends in Belfast to
provide him with lodgings and some money on which to live.
The selection of someone – as Dr Christopher Woods of the
Royal Irish Academy points out – who was virtually dyslexic to
be a librarian may not have been inspired. However, Russell
and Templeton were firm friends and the compilation of the
library's second catalogue was no doubt congenial work for
both men.

On 1 January 1795, a revision of the rules of the Belfast
Society for Promoting Knowledge was tabled in the society's
house in Ann Street, accepted by the assembled members, and

it was ordered that these rules – forty-six in number – be published in the catalogue. Rule number two set out the purpose of the society, and reflected the influence of Franklin's Philadelphia library. It read:

> The object of this Society is the collection of an extensive library, philosophical apparatus and such productions of nature and art as tend to improve the mind and excite a spirit of general inquiry.
>
> The Society intends to collect such materials as may illustrate the antiquities, the natural, civil, commercial and ecclesiastical history of this country . . . Donations of books, models of machinery, specimens of minerals, animals and plants will be thankfully received, and all communications, relative to arts, natural philosophy and literature, addressed to the Secretary for the time being, will be respectfully attended to.[5]

This rule, setting out the serious nature of the society's collecting policy, harks back to an earlier rule of March 1792, which stated that all future members of the committee of the society should, upon admission, sign a declaration that while they were in office, they would: 'Not consent to the choice or purchase of any common novel, or farce, or other book of trivial amusement.'[6] This proscription of works of fiction arose from an eighteenth-century belief that fiction was at best a waste of valuable time, or at worst, immoral.

Rousseau in his *Confessions*, described how he had early become addicted to the reading of novels – and the consequence thereof:

> My mother had possessed some novels, and my father and I began to read them after supper . . . Soon my interest in this entertaining literature became so strong that we read them by turns continuously, and spent whole nights so engaged . . . In a short time I acquired, by this dangerous method, not only an extreme facility in reading and expressing myself, but a singular insight for my age into the passions. I had no idea of the facts, but I was already familiar with every feeling. I had grasped nothing; I had sensed everything. These confused emotions which I experienced one after the other, did not warp my reasoning powers in any way, for as yet I had none. But they shaped them after a special pattern,

giving me the strangest and most romantic notions about human life, which neither experience nor reflection has ever succeeded in curing me of.[7]

Not for the practical citizens of Belfast such a fate. Consequently, the encyclopaedias, the journals of both Houses of Parliament, and the learned journals of the day rubbed shoulders with books on medicine, natural history, travel, politics, chemistry, music, religion and *belles lettres*. These books included: Adams on *The microscope*, quarto, with a folio volume of plates; Alison on *Taste*; Arbuthnot's *Tables of coins, weights and measures*, duodecimo; Beaufort's *Map of Ireland*, on rollers; Bergman's *Physical and chemical essays*, three volumes, octavo; Bland's *Treatise on military discipline*, octavo; Curry on *Apparent death*, octavo; *Direction de fortification*, par Vauban, duodecimo; Dundas on *Military tactics*; Euclid's *Elements*, octavo; Foster's *Account of Cook's voyage*, two volumes, quarto; Gibbon's *History of the decline and fall of the Roman empire*, twelve volumes, octavo; Hume's *Essays*, two volumes, octavo; an Irish *Bible*, quarto; Johnson's (Dr Samuel) *Works*, six volumes, octavo; Keogh's *Irish herbal*, quarto; Lavater's *Aphorisms on man*, duodecimo; Montesquieu's *Works*, four volumes, octavo; *Nautical almanac*; Pages's *Travels*, octavo; Rutty's *History of Dublin*, two volumes, octavo; Smith's *Optics*, quarto; *Tracts on bleaching*; Townsend's *Travels in Hungary and Spain*; Voltaire on *Toleration*, duodecimo; White's *Voyage to New South Wales*, quarto; Wollstonecraft's *Vindication of the rights of woman*, octavo; and Young's *Travels in France*, two volumes, octavo. These were the books and the *type of book* in the catalogue of the Belfast Society for Promoting Knowledge in 1795.

But how can we judge the effect of these books: how can we estimate the achievement of the society when it stated: 'The object of the society is the collection of an extensive library [which will] . . . improve the mind and excite a spirit of general inquiry'? One effective gauge is through the letters and journals of John Templeton. Templeton was a man of independent means who was able to devote his life to his chosen interests, primarily botany, science and literature. He was a warm-hearted and faithful friend, who did much for the development of educational establishments, practical research and philanthropy in Belfast. Through his letters and journals we can glimpse the effects of a well-selected library on an enquiring mind.

Writing to Thomas Russell in September 1797, in jail in Dublin for his political activities, Templeton comments on his current reading material – and provides a faintly damning critique of Staunton's *Embassy to China*, a two-volume work published in 1797. He writes:

> I have been engaged some time with the Embassy to China. It is a book, I think, that relates a number of facts, for I believe we may rely on the truth of most things mentioned, on Staunton's own authority; for he appears a man void of the ambition of shining as a literary man . . . I am sorry to find there was no man to be found better qualified to give us an account of so interesting a country . . .[8]

In replying, Russell mentions Tytler's *Historical Register*, and in doing so, demonstrates the immediacy and utility of such works:

> I was much concerned at that part of your letter which mentioned McDonnell's illness, the consequence of the Fever Hospital . . . Mr Tytler observed that . . . infection was of a sluggish nature, and clung to the walls, bed-clothes, etc. rather than occupied the centre of the room, and therefore it should be taken near the bed; if this was analysed carefully, it might be of service in epidemic disorders . . . I wish you would take care of Tytler's Historical Register, as there is no other extant, and I want to have a thing about lightening, and two or three other articles reprinted.[9]

In January 1798, Templeton again writes to Russell about his reading material and mentions Russell's interest in mineralogy:

> I have lately read Townsend's Travels . . . with great satisfaction . . . I find from the author that mineralogists are divided into two sects – Neptunists and Vulcanists. Dr Townsend is of the first sect, which I think is greatly increasing in numbers; this will, no doubt, give you great pleasure, as I know you belong to that class . . .[10]

Templeton was a serious, practical scientist, specialising as he did in botanical research. An entry in his journals for 9 December 1806, taken from Lavater's *Aphorisms*, sums up his attitude to all scientific research. It reads: 'He is not a step away from real greatness who give[s] to his own singular experiments neither more nor less importance than their own nature warrants.'[11] Reflecting on religion on Christmas day in the same year, after reading Fischer's *Travels through Spain*, Templeton writes in his journal: 'Most systems of religion are but the FIRST essays of reason. Formed in ignorance and weakness of mankind, they must lose some part of their authority as soon as the powers of the mind begin to unfold'.[12]

The scientific and literary journals being published in London and Edinburgh, and containing the most up-to-date discoveries and theories, were read enquiringly by Templeton, who sifted and commented upon their content. Early in 1807 he wrote: 'Read the Edinburgh Review of Bailey the Astronomer and Mayor of Paris . . . Posthumous works which give some of the most striking features of the beginning of the French Révolution'. From the same journal he gleaned some useful culinary and botanical information: 'The French use Plantago Mantana (sic) for a pickle and salad; and sometimes boil the leaves in soup'.[13] Always his abiding scientific interest in botany guided his reading: 'Read the Annual Reviewer's account of Sir J[oseph] Banks' paper on the mildew of wheat. He seems to give a good view to the effect – but never mentions his idea of the cause'. Templeton goes on to outline his own theory on the matter:

> From my observation it appears that the wheat receives the seed of mildew . . . from Agrostis Stolonifern principally, but also from Poa Pratensis and Trivalis etc., as I have constantly observed it upon the grasses even when there was none on wheat. But it seems to me that it is only when the wheat is in a state fit to receive it, that it is inflicted; the time when wheat is liable to mildew is when the [straw] is beginning to turn yellow.[14]

On 2 February 1807, Templeton is 'busy with Mr Dubour-dieu's new map of County Antrim'; for Templeton's extensive topographical knowledge of his native county had been used to provide much relevant information for Dubourdieu's statistical survey of county Antrim. Later that month, Templeton read and reflected on the essence of courage and freedom, as described by a writer in the *Annual Review*. He wrote in his journal: 'Military morals are closely connected with military manners and habits. Indeed, lewdness throughout animal nature is allied to courage and the gelding is a spiritless beast. Religion is not favourable to courage, half of its essence consists in inspiring fears of the mind'. Addressing national characteristics, he added: 'The Russians are the bravest, the hardiest, the best of soldiers, but they are not the most humane. The French excel in military virtues, but not in justice and humanity. The Irish are splendidly courageous, they have much humanisation to acquire'.

On the subject of freedom, he wrote: 'Experience shows that any diminution of the freedom of a people necessarily vitiates their morals. Montesquieu, a most acute observer of men, distinctly perceived this. He informs us that virtue is indispensable in a free government – and altogether unnecessary and extremely dangerous in a despotism'.[15] Templeton's own political feelings were close to those of Russell and their contemporary Henry Joy McCracken, but tempered by his abiding love of nature and humanity. To better the lot of his fellows was ever his motivation, and his reading informed his thinking in most practical ways.

Conscious of the unsanitary and dangerous state of the streets of Belfast, Templeton formulated a plan for supplying clean water to the inhabitants of that town. He quotes some of the agents that can spoil a water supply and those with remedial properties. These he took from Fourcroy's *Elements of chemistry*, published in English translation in 1785:

> In order to have good water, Fourcroy says it is necessary that no common sewers or drains should pass into it, that its current should not be impeded or rendered slower by obstacles, or by water being drained off in too great quantities; that the watering of hemp or the washing of clothes in soapy [water] should not be performed in it . . . To correct these bad qualities, several methods are employed, entirely grounded on chemical or physical considerations. Agitation by means of mills or causing it to pass through the air in the

form of jets, cascades, etc. These methods facilitate the
evaporation of noxious gas and putrid spiritus nectar . . .
cause impurities to subside by uniting them into larger
masses, and occasion the absorption of a proper quantity of
atmospheric air.[16]

To complement his scientific, philosophical and historical
reading, Templeton had a deep and critical interest in contemporary theatre and literature. His journals record attendance
at theatrical productions in Belfast and further afield. In 1810
he went to: 'The theatre at Larne to see the tragedy of Douglas,
performed by a company of Scottish actors'.[17] Ten years later
he went to see Mrs Siddons perform in *Damon and Pithias*;
and remarked in his journal: 'In it there are the finest expressions of patriotic feeling, but what forms the most prominent
features of the whole piece is the sublime enthusiasm of a
virtuous friendship'.[18]

Among others, he read the published works of contemporary Irish playwrights such as James Sheridan Knowles. He
had this to say of Knowles' new tragedy, *Caius Gracchus*: 'In
the dialogue we have a little too much of the flippancy of the
modern Italians. The wife of Caius has a little too much gentle
tenderness, and even Cornelia falls much below her historic
character'.[19] He was equally interested in contemporary novel-
ists. Commenting on the introductory letters which set the
scene in Lady Morgan's most famous work he wrote: 'Began
reading Miss Owenson's *Wild Irish Girl* – the feelings of a mind
not entirely deprived of natural sensibilities, but satiated with
dissipation are finely portrayed in the first letters'.[20]

Because of the resolution of the committee of the Belfast
Society for Promoting Knowledge to exclude 'any common
novel, or farce, or other book of trivial amusement', it is
reasonable to suggest that Templeton had his own library of
contemporary literature. Certainly, he epitomised the
cultured Georgian gentleman, intent on self improvement and
the improvement of the society in which he lived. John
Templeton died on 15 December 1835, much lamented by his
family and friends.

John Killen

Notes

1. P.R.O.N.I., Drennan letters, No. 345, Mrs Martha McTier to Dr William Drennan, 28 Oct. 1793.

2. William Drennan, *Fugitive pieces in verse and prose* (Belfast, 1815).

3. Drennan letters, No. 345.

4. *Belfast Newsletter*, 18-22 Oct. 1793.

5. Linen Hall Library: Minutes of the Belfast Society for Promoting Knowledge, 1 Jan. 1795.

6. Minutes of the Belfast Society for Promoting Knowledge, 7 Mar. 1792.

7. Jean-Jacques Rousseau, *The confessions of Jean-Jacques Rousseau*, translated by J.M. Cohen (Harmondsworth, 1953).

8. Richard Robert Madden, *The United Irishmen: their lives and times*, 3rd series, ii (Dublin, 1846), p. 189.

9. Madden, *United Irishmen*, 3rd series, ii, pp 192-193.

10. Madden, *United Irishmen*, 3rd series, ii, p. 195.

11. Ulster Museum, Journals of John Templeton, 9 Dec. 1806.

12. Journals of John Templeton, 25 Dec. 1806.

13. Journals of John Templeton, 18 Jan. 1807.

14. Journals of John Templeton, 26 Jan. 1807.

15. Journals of John Templeton, 18 Feb. 1807.

16. Journals of John Templeton, 28 Mar. 1807.

17. Journals of John Templeton, 31 Aug. 1810.

18. Journals of John Templeton, 26 July 1821.

19. Journals of John Templeton, 11 Dec. 1824.

20. Journals of John Templeton, 21 Dec. 1806.

The Kilkenny Circulating-Library Society and the growth of reading rooms in nineteenth-century Ireland

Marie-Louise Legg

A T THE BEGINNING OF THE nineteenth century, the rising numbers of professional men, middle-class families and well-to-do tradesmen in provincial Ireland were starved of literature. This was due, in part, to the high price of books and newspapers but mainly because there was almost nowhere to buy them.[1] Outside Dublin, even by the middle of the century, there were few bookshops. Shops in villages might have kept a small stock of cheap literature, and pedlars carried some books but their quality would probably have been poor.[2] Many provincial newspapers founded before 1851 were run by stationers and patent medicine vendors who also sold books.[3] James Grant, an Englishman travelling in Ireland in 1844, noticed that it was almost impossible to buy books, and Thomas Davis believed that there were ten counties in Ireland without any bookshop.[4] In 1849, a parliamentary committee considering the provision of public libraries heard that seventy-three towns in Ireland, with an average population of 2,300 people, had no bookshop.[5] This evidence may have ignored the bookshops in towns such as Dundalk, which twenty years earlier had a number of bookshops.[6] In 1860, W.H. Smith and Son began the first subscription library in Ireland but this service was not easily available to many readers in the more remote countryside, and certainly not to the poor.[7]

In 1851 it was calculated by one observer that between 1811 and 1849, 30,000 Irish adults had learned to read. In 1841 47 per cent of the population over the age of five claimed to be able to read.[8] To meet this growing demand for books, people banded together to make books available both for

109

themselves and for a wider audience. Five main motives impelled them. The first was self-serving: groups of local gentry paid regular subscriptions to obtain and circulate books for and among themselves. With her neighbours, Elizabeth Smith of Baltiboys, county Wicklow founded such a small private reading society with her neighbours in 1840. The second motive was to improve the training of artisans through the provision of education in local clubs and mechanics' institutes. This was joined with the third, the inculcation of virtue and social conformity. In this spirit, landlords founded libraries for their tenants and servants. The fourth was the common desire to create a measure of civic and national pride, and this was the impulse behind the founding of reading rooms by the movements for temperance and repeal. The instillation of virtue was joined to the fifth motive, the need to foster the spirit of nationalism. All these groups may have desired to improve the quality of books available where the stock in the existing provincial bookshops may well not have met the moral and political beliefs of both the local gentry and the leaders of social and national reform.

Reading rooms were founded by employers for their factory workers, by the workers themselves and by the church. Moral improvement abounded: Lord Roden founded a library for his tenants at Bryansford in 1836, believing it would be 'spiritually uplifting.' William Johnston bought Kildare Place Society books for his tenantry at Ballykilbeg. Protestant reading societies were founded to be a force against ignorance. Elizabeth Smith, who also had a lending library for her husband's tenants, said that her objective was the cultivation of 'the sober conviction of rational intelligence and *Lending Libraries* are to be among our tools.'[9] Its stock was made up of titles chosen from *Chambers Journal* and the *Penny Magazine*.[10] During the winter of 1842, twelve of their tenants met in the evenings, when the schoolmaster read aloud and the women knitted.

Libraries were started by mill owners for their employees: the Annsborough Library and Reading Society was founded by Murlands in 1865 and the Hillsborough Linen Company established both reading and recreation rooms for its employees in 1888.[11] In Bangor, county Down, it was hoped that the working men would be improved by the reading room, inaugurated

110

there in 1853.[12] Ports such as Belfast had reading rooms for sailors who could not see newspapers regularly.[13] New mechanics' institutes included a library and reading room for the use of artisans. A survey in 1852 found that 50 per cent of the members of mechanics' institutes were shopkeepers and their assistants and 25 per cent were members of trades: carpenters, masons, workmen and mechanics.[14] At the first meeting of the Clonmel Mechanics' Institute in February 1842 it was resolved that its aim was to benefit employer and worker alike by improving the skills and technical knowledge of men working in the town's cotton factory, corn mills, breweries and distilleries.[15] In 1865 the directors of the Belfast Mechanics' Institute (which became the Belfast People's Reading Room that year) included two lappers, a designer, a lithographer, a farrier, a founder, an embosser, a tailor, a painter, a fireman, two engineers, a machinist, an engraver, a printer and a cooper.[16] These men were the 'new and noble aristocracy appearing in the shops and warehouses . . . the aristocracy of mind . . .' about whom the Revd Dr Cumming addressed the Young Men's Christian Association in 1854. They were, he said, 'ready to take the "shine" out of the great aristocracy that preceded them.' The report of Dr Cumming's sermon in the Fermanagh *Impartial Reporter* was accompanied by a poem, 'The New Aristocracy', which celebrated the spread of reading among the working classes of Ireland as a mark of their rise in society.[17]

Elizabeth Smith's indoor communal reading mirrored the groups of peasants gathered in the open air who listened to the repeal papers read aloud during the 1840s. This passion for listening to the printed word was reflected in Irish nineteenth-century genre paintings. Three paintings of peasants listening to newspapers being read aloud are Howard Helmick's 'News of the Land League', Erskine Nicholl's 'The Ryans and Dwyers, Calumniated men' and Charles Lamb's 'Spreading the News'. Grant, the English traveller, witnessed such scenes and reflected that it was hardly surprising that the Repeal question had made such amazing progress.[18] Indeed it is possible that reading the Repeal press in the open air was the only way it could be heard. As will be seen in the case of Clonmel, the need for newspapers and newsrooms was frequently raised. But in the first half of the century newspapers were often kept out of the new libraries because they were thought to inflame political sentiment.[19]

In 1850 Dr Croke of Cashel spoke of having the 'general interests' of Ireland as his object when he founded the Charleville Reading Society. He recognised that 'general agitation in one shape or another' was inevitable, but he judged that no such agitation could succeed if people were ignorant of their duties and their rights as citizens. Popular education would improve the national character and act as a 'powerful auxiliary' to a new national movement.[20] Two movements had seen reading rooms as central to their programme of education and reform. These were Father Mathew's campaign for temperance and the Loyal National Repeal Association. Father Mathew had encouraged virtue and respectability by linking education to the teaching of social conformity. Preaching the message of temperance was not just an end in itself; the aim was to provide a different and morally improving life in order to occupy otherwise idle hands and minds. Father Mathew believed that his crusade should provide men with a meeting place as an alternative to the public house. He encouraged the opening of libraries and reading rooms and pressed for the reduction of duties on paper. Writing in 1844, James Grant attributed the growing taste for reading and the establishment of mechanics' institutes and reading societies to the influence of temperance.[21]

The leaders of the movement for the repeal of the Act of Union also believed that reading rooms were an essential component of its programme to spread the support of moderate constitutional reform. The Repeal enrolment certificate stated that its 'first principle' was to 'preserve and increase the VIRTUE of the people.'[22] Thomas Davis saw that the temperance societies' model of instruction and moral reform could be used as a way to put over the repeal programme. The Repeal reading rooms, founded from 1844 onwards, joined 'the great national question of repeal' to creating, in Davis's words, 'a brave, modest, laborious, and instructed People.'[23] If 2,000 enrolled repealers subscribed 1s. a year, a room would be set up in the locality and run by the committee of the Repeal Association and the local clergy. Davis urged that every parish should have such a room, provided with books, maps, prints, models and specimens in order to educate members in the history and geography of Ireland.[24] Were such a room in each village, he wrote, there would gather a 'knot of young men who had abjured cards, tobacco, dissipation and . . . laziness.'[25] However, although the rules for the new rooms emphasised the importance of education, the main business at the regular meetings of the local Repeal committee was to do Repeal business: receive the rent, collect signatures for parliamentary petitions and register voters. Such local Repeal business may have had the effect of side-lining the primacy of education, for Davis became concerned about the quality of some village rooms, which were ill-managed, their school-rooms almost unused, with 'few or no books.'[26] Repeal Association inspectors, however, believed that the new rooms did have a moral effect. In Cashel, card-playing was said to have been entirely given up, dance houses were less frequented in Trim, and examinations in history and science were said to be preferred to frequenting the public house.[27]

Outside Dublin, Belfast and Cork, the membership of the twelve mechanics' institutes which possessed libraries ranged in size from sixteen members in Portaferry to 300 in Waterford.[28] The largest library, the Limerick Institute, had 4,200 books and the smallest, in the Young Mens' Institutes in Garvagh and Kilrea had 100. The demand for books can be broadly assessed by dividing the number of books issued by the libraries of eleven provincial institutes by their membership and comparing these figures with the figures provided for institutes in Dublin, Belfast and Cork. Compared to an average of 5.89 books issued annually to each member of institutes in Dublin, Cork and Belfast, the provincial libraries in the smaller towns issued an average of 16.45 titles. These figures, however crude, underline the absence of good local bookshops in the provinces.

Reading rooms were financed by the sale of shares, by subscriptions and by selling old stock. In 1851, subscriptions ranged from 6s. a year in Downpatrick to 40s. a year in Limerick. Many societies had concessions. Working members of the Cork Protestant Operative Association paid 2s., less than half the annual subscription of 5s. Apprentices and children were admitted at half price to the Clonmel Mechanics' Institute.[29]

Auctions of old stock in order to finance the purchase of new books and newspapers was common. In 1841 Elizabeth Smith had a luncheon party for twenty-four people when her reading society raised £27 by auctioning books that had been bought over the previous year.[30] In the local libraries, newspapers were kept for a number of days in the newsroom and then sent to the purchaser who had been successful at auction. In 1858 a year's supply of the London *Times* had originally cost the Kilkenny Circulating-Library Society £7.16s.0d. It was sold by the Society for £3.1s.0d.[31] Some societies raised money to finance their work through public lectures on husbandry and science.[32]

The Kilkenny Circulating-Library Society was founded in April 1811. The founders included Edward Denroche, proprietor of the *Kilkenny Moderator*, the Revd Andrew O'Callaghan, headmaster of Kilkenny College, the Revd Peter Roe, incumbent of St. Mary's, Kilkenny and John Prim, general printer and stationer, who was the father of John Prim the antiquarian.[33] Their politics were conservative.[34] Their aim appears to have been to create a local lending library for themselves and those like them which, from the titles of the books they bought, would emulate the library of an Ascendancy landlord. Each proprietor of the society, as the shareholders were called, owned a 20 guinea share. Ordinary subscribers paid a small annual sum. The corporation allowed the society to have its reading and conversation rooms in the Tholsel. The librarian was paid an annual salary of £50 and a porter was hired to sweep the rooms, take care of the fires and candlesticks, open the front door and keep the newspapers tidy.[35] The opening hours of the reading room were from 10am to 5pm, and those of the newsroom from 7am to 8pm; hours suitable for working men.[36] The books first proposed for acquisition in 1811 concentrated on natural history, philosophy, ancient history, travels and standard works of reference. This first list included Sir Laurence Parsons, *Defence of Irish history* and Ledwich's *Antiquities of Ireland*. Two months later there appears to have been some thought on the need for books about Ireland. The next list of titles included James Ware's *Antiquities*, Walter Harris's *Hibernia*, a history of the rebellion, Grattan's speeches, and Molyneux's *Natural history of Ireland*, together with three volumes of Irish pamphlets.

Charlotte Brooke's *Reliques of Irish poetry* was bought in 1812.[37] The society even-handedly subscribed to both the *Edinburgh Review* and to the *Quarterly Review*. In the first year, the library had acquired 1,094 volumes by purchase and donation.[38] There were problems in ordering the titles they planned because of the difficulty of buying them in Ireland (possibly another indication of the inadequacy of booksellers) and they were forced to consider sending to England for much of their stock.[39] The earl of Ossory directed that his library should be examined and his duplicate books should be given to the society.[40] By the annual meeting in 1814 there were seventy-four proprietors, seventy-one subscribers and thirty-two people nominated to be able to use the separate circulating library.[41] From the start, the intellectual nature of the society's stock did not suit some members' needs and there were repeated requests for newspapers which would provide information on local commerce and market prices.[42] The conduct of the newspaper readers was a problem. Newspapers encouraged conversation, and although newspapers were supposed to be kept in the conversation room, they must have crept into the reading room, because a resolution was passed in 1812 to keep them out in order to ensure silence.[43] Despite, or perhaps because of, the high share prices and the cost of subscriptions, the library committee was constrained on a number of occasions from buying stock.[44] However, in 1820 the society received £150, the first instalment of an annuity from the Joseph Evans Trust, a local charity.[45] The Evans trustees proved fickle friends, and soon their payments began to fall behind. By 1836 they owed the society over £550, and to raise money a proposal was made by the committee to sell off volumes of periodicals. This was roundly denounced as threatening the only library in Kilkenny which contained European literary history and criticism.[46] Problems with the payment of the Evans annuity lasted over twenty years and at one point the mayor of Kilkenny threatened to take the case to the High Court.[47]

At some point in the decline of their fortunes, the library and newsroom moved from the Tholsel to the Coal Market, which appears to have proved unsatisfactory. By 1844 the institution had deteriorated to such an extent that it had become 'just a newsroom' and it was decided to move it to a central part of Kilkenny so that it could be 'conducted in a more respectable manner.'[48] The salary of the librarian was reduced and the committee was forced to beg for free additions to its stock. The proprietors of the local newspapers were now prevailed upon to supply their papers free and the marquis of Ormonde and the county MPs were asked to donate parliamentary reports.[49] A threatened sale of the society's rooms in 1860 was averted when the payment of the Evans Trust annuity was resumed.[50]

There is little information on the nature of the society's membership, but there are some indications in the minutes that by the mid-century the political allegiance of the people who ran and used the society's rooms had begun to change. One of the society's active figures from the 1830s onwards was Robert Cane, a wealthy doctor whose patients came from the gentry of Kilkenny and the surrounding area.[51] An energetic member of the campaign for repeal, he was twice mayor of Kilkenny and presided over the confederate debate in 1848. In 1857 Cane founded a weekly journal dedicated to 'national literature', *The Celt*. Like the movements for temperance and repeal, *The Celt* advocated the inculcation of virtue and love of country. Cane commissioned articles from the Fenian, C.J. Kickham, and from William Kenealy, editor of the *Kilkenny Journal*. (The *Journal* was a long-established liberal paper which proclaimed 'Ireland for the Irish' on its masthead). Kenealy, who wrote poetry for *The Nation*, was a proprietor of the society from at least 1859. The influence of both Cane and Kenealy, neither of them Fenians but both warmly sympathetic to the promotion of Ireland's cause, can be perceived in the changes in the library stock. From 1847 the committee resolved to discontinue subscribing to some British papers and take Kilkenny papers instead.[52] In 1861 they decided to buy Irish guidebooks and books about Kilkenny and its surrounding countryside. These included such titles as Robert Cane's history of the Williamite wars, Prim and Graves's history of St. Canice's Cathedral, the works of John Banim and the transactions of the Kilkenny Archaeological Society, founded in 1849 by the younger John Prim and the Revd James Graves.[53] The library also began to subscribe to the publications of the Irish Archaeological and Celtic Society and the Ossianic Society. A large number of English books were sold, including all the works of Walter Scott, bought in the 1830s, and guides to various English counties.[54]

The problems faced by the Kilkenny Circulating-Library Society over maintaining its income were common. Secretaries and treasurers defaulted with the funds; the price of keeping the stock up to date, as we have seen, was prohibitive. As the stock declined so did the number of subscribers.[55] Workers felt diffident about entering the rooms, lacking suitable dress and price of subscriptions. Readers began to be more demanding. In 1847, the *Tipperary Free Press* drew attention to a fall in the membership of the Clonmel Mechanics' Institute.[56] In a swingeing attack, the newspaper accused the committee of both incompetence and prejudice. The charges were that for many years they had failed to stock scientific books – one of the original objects of the institute – and refused to buy newspapers. Ninety members out of 194 believed that the institute was run in a manner that would not discredit Russian despotism because they had controlled acquisitions with an iron hand. Their accusers deployed a skilful attack on the committee's policies, pointing out that Goethe's *Sorrows of Werther* acquired in the previous year, could not be classified as science, and that if the *Letters of Junius* were classified as history, why were newspapers excluded. They were, after all, the history of modern times.[57]

Local criticism was one problem. Government opposition was another. Dublin Castle had a long history of resistance to popular reading, and the growing number of reading rooms and newsrooms worried them, and it worried others.[58] In 1798, a reading room in Doagh, county Antrim, and another in Newry, county Down, had been wrecked by the yeomanry. The marquis of Downshire, who feared that 'reading . . . might set the good people of Hillsborough to think', closed his local book club.[59] Despite Father Mathew's efforts to avoid political questions,[60] the police believed that the temperance movement was a political hotbed and that its reading rooms were a focus of radical politics. A temperance reading room in Tipperary was said to supply newspapers preaching 'violent politics.'[61] Resident magistrates regularly sent reports to Dublin Castle about what they perceived to be the influence of popular literature, supported by copies of seditious ballads and cuttings from newspapers.[62] In 1849, Repeal reading rooms across Ireland were ordered to be closed, amid comments by local resident magistrates on the influence 'inflicted upon a mercurial People by . . . inflammatory and seditious essays' and the 'poisonous publications . . . read at all the cheap reading rooms on Sunday.'[63] Almost immediately there were protests by the clergy that the exiled readers had transferred their custom to the public houses.[64]

The political events after 1870 brought a new recognition of the importance of reading rooms to spread the cause of nationalism. Writing the history of Young Ireland in 1880, Gavan Duffy recalled that its greatest supporters had been 'the reading men': the tradesmen, clerks and shopkeepers who had been educated in the reading rooms of the Repeal Association.[65] A series of letters in *The Nation* in 1878 now renewed the link between temperance, nationalism and the provision of reading rooms. In the 1880s the Land League founded reading rooms in conscious imitation of their predecessors; these were seen to be the true 'heirs at law' of Thomas Davis's Repeal reading rooms.[66] The possibilities of reading rooms took on a new life with the formation of the Gaelic League. Village libraries were seen as a means to revive the Irish language and provide classes to study Irish history and customs.[67]

The nineteenth-century reading rooms survive in the county libraries of today. When the committee of the Kilkenny Circulating-Library Society received the first monies from the Joseph Evans Trust in 1820 they believed it would give the library 'permanence and importance.'[68] They were proved to be right when, with the support of its members, the Circulating-Library's stock became part of the new Carnegie Library when it opened in Kilkenny in November 1910. Carnegie himself had provided that grants for libraries were only available when sites were donated by local landowners and the new library was built on a site in John Street donated by Ellen, Lady Desart. The rules for the new library echoed earlier regulations, but the building included a reading room for women. But women could only use the room especially provided for them, and newspapers could only be read in the reading room: open exclusively to men. Unusually, the new library building contained a gymnasium, which had been included by Kilkenny Corporation in order to attract monies available under a gymnasium act.[69] The terms of Carnegie's grant to Kilkenny maintained the nineteenth-century tradition of local landowners' involvement in the support of education and self-improvement for Kilkenny's inhabitants. The great difference was that, unlike the subscription library of the past, the new library was free. The corporation now bore the cost of the library's upkeep – making available to all what had until then been a provision available only to those who could afford to pay.

Marie-Louise Legg

Notes

1. A 3-volume novel cost 31s.6d. L.M. Cullen, *Easons: a history* (Dublin, 1989), p. 189. Cullen does not give a date for this price, but it was probably the mid-century.

2. Niall Ó Ciosáin, *Print and popular culture in Ireland 1750–1850* (Basingstoke, 1997), pp 59–60.

3. Marie-Louise Legg, *Newspapers and nationalism: the Irish provincial press 1850–92* (Dublin, 1998), appendix: newspapers in print, 1850–92.

4. J. Grant, *Impressions of Ireland and the Irish* (London, 1844), pp 168–169; Thomas Davis, 'Schools and study', in *Essays and poems with a centenary memoir* (Dublin, 1945), p. 86.

5. T. Cliffe Leslie, *An inquiry into the progress and present condition of Mechanics' Institutions*, part i (Dublin Statistical Society, 1852), p. 10.

6. According to J. Pigot & Co., *The commercial directory of Ireland, Scotland and the four most northern counties of England for 1820–1 & 22* (Manchester, 1820); *Pigot and Co's city of Dublin and Hibernian provincial directory* (Manchester, 1824); *Slater's national commercial directory of Ireland* (Manchester, 1846), Dundalk had three booksellers in 1820 and four in 1824 and by 1846 they had six booksellers. I am grateful to Máire Kennedy for drawing my attention to this information.

7. Cullen, *Easons*, p. 59.

8. J.W. Hudson, *History of adult education* (London, 1851), p. 23; Joseph Lee, *The modernisation of Irish society* (Dublin, 1973), p. 13.

9. 30 May 1842. Patricia Pelly and Andrew Tod (eds), *Elizabeth Grant of Rothiemurchus: the Highland lady in Ireland, 1840–1850* (Edinburgh, 1991), p. 110.

10. Pelly and Tod (eds), *Elizabeth Grant*, p. 145.

11. J.R.R. Adams, *The printed word and the common man: popular culture in Ulster, 1700–1900* (Belfast, 1987), p. 39.

12. Adams, *The printed word*, p. 128.

13. In 1877, the Belfast Sailors' Institution and Workmen's Reading rooms had a reading room and circulating library. *The Belfast and province of Ulster directory for 1877* (Belfast, 1877).

14. Leslie, *An inquiry*, p. 8.

15. Kieran Byrne, 'Mechanics' Institutes in Ireland before 1855', M.Ed. thesis, University College Cork, 1976, p. 174.

16. The Belfast Mechanics' Institute and the Belfast Working Men's Institute, P.R.O.N.I., D1769/24/2.

17. 'The new aristocracy' in *The Impartial Reporter and Fermanagh Journal*, 19 Apr. 1854.

18. Grant, *Impressions*, pp 171–172, 200–201.

19. Dublin Literary Society Laws and Regulations revised 1863, N.L.I., MS. 328, p. 3.

20. *Limerick and Clare Examiner*, 11 Sept. 1850.

21. Grant, *Impressions*, pp 250–251.

22. H.F. Kearney, 'Father Mathew: apostle of modernism' in Art Cosgrove and Donal McCartney (eds), *Studies in Irish history presented to R. Dudley Edwards* (Dublin, 1979), p. 167.

23. Thomas Davis, 'Self-education' in *Essays,* p. 66.

24. Davis, 'Schools and study' in *Essays*, p. 82; Margaret Barnes, 'Repeal reading rooms' in *An Leabharlann*, xxiii, no. 2 (1965), p. 53.

25. Davis, 'Schools and study' in *Essays*, p. 83.

26. Davis, 'Schools and Study' in *Essays*, p. 86.

27. Barnes, 'Repeal reading rooms', p. 55.

28. Table of Mechanics' and Literary Institutions in Hudson, *History*, pp 236–237.

29. 'Borough Directory', in *Thom's Irish almanac and official directory, 1850* (Dublin, 1850).

30. 20 August 1841. Pelly and Tod (eds), *Elizabeth Grant*, pp 73–74.

31. The Society raised £17.11s.0d. in this way in 1850. Minutes of 7 October 1850; 30 Mar. 1858. Kilkenny County Library, Kilkenny Circulating-Library Society, minute book 4. (The archives consists of 5 minute books running from Apr. 1811 to 1911, a suggestion book and an undated catalogue. I am greatly indebted to Declan Macauley of the Kilkenny County Library for having drawn my attention to this source.)

32. Kearney, 'Father Mathew', p. 166; Hudson, *History,* pp 236–238.

33. Minute of 6 Apr. 1811, Kilkenny Circulating-Library Society, minute book 1.

34. The sons of both Edward Denroche and John Prim edited the *Kilkenny Moderator*, a conservative weekly newspaper in the 1850s, Legg, *Newspapers*, appendix.

35. Minutes of 6 and 30 Sept. 1811, Kilkenny Circulating-Library Society, minute book 1.

36. Laws and Regulations of the Society, minute of 1 Aug. 1811, Kilkenny Circulating-Library Society, minute book 1.

37. Minutes of 24 Apr. and 10 June 1811; 13 Apr. 1812, Kilkenny Circulating-Library Society, minute book 1.

38. 456 books had been purchased at a cost of £136.6s.6d. and £15.5s.10d. had been spent on periodicals. 163 volumes had been donated. Minute of 30 Sept. 1811, Kilkenny Circulating-Library Society, minute book 1.

39. Minute of 29 Sept. 1812, Kilkenny Circulating-Library Society, minute book 1.

40. Minute of 29 Sept. 1814., Kilkenny Circulating-Library Society, minute book 1.

41. These nominees seem to have been those who used the reading room but did not borrow books. Minutes of 29 Sept. 1814, 29 Sept. 1817 (Kilkenny Circulating-Library Society, minute book 1 and minute book 4).

42. Minutes of 29 Sept. 1818 and 30 June 1858, Kilkenny Circulating-Library Society, minute book 2 and minute book 4.

43. Minute of 14 Mar. 1812, Kilkenny Circulating-Library Society, minute book 1.

44. When the *Waterford Chronicle* was ordered in 1818, *Carrick's Dublin Journal*, the *Philosophical Magazine* and the *Army List* were discontinued. Minute of 29 Sept. 1818, Kilkenny Circulating-Library Society, minute book 2.

45. Minute of 30 Sept. 1820, Kilkenny Circulating-Library Society, minute book 2.

46. Minute of 29 Sept. 1836, Kilkenny Circulating-Library Society, minute book 2.

47. Minute of 9 Oct. 1854, Kilkenny Circulating-Library Society, minute book 4.

48. Minute of 17 Dec. 1844, Kilkenny Circulating-Library Society, minute book 4.

49. Dr Robert Cane to the committee 3 Feb. 1845; minute of 3 Nov. 1845, Kilkenny Circulating-Library Society, minute book 1.

50. Abstract of receipts and expenditure for six months 29 Sept. 1859–25 Mar. 1860. During this period the Society received £92.6s.2d., Kilkenny Circulating-Library Society, minute book 5.

51. Cane joined the Society's committee in 1834. Minute of 13 Oct. 1834, Kilkenny Circulating-Library Society, minute book 1.

52. Minutes of 13 December 1847, 28 Mar. 1848 and 29 Sept. 1859, Kilkenny Circulating-Library Society, minute book 4.

53. John Banim (1798–1842) was born and educated in Kilkenny. Minute of 22 Mar. 1861, Kilkenny Circulating-Library Society, minute book 5.

54. Minute of 22 Apr. 1861, Kilkenny Circulating-Library Society, minute book 5.

55. Members of the Clonmel Mechanics' Institute complained that their newsroom was 'cold and cheerless', and had old and defaced copies of periodicals. Leslie, *An inquiry*; *Tipperary Free Press*, 18 December 1847.

56. The membership had dropped from 415 members in 1845 to 241 in 1846 and 194 in 1847. *Tipperary Free Press*, 18 Dec. 1847.

57. In 1842 the Dublin Mechanics' Institute had refused to stock novels. Mary Casteleyn, *History of literacy and libraries in Ireland* (Dublin, 1984) pp 154–155; *Tipperary Free Press*, 18 December 1847.

58. Kevin B. Nowlan, 'The origins of the press in Ireland' in Brian Farrell (ed.), *Communications and community in Ireland* (Dublin, 1984), pp 9–10.

59. Adams, *The printed word*, pp 38, 39.

60. Kearney, 'Father Mathew', p. 165.

61. Statement by a police inspector, quoted in Kearney, 'Father Mathew' p. 174.

62. There was a high level of concern between 1829 and 1848. Maura Murphy, 'The ballad singer and the role of the seditious ballad in nineteenth-century Ireland, Dublin Castle's view' in *Ulster Folklife*, xxv (1979), p. 80.

63. Confidential report on the state of the lately disturbed districts, 8 January 1849, P.R.O., CO904/9.

64. A request by a Cork clergyman to reopen a newsroom to keep men out of public houses was refused by the local resident magistrate, P.R.O., CO904/9.

65. C. Gavan Duffy, *Young Ireland: a fragment of Irish history* (Dublin, 1880), p. 175.

66. J. Pope-Hennessy, 'What do the Irish read?' in *Nineteenth Century* xv (June 1884), pp 925–926.

67. Revd J. O'Donovan, 'Village libraries' in *Irish Homestead*, vi, no. 1, 20 January 1899.

68. Minute of 30 Sept. 1820, Kilkenny Circulating-Library Society, minute book 1.

69. Brendan Grimes, 'Carnegie Libraries in Ireland' in *History Ireland*, vi, no. 4 (1998), pp 27–28.

Fiction available to and written for cottagers and their children

Rolf Loeber and
Magda Stouthamer-Loeber

ALTHOUGH POPULAR LITERATURE in Ireland has increasingly become a focus of study,[1] relatively little is known about books produced for peasants and cottagers in the eighteenth and nineteenth centuries, which have often been kept artificially outside of literary studies.[2] More needs to be known about these groups of readers, especially since they constituted the majority of the Irish population. This essay will focus on the period from the 1770s to 1850s, when the Irish language declined significantly and the English language became increasingly popular.[3] During this time the English language rapidly replaced Irish as the medium of instruction in the hedge schools.[4] In the rural districts of Waterford, Cork, Kerry, and Galway, English was called 'the new tongue', and was increasingly adopted.[5] Much of the increase in literacy was among the largest population group, the cottagers. Richard Lovell Edgeworth, one of the Commissioners of the Board of Education in Ireland, stated in 1811 that 'for one person that could read or write twenty years ago, there are now twenty'.[6] Remarkably, in this period reading in the English language by cottagers dramatically increased, partly because of a lack of printed books in Irish.[7] Therefore, the focus of the paper is on English fiction available to and written for cottagers and their children.

There are several problems in understanding the literature available to and written for this segment of the population. Their books were often cheap and perishable productions. Poverty, dampness, and emigration all helped to eradicate whatever literature was kept in cottages. Moreover, since many of the books were published for and read by cottagers' children, they may have suffered like most children's books. No contemporary lists or catalogues are known of book holdings in cottages, and to date we have been unable to locate a comprehensive collection of Irish popular fiction representing the books available to cottagers.[8]

Cottagers are defined as tenants, day-labourers, and servants as well as their families usually living in cottages on estates. They are often known as peasants or, in contemporary terms, 'the lower classes'.[9] The latter category does not distinguish between the poor living in the country and those living in the towns, but it should be understood that literature produced for cottagers could also apply to the urban poor. It should be noted that cottagers were mostly Catholics, with a minority being Protestants. Our definition of literature excludes religious works, academic school books, primers and printed ballads. We concentrate on popular fiction produced in Ireland rather than such books produced in England or the United States for the Irish market.

Our focus is on popular books, that is relatively inexpensive books, consisting of either (a) chapbooks printed in a single sheet, folded in eight to produce sixteen pages, folded in twelve to produce twenty-four pages, or folded in sixteen to produce thirty-two pages, in a size of about 5½ by 3½ inches. The chapbooks were sold for a few farthings, but often costing 1*d*.; or (b) chapmen's books, i.e., dearer books of about 140-180 pages, printed on more than one sheet, usually covered with a paper wrapper or in a sheep-leather binding and priced at about 6*d*. Frequently books in both of these categories constituted abridgements of longer, and as we will see, usually much older works.[10] Pederson characterised their contents as follows: 'Often chapbooks present either a fantasy landscape or a world turned upside down: a world of giants and witches, of poor but valorous heroes, of scheming wives and successful crooks. Above all they are hostile to respectability: to industry, chastity, piety, and other bourgeois virtues'. Such stories often feature seduction, rape, and sexual 'meddling', and are often misogynist and always forthright about sex. The stories were related to amuse without any polemical or political intent and lacked moral messages. Chapbooks often contained much humour, and presented 'a fictional world where the sexual and social order was fluid and changeable.'[11] The following is mainly a bibliographical essay, illustrated by descriptions of the contents of books wherever known to us. We will show that the history of Irish popular books must be both the history of the reader *and* the history of the financial sponsors of such books.

The belief that children and adults should be able to read was not universally held in eighteenth- and nineteenth-century Ireland. Dewar relates that some people were opposed to educating the Irish poor, on the grounds 'that it is dangerous to enlighten the inferior orders lest they become discontented with their condition'.[12] For example, Richard Lovell Edgeworth reported to the Board of Education in 1808 that 'I have been told, that in some schools the Greek and Roman histories are forbidden; such abridgements of these histories, as I have seen, are certainly improper; they inculcate democracy, and a foolish hankering after undefined liberty: this is particularly dangerous in Ireland . . . For their amusement, stories inculcating piety, and morality, and industry, should be admitted. But every thing that leads to restlessness and adventure should be carefully avoided.'[13] The notion that the peasantry might increasingly become aware of democratic principles leading to social change, was quite realistic. As one fictional character, 'Ned of the Hill', in the novel *Blue-stocking Hall*, set near Killarney, said in 1827: 'Education seems to be declining among the *heads* of the community, as much as it is flourishing amongst the *tails*, and, before long, it will be found that the *tails* will take the post where the *heads* are now.'[14] Remarkably, the Commissioners of the Board of Irish Education recognised in 1825 that the issue was not whether they could decide to provide education for the 'lower classes' leading to 'evil rather than to good'. Instead, the Commissioners acknowledged that the lower classes were 'actually obtaining [education] for themselves'.[15]

Another perceived danger was that reading about criminal activities would cause people to become delinquent themselves. For example, R. Bell, who had testified before the commissioners inquiring into the state of education and schools of Ireland in 1788, wrote that when juveniles perused such books as *The History of the Irish rogues and rapparees*

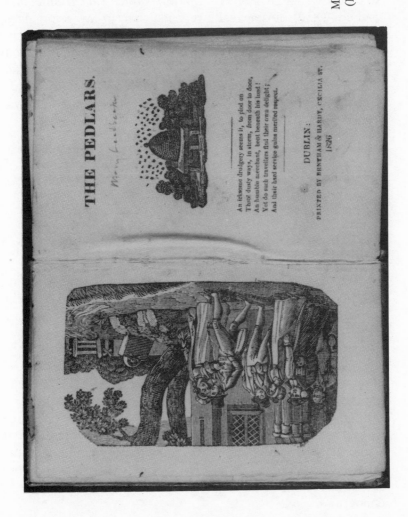

Figure 5: Title page
and frontispiece of
Mary Leadbeater's *The pedlars*
(Dublin, 1826). Printed for the
Kildare Place Society.

[sic], *The Adventures of Captain Phreny* [sic, Freney], and of *Redmond O'Hanlon*, they become:

> familiarised to offences of the most violent and atrocious nature; and were taught to look upon robbers, incendiaries, murderers, and violators of women, as objects of admiration. The transition from theory to practice was but short.- And crimes proceeded more frequently from an inherent depravity in the perpetrators, than from that desire of gain which constitute their origin in most other countries.[16]

A landowner, in George Brittaine's *Irishmen and Irishwomen* (Dublin, 1830), nostalgically recalled that 'in my young days, the people were quiet, and loyal, and civil and orderly; yet, not one in fifty could sign his name, or distinguish one letter from another . . . [But now] the whole world is going to school, and, of consequence, is growing worse and worse every day.'[17] However, these views were not universally shared. Dewar argued that:

> reading cannot possibly injure the morals, since there are few who can read; and yet, the enemies of education, so far from discovering any superior innocency of manners, will find the perpetration of crimes much more frequent, because the moral feelings are perverted by the deadly influence of a baneful superstition. – The truth is, reading is the chief security of the poor against moral, political, and religious error. The contamination is always in their way; is it not proper, then, to provide an antidote?[18]

Another argument in favour of reading was expressed in the periodical *Captain Rock in London* in 1825. It asked the question, 'how could the government expect the Irish to obey laws, [while] not being able to read them?'[19]

Some held the point of view that even literature as a form of relaxation was unnecessary for labourers. As a character in the novel *Blue-stocking Hall* stated: 'A man who works for a shilling a day, eats his potatoes, and lies down to be refreshed by sleep for the morrow's labour, had no need of literature. It would neither make him happier or better, unless he read the Bible.'[20] It was not merely the act of reading for relaxation but the accompanying unchristian thinking that became a concern.

In some respects the discussions about the lack of desirability of Irish cottagers reading and becoming educated was irrelevant. The most influential group of individuals – Irish publishers – probably did not need convincing that stimulation of reading would be economically advantageous to all professions involved in the production of books. The main questions posed by this essay are: what popular literature was available and written for cottagers in the eighteenth century? What was the thrust of such books, and how widespread was their distribution among cottagers and their children?

Overall, Protestants, even those from an Irish background, severely criticised the literature available to peasants and to children in general. One of the earliest recorded denunciations of literature for youth was expressed in 1788 by Mathew Carey, the Dublin printer who had left Ireland four years earlier to settle in the United States. He referred to 'the vile tales and burton books, whereof thousands are annually disseminated throughout Ireland, and which corrupt the taste (and may I not add, the morals) of the youth of both sexes.' Specifically, he referred to:

> a large proportion of the reading of young people . . . for amusement was confined to *Don Bellianis of Greece*, *Gesta Romanorum*, the *Seven Champions of Christendom*, the *Seven Wise Masters of Greece*, *Guy Earl of Warwick*, etc., etc.; and for the improvement of their morals and manners, the *History of the Pirates*, and of the *Irish Rogues and Rapparees*, etc. etc.[21]

Burton books were chapman's books named after R. Burton, the pseudonym of Nathaniel Crouch, a London publisher and hack writer, who adapted major books for the popular market.[22] They could be purchased for about 6*d*. a piece. Dr Whitley Stokes who criticised burtons in 1799, stated that there were about eighty such chapmen's books on the market, which formerly could be purchased at 6½*d*, but then cost 8*d*. and were 'sold' (i.e., produced?) by six or seven persons in Ireland. Stokes distinguished between the following categories: histories of robbers and pirates; books of chivalry; books of witchcraft and gross superstition; indecent books.

These categories constituted about two-thirds of the chapmen's books. The remainder consisted of useful or innocent books of voyage, travel, history or novels. Stokes warned that 'the mischief' done by the other categories of chapmen's books 'will be acknowledged', and stated that one should not think that romances were innocent, because such works 'contribute greatly to keep alive a false admiration of courage, a spirit of war and revenge, and a love of adventure so incompatible with the happiness of mankind.'[23] Many others echoed similar sentiments. For example, the Protestant Bishop Magee, in a sermon of 1796 to the Association for Discountenancing Vice and Promoting the Knowledge and Practice of the Christian Religion, disapproved of 'The pernicious tendency of most of the cheap publications, commonly entitled story books and ballads, which formerly constituted almost the whole of the literary entertainment of the lower classes.'[24]

References to the unsuitability of the reading matter available to young people also began to appear in fiction books. For example, a father in *The Pedlars* (Dublin, 1826; Figure 5), told his son that:

> In my young days, there was a great dearth of good books for young persons. There were fairy tales enough, and histories of noted robbers; but what profit could be derived from nonsense concerning things which never had existence, or from accounts of people, who were a terror to their neighbours, and at last met the punishment which their crimes deserved.[25]

Carleton, writing in a Protestant mode of thinking in 1830, echoed a similar sentiment, and stated that the hedge schools had teachers whose knowledge was 'directed to evil purposes'. Particularly:

> disloyal principles were industriously insinuated in their minds by their teachers. The matter placed in their [the pupils'] hands was of a most inflammatory and pernicious nature, as regarded politics; and as far as religion and morality were concerned, nothing could be more gross and superstitious than the books which circulated amongst them. Eulogiums on murder, robbery, and theft, were read with delight.[26]

Criticism of the chapbooks came from several quarters. The Hibernian Bible Society called the books available in hedge schools 'foolish legends which poisoned the minds of youth'. The Report of the Commissioners of Irish Education of 1825 quoted a report from 1812, stating that poverty and bad teachers prevented the acquisition of books fit for children to read. As a result, children's minds 'are corrupted by Books calculated to incite to lawless and profligate adventure, to cherish superstition, or to lead to dissension or disloyalty'.[27]

Remarkably, contemporary authors often did not refer to the bad influence of libertine or sexual adventure books or label them as being unsuitable for children, even though these books may fall under the heading of books perverting the morals of juveniles. However, attitudes toward sex in books may have become more restricted over the period we are discussing. We find that the commissioners investigating the disturbances in 1824 repeatedly questioned witnesses if they had seen copies of *Moll Flanders* in schools.[28]

The chapbooks were produced in very large quantities. A writer in *The Dublin and London Magazine* in 1825 reported that:

> The number of sixpenny or Burton books annually sold, was formerly immense. Four booksellers in Dublin used to deal exclusively in them, and one had four presses constantly employed, and published on an average fifty thousand annually; besides these there were presses in Cork and Limerick employed in no other work. It was supposed that in this way three hundred thousand were every year printed and circulated.[29]

The chapman's books were much used for teaching reading in Irish schools. Isaac Heron, who was born in Coleraine in 1735, recounted that when he attended school he read chapbooks, such as *Valentine and Orson*, *Parismus*, *The life of Jack the giant killer*, and the *Tale of Robinson Crusoe*.[30] Records of books available in schools in Ireland in the eighteenth century are extremely scarce. It is not until 1824 that a long list was drawn up of books available in schools in counties Donegal, Kildare, Galway, and Kerry.[31] A category called 'Works of Entertainment, Histories, Tales, &c.', which excluded religious books and the books published by the Kildare Place Society, included an amazing variety of 302 titles. Since the list does not contain publishers' names or dates of publication, it is mostly impossible to trace the origin of publication of the volumes. Although we can presume that chapbooks were represented, this is hard to discern; however, some of the books in the list are only known from editions that were more substantial and expensive than chapmen's books.

The parochial returns of 1824 show that many parents were far too poor to even buy food or clothing, let alone to purchase books for their children.[32] However, many records show that parents, and less often children, were the main purveyors of children's reading material in schools. As Justin McCarthy recounted in 1824: 'The practice in the country schools is, when the parent sends his child to school, he buys any book that he finds, no matter what.'[33] On the other hand, children such as the young Carleton are known to have scavenged for books at their own home or that of others, and to have taken their finds to school.[34] James Glassford, one of the inspectors of schools, noted in 1825-26 that 'children bring what they have or can find; religious, political, dramatic, and in fragments or leaves; and are allowed to read and spell from whatever they so produce.'[35] Given that cottagers' children rarely would have had money to purchase books, we can assume that most of the books they brought to school were derived from the possessions of the older generations, particularly parents, who purchased either new or second hand books from pedlars and grocers.[36] However, the older generations had a higher rate of illiteracy than their children. Those parents who could read may have been able to make judicious choices of what their children could or should read. Parents' provision of books for schools was, of course, less straightforward when such parents could not read. Did such parents keep books even if they were illiterate? Judging from William Carleton, this was indeed the case in the county Tyrone village where he grew up. He characterised himself when young as 'an insatiable reader of such sixpenny romances and history books as the hedge-schools afforded'.[37] His great hunger for books, made him go through the greater part of the parish 'hunting for books of entertainment', and he:

ransacked almost all the old cupboards and boxes in the parish . . . Although the state of education was, at the period of which I write, very low, and knowledge scanty among the people, yet it is surprising what a number of books, pamphlets and odd volumes, many of these works of fiction, I found among them. If you examined the number of Catholic families in the parish, you would find that one half of them could not read; yet several of these utterly illiterate persons had many of the works I have alluded to, most carefully laid up, under the hope that some young relation might be able to read them.[38]

Nowadays it is difficult to sense how scarce books were in Ireland at the beginning of the nineteenth century. One school-master, Thady O'Conolan (better known as Thady Connellan), teacher at a classical 'seminary' in county Sligo, noted that 'This is the only Homer I have; and though seven boys read out of it daily, it never causes a moment's dispute'.[39] Trotter .complained in 1812 that Irish youth could not get 'English books to read. . . Books in Irish are not to be had.'[40] Glassford in his travels in the 1820s found that one boy in a Catholic school in the town of Wexford had been reading Fielding's *Tom Jones* 'for five years'.[41] Incidentally, this book also impressed William Carleton as a child. When visiting the house of fellow-student in 'a wild mountainous district' of county Tyrone, 'I saw for the first time an odd volume of *Tom Jones*; but I have not the slightest intention of describing the wonder and the feeling with which I read it. No pen could do justice to that. It was the second volume; of course, the story was incomplete, and, as a natural consequence, I felt something amounting to agony at the disappointment – not knowing what the *dénouement* was.'[42]

This combination of the scarcity of books and the lack of ability of parents to judge the appropriateness of the books for children, may partly explain the availability of 'unsuitable' literature in schools.[43] In fact, the types of books brought in by students sometimes determined the students' academic assignment. For example, an English teacher visiting a national school at Clifden in county Galway in 1841, remarked that the students brought their own books, 'and the master is obliged to class them, not according to their proficiency, but according to the books they bring'.[44]

Aside from Adams' seminal study of popular books in Ulster, few studies have examined such books published in Dublin.[45] However, insights into popular literature printed in Dublin in the second half of the eighteenth century can be gleaned from advertisements. Table 1 presents a list of fifty-three popular fiction books advertised by Richard Cross, a Catholic bookseller, printer and publisher, and later a United Irishman, who worked in Dublin from 1757 to 1809.[46] He 'printed and sold' the advertised works at his establishment at 29 Bridge Street, 'where country merchants, and dealers may be furnished at the most reasonable rates, with the greatest variety of all kinds of books, neatly and strongly bound'. Although the advertisement is not dated, internal evidence suggests a date sometime between 1779 and 1786.[47] The dating of the actual books is severely hampered by their extreme rarity, with only six out of the fifty-three titles (11.3 per cent) known from existing copies.[48] The surviving copies are small, in a duodecimo format, measuring about 3½ by 5 inches. All the books were in English, reflecting the fact that Dublin Catholic printers were, as Ó Ciosáin says: 'English speakers in an anglophone environment, and were therefore not able or inclined to supply a chapbook literature in the Irish language'.[49]

There are several reasons to believe that the Cross list is a fairly representative sample of the popular fiction books distributed by chapmen and pedlars at the end of the eighteenth century. First, several of the volumes (called 'Valentines, Montelions, Reynards, Troys, Parismus, Fortunatus, Gesta Romanorum, Wise Masters, &c.') were listed among the stock in 1719 of James Malone, a Catholic bookseller.[50] Further, several volumes were mentioned by Mathew Carey (see above), and just under half of these titles (47.2 per cent), were also advertised as chapmen's books by James Magee in Belfast in the 1750s and 1770s. Secondly, the majority of the titles listed by Cross feature in individuals' recollections of having seen or read such popular fiction sometime in the first part of the nineteenth century.[51] Further, twenty-seven of the titles advertised by Cross were also included in the long list of books in Irish schools published by the Commissioners on Education in 1825.[52] Lastly, many of the titles published by Cross were also available among books distributed by chapmen

134

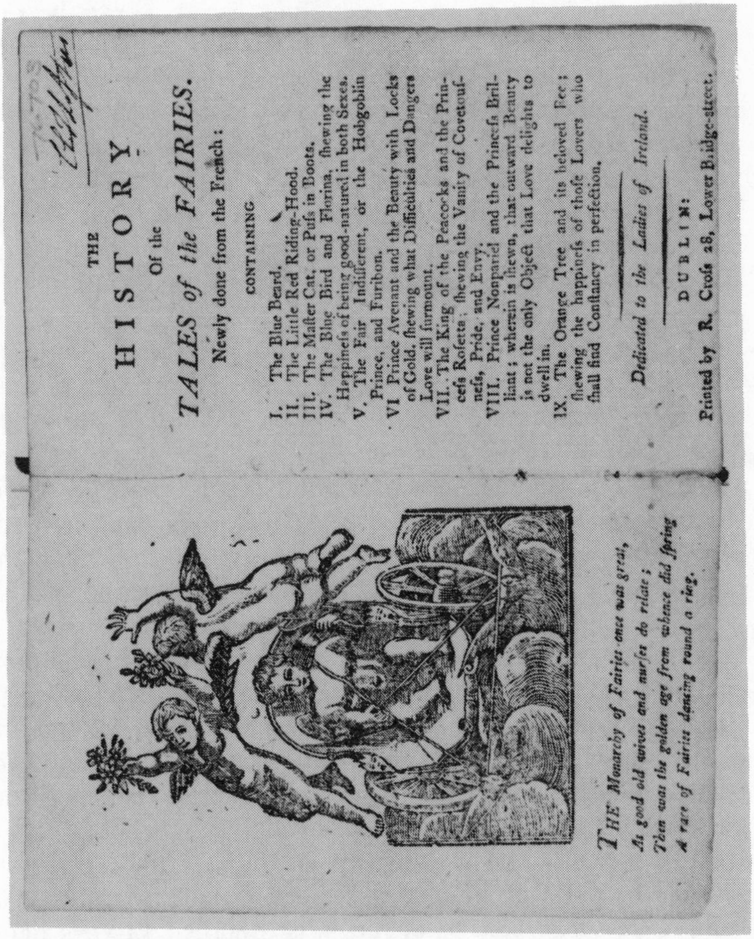

THE Monarchy of Fairies once was great,
As good old wives and nurses do relate;
Then was the golden age from whence did spring
A race of Fairies dancing round a ring.

THE
HISTORY
Of the
TALES of the FAIRIES.
Newly done from the French:
CONTAINING

I. The Blue Beard.
II. The Little Red Riding-Hood.
III. The Master Cat, or Puss in Boots.
IV. The Blue Bird and Florina, shewing the Happiness of being good-natured in both Sexes.
V. The Fair Indifferent, or the Hobgoblin Prince, and Furibon.
VI Prince Avenant and the Beauty with Locks of Gold, shewing what Difficulties and Dangers Love will surmount.
VII. The King of the Peacocks and the Princess Rosetta, shewing the Vanity of Covetousness, Pride, and Envy.
VIII. Prince Nonparail and the Princess Brilliant; wherein is shewn, that outward Beauty is not the only Object that Love delights to dwell in.
IX. The Orange Tree and its beloved Bee; shewing the happiness of those Lovers who shall find Constancy in perfection.

Dedicated to the Ladies of Ireland.

DUBLIN:
Printed by R. Cross 28, Lower Bridge-street.

Figure 6: Title page and frontispiece of *The history of the tales of the fairies* (Dublin, [1780s?]).

in England at an earlier date.[53] Thus, it is likely that many of the Dublin editions of such books were in fact reissues of English editions, probably as abridgements of the original works, similar to the abridgements published in England.[54]

The first notable feature is the preponderance of older literature published before 1732. The list contains a few medieval and late medieval tales of continental origin (such as *Reynard the fox*, *History of Fortunatus*, *Valentine and Orson*, and *Aesop's fables*),[55] and some sixteenth-century works (*Seven wise masters*, Forde's *Parismus*, Johnson's *Seven champions*, *Don Belianis*, and the *Destruction of Troy*). Further, several seventeenth-century works are mentioned (*Argalus and Parthenia*, *Montellion*, *Mary Stuart* (based on a translation from the French), Head's *English rogues*, *Cynthia*, and two of Bunyan's works: his *Pilgrim's progress*, and *Solomon's temple spiritualised*), and Nathaniel Crouch's *Drake's voyages*.

The largest block of books, however, were works of fiction first published in English between 1707 and 1731: Swift's *Gulliver's travels*, Aubin's *Noble slaves* and her *Lady Lucy*, Ward's *Female policy detected*, *Boyle's voyages*, Defoe's *Robinson Crusoe* and his *Moll Flanders*, two of Crouch's works (including *Nine worthies*, and *Winter evening entertainments*), *Laugh and be fat*, and *History of the pirates*, and three translations from the French: *Zulima or pure love*, Madame d'Aulnoy's *Tales of the fairies* (figure 6), and Voltaire's *Charles the XIIth*.[56] In comparison, relatively few of the more 'modern' novels first published in England between the 1730s and the 1770s found their way into the chapmen's collections,[57] with the exception of *Ascanius* (which deals with the Young Pretender), and the *Seven wise masters* in Cross's list. Remarkably, a new genre of Irish productions appeared from the 1720s onward, including Swift's *Gulliver's travels*, Cosgrave's *Irish rogues*, *Captain Freney*, and the anonymous *Patrick O'Donnell*, while Aubin's *Lady Lucy* was partly set in Ireland. It may come as a surprise that the Cross list of titles can be linked to the availability of books in the Irish countryside. Several surveys of Catholic and Protestant schools in parts of Ireland were undertaken by individuals from 1795 onward. One of the most detailed surveys dates from 1824 and covered the dioceses of Kildare and Leighlin, while another survey covered schools in counties Donegal, Kildare, Galway and Kerry in that year. In addition, authors like William Carleton reported on the titles of books available in schools in county Tyrone (for details of the surveys see microfiche at the back of this volume). The surveys mention many titles of books available in schools, but are not exhaustive. Nevertheless, the information makes it possible to identify Catholic and Protestant schools in which titles mentioned in Cross's list of chapbooks were used (this does not preclude the presence of editions other than those published by Cross in the schools). Prior to the advent of public education parents often supplied reading material for their children to read in schools, because of this records of books available in schools give us access to cottage literature. Our analysis of the surveys shows that during the period 1795–1830, two thirds (66 per cent) of the books advertised by Cross were present in schools, mainly in the Irish countryside, and many in schools with Catholic teachers.[58]

We can assume with some caution that works noted as present in several schools were probably more common and more widely read than books only known from a single school.[59] The most popular books were medieval and early modern romances and tales, including the *Seven champions* (eleven schools), the *Seven wise masters* (ten schools), *Valentine and Orson*, *Aesop's fables*, and *Don Belianis* (each nine and seven schools, respectively).[60] The next most popular group were tales of robbers (*Irish rogues*, and *Captain Freney*, each in six schools).[61] Sexually explicit novels were found in few schools, such as *Fair Rosamond and Jane Shore* (three schools), *Moll Flanders*, *Ovid's Art of love*, *Garden of love* (each in one or two schools), and *Female policy detected* (only in a single school).[62] Not surprisingly, tales with some Irish content were among the more widely available books, featuring either Irish saints or robbers (e.g., *Don Belianis*, *Seven champions*, *Irish rogues*, and *Captain Freney*, in six to eleven schools). The major genre of gothic novels, which was highly popular in eighteenth-century England, could not be found in Cross's list. As Adams remarked, from 1740 onwards, 'during one of the great periods of novel-writing in the English language (by such authors as Samuel Richardson), the unsophisticated provincial readers of Ulster, and presumably elsewhere in Britain and Ireland, were avidly consuming material produced before the true birth of the genre in 1740.'[63] Although we do not know which editions and what dates the above books found in schools were, older editions did survive. A priest found 'a very old tract' of the *Irish rogues*, 'introduced rather privately for the second or third time by one of the children' at a Catholic school at Ballynakill (county Laois) in 1824 and had it instantly removed.[64]

Which titles were the most popular as shown by sources other than the school lists? The weekly, *Captain Rock in London*, mentioned in 1825 that *The seven champions* was one of the 'hedge [school] classics'.[65] Remarkably, the preface of the copy of *The seven wise masters*, owned by Samuel Pepys in London in the late seventeenth century, claimed that, 'of all Histories of this nature, this exceeds, being held in such esteem in *Ireland* that it is of chiefest use in all the *English* schools for introducing Children to the understanding of good Letters'.[66] Thus, there is some support for the contention that the *Seven champions* and the *Seven wise masters* were among the most popular books in Irish schools, with the popularity of the *Seven wise masters* extending over at least 150 years. Finally, Thomas Crofton Croker observed in the 1820s that the most popular book among the Irish peasantry in Munster was the *Irish rogues*,[67] which was noted in six schools in our survey. Chapmen's books which challenged the political order, such as those by Thomas Paine, were widely disseminated in Ireland.[68] Leonard McNally stated in 1795 that in Cork Paine's works were read by every schoolboy. However, our survey shows that publications by Paine did not show up among the titles noted by visitors to Irish schools in the period from 1795 to the 1830s.

A wide variety of chapmen's books were available in schools, particularly in schools having a Catholic teacher. The reading material reflected the availability of chapmen's books as advertised and as produced by Cross in Dublin and by Magee in Belfast and, to a lesser extent, by other publishers in the 1770s and 1780s. The desirability of the contents of the books for children was certainly an issue which drew contemporary comment. Although *Reynard the fox* contained some coarse passages, it could be well adapted for juveniles. *Aesop's fables* and *Gulliver's travels* elicited no known protests. However, the majority of the books listed by Cross were considered unsuitable reading material for children. Further, many of the books listed by Cross were far from suitable for children *learning* to read.

A new style of fiction emerged in the late eighteenth century, sponsored by religious societies who published tracts in an attempt to replace the books distributed by chapmen. Initially such fiction, written for the lower classes, consisted of moral, Christian tales. The publications were designed so as not to be distinguishable from ordinary fiction sold by chapmen, other than by their more outspoken moralising content. Hislop characterised the tract society literature as major attempts 'at social planning through propaganda' to influence the lives of the common people.[69] These attempts differed from those of the United Irishmen in the 1790s.[70] Whereas the United Irishmen utilised newspapers and ballads the Protestant societies produced chapbooks and chapmen's books.[71] And while the United Irishmen targeted adults and book societies the Protestant societies focused on young people and schools.

From the 1790s to about 1850 a plethora of charitable societies emerged.[72] The tract society which pioneered this form of publication from/the 1790s onward was the Association for Discountenancing Vice and Promoting the Knowledge and Practice of the Christian Religion.[73] Bishop Magee, after denouncing the cheap popular literature available, stated that the aim of the Association was to attempt:

> to destroy this source of corruption, and to substitute in its place such small tracts as might at once amuse and entertain the lower class of readers, and at the same time insensibly instill into their hitherto untutored minds moral instruction, by representing, under the garb of fable, the happy effects which naturally flow from the observation of the laws of Christian morality, and the destructive consequences of their violation.[74]

These productions were limited to chapbooks, usually of a single sheet folded into twenty-four pages, and do not appear

to have included the larger chapman's books. Thus, the booklets were meant to compete at the least expensive level of the
popular market. Content-wise, their publications were domi-
nated by moral themes cast in fictional accounts, sometimes
after real life events.[75] The association produced twenty-four
tracts by 1796 of which 150,000 copies were printed.[76] Many
of the volumes were copied from English editions of similar
works by the English authoress, Hannah More, who through
her booklets hoped 'to improve the habits and raise the principles of the common people . . . and abate their relish' for the
critiques of monarchy and aristocracy by radical reformers
such as Thomas Paine.[77] For example, her *The history of Mr.
Fantom, the new-fashioned philosopher, and his man William*
(Dublin, [c.1797]; figure 7) railed against the dangers of political innovations as expressed in the works of Godwin.[78] As far
as we have been able to ascertain, no original works by Irish
authors were published by the association.[79]

In the early decades of the nineteenth century, Ireland
became the operating ground for nine Protestant tract societies. Most of the Protestant tract societies seem to have
produced non-fictional, religious books only. Our focus here is
on the four societies that published fiction books. The earliest
organisations to print fiction were the Belfast Religious Tract
Society and the Dublin Religious Tract Society, both of which
started publishing tracts in the 1810s. Three copies were
produced for the Belfast society, and forty-eight by the Dublin
society in their first year of existence. Examples of the anonymous Belfast publications were: *The advantage of reading the
scriptures, exemplified in the history of James Byrne* (Belfast,
1816), *The history of Mary Watson and Jenny Mortimer*
(Belfast, [c.1816]), and *The history of little Jane, the young
cottager* (Belfast, 1816).

One of the first to broach the idea of replacing chapmen's
books by more didactic volumes was Dr Whitley Stokes in a
pamphlet published in Dublin in 1799. He wrote that to
counter the existing chapman's books:

> The subjects on which books should be written for the poor
> are, the different branches of natural history . . . illustrated
> with wooden cuts, and calculated to come to one shilling and

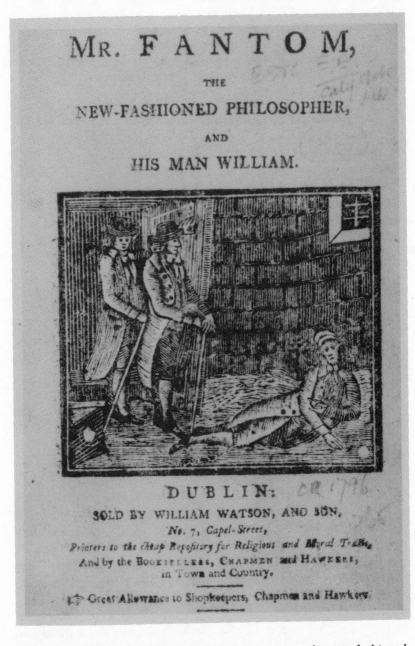

Figure 7: Title page of [Hannah More], *Mr. Fantom, the new-fashioned philosopher, and his man William* (Dublin c. 1797).

sixpence a volume . . . Books on farming, not on the management of fifty, but of two or three acres; on the domestic
animals; on domestic manufacture, as many of these books
should be kept within sixpence halfpenny . . . Besides . . .
abridgements of voyages and travels are of great use, by
turning the spirit of enterprise to a laudable purpose.[80]

Richard Lovell Edgeworth reacted strongly against unsuitable
literature, such as *The life and adventures of James Freney*.
In 1811 he advocated putting 'good books . . . that shall enter-
tain and instruct . . . into the hands of the children of the poor,
and they will soon form a taste that must disdain such disgust-
ing trash.'[81] Stokes' and Edgeworth's farsighted views were
soon realised. The founding of the Cheap Book Society by
Protestants led to the production of two books for children:
The shipwreck of the Antelope Packet on the Pelew Islands
(Dublin: Graisberry and Campbell, 1815, no known copy), and
A description of animals (1816, probably not published).[82]
The society merged in 1816 with the Society for Promoting the
Education of the Poor in Ireland (later known as the Kildare
Place Society, in reference to the location of their
headquarters). The Kildare Place Society began to produce
books similar in format to the 'burtons' which they were
designed to replace (such as title page, binding, and
woodcuts).[83] It was later noted that the society 'became sensi-
ble of the absolute necessity of expelling from circulation, the
pernicious works which have been above adverted to, as
constituting the class books of the Hedge-schools.'[84]

In contrast to the chapbook format of the Association for
Discountenancing Vice published in the 1790s, the preferred
format of the Kildare Place Society were more substantial,
though still slim books. They were produced by folding sheets
in eighteen leaves or thirty-six pages, at a standard of five
sheets of 180 pages, but variations were allowed, producing
booklets measuring about 3½ by 5 inches, similar to the
format Cross had used at the end of the eighteenth century.
However, it was recognised by the publication committee that
the market teemed 'with works of an improper description that
are of smaller size than those which we have compiled', so
they suggested producing two sheet books of seventy-two
pages, which the committee thought would appeal to 'many

people in the lower class whose means are inadequate or who otherwise disinclined to purchase a five sheet burton'.[85] However, the society never competed with single sheet chapbooks of twenty-four or thirty-six pages. Thus, the society did not attempt to compete with the lightest and least expensive popular literature, usually costing 1*d.* but, instead, focused on the more expensive literature of a popular kind, costing in the 6*d.* range.

Unlike earlier tract societies, the society's principal aim was to disseminate tracts to children in schools either by direct grants to schools or by selling the booklets through the channels of the chapmen and pedlars travelling in the country. In terms of the schools, the Kildare Place Society's approach was two-pronged, the financial sponsoring of schools and the provision of reading material for the children.

The titles produced by the Kildare Place Society make it clear that some of the older chapmen's books were found to be less objectionable, or even desirable for children. *Robinson Crusoe* (Dublin, 1817) and *Aesop's fables* (Dublin, 1821) were reprinted in direct competition with the existing chapmen's versions of the same titles. By publishing many other reprints, often purged of improper episodes, the society carved out its own market. The society published books on natural history, from 1818 onwards, for which there was no precedent in the British popular literature market.[86]

Most importantly, it commissioned original works by Irish authors. The most industrious author was the society's secretary Charles Bardin, who between 1818 and 1820 was responsible for twenty-six new titles (mostly compilations from existing works).[87] Women authors were encouraged, including the Quakers, Mary Leadbeater and Abigail Roberts, each of whom anonymously published original works.[88]

Maria Edgeworth's books for children were not included in the society's list, either because her works were aimed primarily at a middle class audience,[89] or because of the need to deal with English copyright.[90] However, the Drogheda 1802 edition of her *The parent's assistant* has an advertisement stating that the reprint was authorised by the London publisher, Mr. [John] Johnson, who permitted 'a Thousand Copies of this cheap Selection to be printed, for the Use of the

Country Schools in Ireland.'[91] Edgeworth's works are rarely mentioned in the survey of schools in the Dioceses of Kildare and Leighlin in 1824.[92]

Whereas most Kildare Place Society's titles did not specifically target readers in cottages, some works such as *Miscellany or an evening's occupation for the youthful peasantry of Ireland* (Dublin, 1818) and *The cottage fireside* (Dublin, 1821) did. These volumes advocated the eradication of such immoral and undesirable habits among the peasantry as intemperance, sloth and lack of foresight. The books urged cottagers to endeavour to replace these human weaknesses by 'honesty, gentleness, kindness, and a respect for religion'. In addition, at least five of the Kildare Place books encouraged economic planning by saving money and lodging it in savings banks.[93]

The society pioneered the publication of books with practical, improving contents aimed directly at cottagers. These 'improving' works focused on self-improvements through fictional examples, and covered such areas as agriculture, food consumption, health, housekeeping, and child-rearing.[94] The Revd William Hickey's *Hints for the small farmers of Ireland* (Dublin, 1830) was one of the prime examples of this literature, another was Mary Leadbeater's *The pedlars* (Dublin, 1826).[95]

The superiority of British society over the societies of other lands was another major theme of the Kildare Place books. They encouraged the readers to identify with British government and laws. However, the books were sensitive to the needs of Irish tenants vis-à-vis their landlords. Many were intensely critical of the inactive members of the upper class who pursued self-gratification at the expense of neglecting their tenants. Thus, the books served to fulfil the role of advice and counsel that the landlords in principle could provide cottagers. At the same time, some of the books lauded the precious benefits that the poor enjoyed in their poverty and 'thereby to make them happy with their lot', by sparing them many temptations and trials that were common for the rich, and promising them heavenly rewards.[96]

Another aspect that distinguished the new fiction from the former chapmen's books was the emphasis on real rather than imagined life. Fantasies about unidentified foreign countries, castles, and improbable life stories gave way to tales about existing countries, country cottages, and ordinary lives. Escapes from unimaginable dangers were replaced by escapes from the disadvantages and hazards of day-to-day events.[97] Most of the volumes carried Christian messages, but did not attempt to evangelise or seek conversions. This practical direction found in the literature coincides with a suppression of tales about fairies and superstitions. Further, legendary, heroic tales apparently were not thought suitable for propagation to cottagers through the printed word.

The detailed survey of schools in the Dioceses of Kildare and Leighlin shows that grants for books by the Kildare Place Society were mostly placed in Protestant schools and to a lesser extent in Catholic schools.[98] This implies that Protestant children, and smaller numbers of Catholic school children, were exposed to the books of the society. Further, it is clear that the publications of the Kildare Place Society were. aimed exclusively at the younger generation. Presumably, to optimise distribution, the society supported the establishment of lending libraries in schools rather than issuing the books directly to children. The society apparently never directly attempted to influence the parents, although it may have had an indirect effect because the parents or others in the household may have read the books when brought into the home by the children from the lending library. Adults' opinions, including those of parents and priests, were certainly taken into account by the society, because they could reject the books, and take their children out of schools. Therefore, the content of the books was deliberately kept neutral vis-à-vis the Catholic and Protestant religions, something which was achieved with remarkable success, although not fully. The fact that so few of the books or passages in the books were found objectionable by adults was a sign of the success of the society.

The lending libraries of Sunday schools formed another source from which children drew books. Although such libraries mostly held religious works, they played an important role in the teaching of reading. This became more important as greater numbers of young people were employed during the week in mills and factories.[99]

Moreover, lending libraries were set up by some of the land-lords for their servants and tenants.[100] In 1834 the traveller H. D. Inglis noted that a lending library had been established on the estate of Lord Stanley near Tipperary town, for the benefit of the tenantry with the agent acting as its librarian.[101] The Pakenham estate at Tullynally (county Westmeath), which still has a splendid library for the owner's family, also had a small servant's library at one time.[102] Another landlord, the author William Parnell stated in 1817 that lending libraries provided an alternative to undesirable activities by the cottagers. He wrote that the establishment of lending libraries in Ireland has already been found to check the evil of country people assem-bling 'either at a neighbour's house, or a dancing house, where the conversation and amusement are of a very questionable description'. Without the lending libraries the Irish 'generally being illiterate, or at best possessing no books, they have no means of amusement at home, during the long winter evenings'.[103] Since most lending libraries for the Irish peas-antry were organised by members of the middle and upper classes, a certain degree of control must have been exercised over the reading material.

The Religious Tract Society, which operated from London also served the Irish market. In addition the Religious Tract and Book Society for Ireland probably started in the early 1820s and had Charlotte Elizabeth Tonna as one of its prolific authors (she is better known under her pseudonym of Char-lotte Elizabeth). Examples of her work include: *Anne Bell; or, the faults* (Dublin, 1826), *The simple flower* (Dublin, 1826), and *Philip, and his garden* (Dublin, 1827).[104]

The Dublin Temperance Society (later known as the Hibernian Temperance Society), employed Betsy Shackleton, sister of Mary Leadbeater, to write *Dialogues on whiskey, between John Sheppard, the millright, and Peter Carroll, the cooper* (Dublin, 1832) and *Philip and his friends: or, cottage dialogues on temperance societies and intemperance* (Dublin, [n.d.]). In the 1820s and 1830s two Catholic tract societies sprang up, which will be discussed later. Finally, the Hibernian Gaelic Society, founded in 1843, had plans to publish fiction in the Gaelic language, but the society failed to flourish.[105]

The tract literature was supplemented by a variety of other publications written for cottagers, but not known to have been sponsored by tract societies.[106] For example, William Carleton in the introduction to his temperance tale, *Art Maguire; or, the broken pledge* (Dublin, 1845) proclaimed his intention to write a series of 'Tales for the Irish people', of which this volume was the first. Subsequently, it was published in Duffy's Library of Ireland. The second volume in the proposed series was the anti-whiteboy story of *Rody the rover; or, the ribbon-man* (Dublin, 1845), which also appeared in Duffy's Library of Ireland.[107] Carleton's objective was for the Irish people:

> to improve their physical and social condition – generally; and through the medium of vivid and striking, but unobjectionable narratives, to inculcate such principles as may enable Irishmen to think more clearly, reason more correctly, and act more earnestly upon the general duties, which, from their position in life, they are called upon to perform.[108]

Both volumes may have been commissioned by Protestant individuals or organisations, though it is not clear who they were. The same may be the case for Carleton's *Parra Sastha* (Dublin, 1845; Duffy's Library of Ireland), which he dedicated to 'the people of Ireland . . . to improve their condition', and which was supposedly written for farmers. It even included an appendix, containing instructions on agricultural and other farm matters, copied from Martin Doyle's [Revd William Hickey] *Hints to the small farmers of the County of Wexford* (1830, 4th ed.).

Another improving type of book is Mrs S.C. Hall's *Stories of the Irish peasantry* (Edinburgh, 1840), dedicated to the landlords and tenants of Ireland, which aimed to reconcile landlords and peasantry. Many of the stories are meant to show the peasantry that their present condition is due to defects in the national character, such as drink, early marriages, laziness and superstition, as can be seen by such story titles as: 'Too early wed!,' 'It's only a drop!', 'Do you think I'd inform?', 'Debt and danger,' and 'The tenant-right.' The publishers (Chambers in Edinburgh) in their introduction rightly stated that 'How far she [Mrs S.C. Hall] may have succeeded in impressing her sound and judicious maxims upon those to whom they were more particularly addressed, it would be difficult, especially at this early period, to ascertain.'[109] The volume was first published in the Chambers' 'People's edition', presumably at a low price.

Some of the privately-published volumes had strong evangelising overtones, such as the anonymous clergyman's *Simple memorials of an Irish family* (London, 1824), and Selina Bunbury's *Cabin conversations and castle scenes* (London, 1827), both set in Ireland and both featuring the benefits of scripture reading.

In a special category were the fiction books written to improve cottagers' household, garden, and farming practices. The least well-known is the *History of Paddy Blake and Kathleen O'More* (Dungannon, 1847), written by Edward Houston Caulfield, 'a country gentleman, . . . for the instruction and amusement of the farmers of Co. Tyrone'. It consists of a prose sketch interspersed with various songs and poems, and tells of the farming of Paddy and the housekeeping of his wife, Kitty, as models of their respective occupations. It presents practical details of farming, and introduces observations on agriculture, chemistry and a variety of other subjects.[110]

The most well-known improving books were written by Mary Leadbeater and the Revd William Hickey. Hickey, through dialogues, concentrated mostly on advice concerning farming and the farm-house (see his *Common sense for common people*, Dublin, 1835). In contrast, Mary Leadbeater, also using dialogues, concentrated more on improvements in day-to-day living arrangements. Among her principal works were *Cottage dialogues*, which appeared in three series between 1811 and 1818,[111] and her *Short stories for cottagers* (Dublin, 1813), and *Tales for cottagers* (Dublin, 1814). It is important to note that these books appeared well before the first publications of the Kildare Place Society.[112]

Whereas all of the above volumes were written by individuals who did not earn their living by menial labour, a remarkable exception seems to have been *The guide to service. The dairy maid* (London, 1843), which, presumably, was written by the dairymaid Mary O'Brien. Set in the barony of Forth (county Wexford), it consists of an instructional and

148

autobiographical story about the life of a dairy maid, who has injured her back and was not able to work anymore. In the story she tells all she knows of being a proper dairy maid for the benefit of other girls who have to go into service and gives specific instructions on how to prepare dairy products.

In many instances, the individual publications and, to some extent, a number of the Kildare Place Society booklets, were cast, to use Hickey's words, in the 'Anglo-Hibernian diction, phraseology, and pronunciation'.[113] Maria Edgeworth, in her advertisement to the reader in Leadbeater's *Cottage dialogues* (London, 1811), calling it 'an exact representation of the *manner of being* of the lower Irish, and a literal transcript of their language'.[114] Such accounts of spoken language could only take place because the author had been in direct contact with his/her characters, and the stories were often based on real people and facts. The use of Hiberno-English by the main characters was an innovation in Irish fiction which may have been aimed at more effectively communicating improving ideas to the cottagers. Also, the Irish settings used in some of the fictional works indicated an acceptance of positive Irish attributes, without introducing the comic Irish element, known from stage plays.[115] Further, some of the fiction was firmly embedded in the Irish countryside, and concerned Irish peasants and customs. This Irishness was expressed without denigration, and often with some admiration. Generally, these publications, although substantially differing in price, were five to six times more expensive than chapman's books and for that reason must have been less accessible to cottagers. For example, Revd William Hickey's *Irish cottagers* (Dublin, 1830) could be purchased at 2s.6d., William Carleton's *Art Maguire* (Dublin, 1845) at 3s., but his *Rody, the rover* (Dublin, 1845) was slightly cheaper at 2s., while the three parts of Leadbeater's *Cottage dialogues* was possibly remaindered initially at 2s. in 1841, and at 1s. in 1855.[116] Also, the books, mostly published in London or Edinburgh, must have encountered distribution problems to the cottagers in Ireland. In the case of works by Hickey and, to some extent the works by Leadbeater, the aim was to sell the works to the landlords, who in turn would distribute them at no cost to their tenants. For example, Hickey mentions in his *Common sense for common people* (Dublin, 1835) that willing landlords usually took 100 copies each, and that 8,000 volumes out of a total printing of 13,000, had been distributed in that manner in its first year of publication.[117]

The extent to which these works were actually read, is impossible to establish. Leadbeater's *Cottage dialogues* was used in a few of the schools in the Dioceses of Kildare and Leighlin.[118] However, Catholic cottagers may have reacted negatively to Protestant individuals not of their own rank advising them on how to conduct their life. Harriet Martineau in 1852 wrote that:

> some years ago, the great authority on Irish peasant life was Mrs. Leadbeater, whose '*Cottage Dialogues*' was the most popular of Irish books till O'Connell's power rose to its height. In the suspicion and hatred which he excited towards the landlords, and the aristocracy in general, works like Mrs. Leadbeater's, which proceed on the supposition of a sort of feudal relation between the aristocracy and the peasantry, went out of favour, and have been little heard since.[119]

This critique was not without foundation. Shared among the various books for cottagers written by individual authors is the notion that the fictional cottagers accept the desirability and stability of the different social strata. The sentiment is well captured by the Irish author Mrs. C.F. Alexander in her well-known hymn '*All things bright and beautiful*,' published in 1848:

> The rich man in his castle,
> The poor man at his gate,
> God made them, high and lowly,
> And order'd their estate.[120]

In Ireland as in England, the tracts tried to reform the morals of the poor as much as their politics, and equality before God was never to be confused with social equality.[121]

Catholics responded to the onslaught of Protestant literature in two ways. Firstly, they participated in the debate about suitable reading material for children, and reacted to Protestant literature by restricting Catholics' access to the books. Secondly, they undertook the task of publishing their own cheap literature for the Irish population. However, financial sponsorship of schools by Catholic religious bodies, compared to sponsorship by Protestant tract societies, was decidedly uncommon in the early nineteenth century.[122]

Some Catholics held the view that tract societies, openly or not, were intent upon converting Catholic children. Thus, even if there were differences in this respect among the various societies operating in Ireland, Catholics often did not distinguish between the societies, and the objectives of the various societies were 'alike in all'.[123] There is substantial evidence that the Kildare Place Society distributed their tracts to Catholic schools, but evidence for the other societies is less clear.[124]

A priest of the parish of Killeigh (county Offaly), reporting on books in schools, admitted in 1824 that 'the only bad and printed papers that I saw these 20 years introduced at the Catholic schools were the foolish, nonsensical, ridiculous tracts sent to them from the Bible Society, which I soon committed to fire.'[125] Catholic children were instructed by the clergy not to accept books from Protestants missionaries. Asenath Nicholson relates that she witnessed one boy saying 'I known this is a Protestant book, and I will not have it'.[126] By at least 1860, Irish Catholic children were advised that one of six categories of bad books were 'Protestant books and tracts'.[127]

Certain Catholic Sunday schools doubled as lending libraries for a parish, such as the one at Killard (county Laois), which contained, among others, thirty-seven volumes of 'Moral Tracts', which were lent for one penny per month. Such tracts could also be found in regular Catholic schools.[128] Dr Doyle in the early nineteenth century established religious libraries in every parish of his diocese of Kildare and Leighlin. Books were lent from these libraries to the heads of families upon their paying a penny a week or fortnight, but the poor received the books gratis.[129]

Protestants criticised Catholic schools for holding on to unsuitable literature for children. For example, Dutton, noting unsuitable books in schools in county Clare, wrote in 1808 that 'it can hardly be expected, that the lives of pirates, dexterous thieves, witches, smugglers, and illustrious prostitutes, can have any but the very worst tendency [on children].'[130] He reproached the Irish clergy, who 'did they pay that attention to the schools, that they ought, such books would not for half a century have continued to disgrace and corrupt the children of their persuasion'; similar arguments were expressed by other Protestant authors.[131] One of the priests reporting on schools in the Dioceses of Kildare and Leighlin in 1824, aware of the criticism that Catholic clergy allowed unsuitable books into the hands of children, denied 'that the Irish Catholic Clergy will put improper books into the hands of their respective flocks'.[132] However, the evidence discussed above on books available in Catholic schools, supports Bell's, Dutton's and Glassford's contention.[133]

Catholics probably saw with dismay the growing numbers of books published by the Protestant tract societies, and wondered why they did not produce tracts themselves. It was not until 1827 that the Catholic Book Society for the Diffusion of Useful Knowledge Throughout Ireland was founded.[134] The Catholic Book Society produced 500,000 volumes in its first five years, and an extraordinary, if not unlikely 5,000,000 by 1837, but because of financial problems was dissolved in 1845.[135] The publications, however, were non-fiction in nature, and fall outside consideration here.[136] The society was soon followed by the Catholic Society of Ireland, which between 1836 and 1840 produced 40,000 volumes, also probably of a nonfictional character.[137] The response of the Catholic clergy to the Protestant onslaught of tracts occurred rather late, and appears to have focused on the production of religious tracts rather than fiction.

The Kildare Place Society pronounced their book publishing business a success. In 1824 the society stated that 'The old trade [in books by chapmen] was accordingly abandoned and the same Hawkers, the same Printers, and, in some instances, even the same Types, which formerly supplied the moral poison, are now employed in the service of the Society.' In less than six years, the society sold about 784,000 volumes.[138] In another publication of the same year, the society claimed that:

> The printing presses in Dublin which formerly teemed with immoral and mischievous publications are now idle, those productions being quite unequal to any successful competition with the Publications of the Society. The consequence is that the Schools and Libraries for the Poor are supplied with

useful and moral publications, to the almost total exclusion of
the pernicious works which formerly so universally
abounded. Increased attention is bestowed by the Committees of the Society to improve the quality of their
publications, works of a lighter and a more entertaining description were necessary at the outset, to supplant the books
which had so long swayed the imaginations and minds of
such of the lower orders as were capable of reading, – but
there is good reason to believe that a better taste has been
produced, and cultivated by the excursions which have been
made by this Society and by other public Institutions.[139]

The suppression of unsuitable popular literature was also
represented in the new fiction. The main character in *The
history of Tim Higgins* (Dublin, 1823) said to the book pedlar
that 'I recollect the time when such as you, had a different
kind of book in your basket: – the history of noted thieves, and
fairy tales and song books; why don't you sell them still?' Upon
which the pedlar replied 'The reason is very plain, because the
people won't buy them; they find it a great deal more useful,
and certainly not less entertaining to read accounts of what
really happened . . . over and above this, the books I now sell
are much cheaper'.[140] Mr and Mrs S.C. Hall, writing in 1843,
stated that 'in recent years, however, a vast improvement in
this respect has taken place; and during our recent visits we
found it difficult to obtain, at any of the low shops in the
suburbs of large towns, copies of the books, of which formerly
they were never without ample supply.' Even the *Life of James
Freney*, with editions 'printed in nearly every town in the
south of Ireland' had become a 'scarce book'.[141]

However, the rosy picture painted by Mr and Mrs Hall was
exaggerated. Glassford was told in 1824 by an inspector from
the Kildare Place Society that in the north of Ireland he 'found
in the shops of the petty booksellers and in the hands of the
people, immoral books of the very worst description, which
were usually supplied from the dealers in Belfast; even those
booksellers of the most respectable class.'[142] This observation
is borne out by the information in Table 1 (microfiche),
showing the re-emergence of chapbooks of an earlier vintage in
Belfast especially during the period 1826-1835.[143] Three types
of popular fiction survived at least until 1850: firstly, books

153

Figure 8: [*Royal*] *Hibernian tales: being a collection of the most entertaining stories now extant* (Dublin, c.1824?).

with Irish contents, such as *Gulliver's travels*, *Lady Lucy*, *Irish rogues*, and *Captain Freney*; secondly, books of sixteenth-century origin, such as *Don Belianis*, the *Seven wise masters*, and the *Seven champions*. The third group were more sexually adventurous books of fiction, including *Fair Rosamond*, *Fortunate and unfortunate lovers*, and *Ovid's Art of love*.[144] We also know from other sources that chapbooks continued to be produced until at least the 1870s, with lists showing many of the older titles still in print.[145] However, because of the inadequate research in the field of popular literature, it is quite likely that other insights will emerge once more of the cheap literature of the period has been identified. Among the later listings by four different authors, the following titles were the most often mentioned: the *Seven champions* (all four authors), the *Seven wise masters*, *Fortunate and unfortunate lovers*, *Tales of the fairies*, *Irish rogues*, and *Freney*, each mentioned by three authors.[146]

In the early part of the nineteenth century, new productions were added to the older range of booklets, including the first known anthology of original Irish legendary stories collected in the Irish countryside, called the *Royal Hibernian tales; being a collection of the most entertaining stories now extant*, which may have first appeared by 1824, and which was announced as containing 'excellent morals' (figure 8).[147] Also, what were called 'penny dreadfuls' began to appear on the market, for example the anonymous, *The mystery of the black convent, An interesting Spanish tale* (Dublin: A. O'Neil, 1814) at the Minerva Printing Office, named after Lane's more famous Minerva Press in London.

The increase in the publication of popular books especially in Belfast by the publisher Joseph Smyth largely coincided with the termination of the parliamentary grants to the Kildare Place Society in 1831. These had provided the financial support for its publishing programme, and the society's circulation of books declined rapidly, with its last volume appearing in 1834.[148] The establishment of the national schools did not lead to a revival in the publication of fiction books for schools; instead more systematic spelling and reading books were produced.[149] An exception is William Hickey's *Agricultural class book; or, how to best cultivate a small farm and garden: together with hints on domestic economy* (Dublin, 1848). As the Commissioners of National Education in Ireland related, 'In order to render the lessons attractive, they have been thrown into the form of a narrative, calculated to arrest the attention of young readers.' The commissioners decided not to compile books for school libraries, but instead they selected from books already printed.[150] Thus, we see the end of the government-sponsored production of fiction in Ireland, replaced by a more strictly instructional literature.

A number of factors limit the scope of the present essay. Many of the chapman's books are not known to have survived and could not be examined, this particularly applies to Richard Cross's works. This survey did not attempt to examine the larger range of titles of chapbooks produced by other eighteenth-century printers and publishers in Dublin and provincial towns. Nor is it possible to gauge accurately the share of the chapman's books on the Irish book market. It is even more difficult to determine the impact of these books on readers, whether in cottages or in other stations of life. Further, our survey of what books of fiction were available in schools in the early nineteenth century was inherently limited by the uncertain quality of visitors' reports. The geographical spread of popular fiction in the English language is also difficult to trace because large parts of the country remained Irish speaking. Finally, although the emphasis here has been upon cottagers as readers, much of the literature available and written for cottagers was also read by members of other classes.[151]

Notes

*Acknowledgments: We are very grateful to the following individuals who contributed in various ways to this chapter and the larger bibliographical work on which it is partly based: Donald Akenson, Seamus Deane, Patricia Donlon, Charles Ginnane, Fiona Fitzsimon, Harold Hislop, Máire Kennedy, M. Pollard, and Kevin Whelan. We thank Eileen Reilly for checking Cross' works in the ESTC, and David Alexander for his comments on an early draft. The larger survey, of which the present survey is part, was financially supported by a grant from Notre Dame University, Notre Dame, IN.

1. P.J. Dowling, *The hedge schools of Ireland* (Cork, [1968]); Gerard Long (ed.), *Books beyond the Pale* (Dublin, 1996); Mary Daly and David Dickson (eds), *The origins of popular literacy in Ireland* (Dublin, 1990); Niall Ó Ciosáin, *Print and popular culture in Ireland 1750-1850* (Basingstoke, 1997); J.R.R. Adams, *The printed word and the common man* (Belfast, 1987); M. Pollard, *Dublin's trade in books 1550-1800* (Oxford, 1989); Mary Casteleyn, *A history of literacy and libraries in Ireland* (Aldershot, 1984); J.H. Murphy, *Catholic fiction and social reality in Ireland 1873-1922* (Westport, CT, 1997), p. 79*ff*; Harold Hislop, The Kildare Place Society 1811-31; an Irish experiment in popular education, Ph.D. thesis, T.C.D., 1990.

2. Authors, addressing Irish readers in the early nineteenth century, but who do not focus on cottagers, include K. Lubbers, 'Author and audience in the early nineteenth century' in P. Connolly (ed.), *Literature and the changing Ireland* (Gerrards Cross, 1982), pp 25-36; D.J. Casey (ed.), *Views of the Irish peasantry 1800-1916* (Hamden, CT, 1977); M. Harmon, 'Aspects of the peasantry in Anglo-Irish literature from 1800 to 1916' in *Studia Hibernica*, xv (1975), pp 105-127.

3. Rolf Loeber and Magda Stouthamer-Loeber, Literary fiction as a mirror of the times. A guide to Irish fiction published in Europe and North America from 1700 to 1900. Manuscript in preparation.

4. Garret FitzGerald, 'The decline of the Irish language' in Daly and Dickson (eds), *The origins of popular literacy*, pp 59-72; D.H. Akenson, 'Pre-university education, 1782-1870' in W.E. Vaughan (ed.), *A new history of Ireland*, vol. v (Oxford, 1989), p. 524.

5. *Appendix to the seventeenth report of the Commissioners of National Education in Ireland,* H.C. 1851, xxiv, p. 135.

6. *Appendix to the fourteenth report of the Commissioners of the Board of Education in Ireland,* H.C. 1812-13, vi, p. 337.

7. D.H. Akenson, *The Irish education experiment* (London, 1970), p. 51.

8. Ó Ciosáin, *Print and popular culture*, pp 13, 17. But see smallish collections in *A catalogue of the Bradshaw collection of Irish books in the University Library, Cambridge* (Cambridge, 1916), i, passim; *Catalogue of the library at Lough Fea* (London, 1872), pp 39-44.

9. They were also known in Ireland as cottiers, which was synonymous with labourers. R. Bell, *A description of the condition and manners as well as of the moral and political character, education, &c. of the peasantry of Ireland* (London, 1804); *Captain Rock in London* (March 19, 1825, p. 22).

10. We follow Adams' definitions (Adams, *The printed word*, p. 33). See also p. 66.

11. Susan Pederson, 'Hannah More meets Simple Simon: Tracts, chapbooks, and popular culture in late eighteenth-century England' in *Journal of British Studies*, xxv (1986), pp 103, 105, 107.

12. D. Dewar, *Observations on the character, customs, and superstitions of the Irish* (London, 1812), [part 2], p. 39.

13. *Memoirs of Richard Lovell Edgeworth, Esq. begun by himself and concluded by his daughter, Maria Edgeworth* (Boston, 1821), ii, pp 257-258, citing the *Appendix to the third report of the Commissioners of Education in Ireland*. Note that the phrase 'this is particularly dangerous in Ireland' in the official version of the appendix was 'is not necessary in Ireland' (*Appendix to the third report of the Commissioners of the Board of Education in Ireland*, H.C. 1809, vii, p. 109).

14. [Miss Chetwode], *Blue-stocking Hall* (London, 1827) ii, p. 54. Similar comments can be found in the novel by [Thomas Ashworth], *Rathlynn* (London, 1864), i, p. 63.

15. Cited in Martin Brenan, *Schools of Kildare and Leighlin 1775-1835* (Dublin, 1935), p. 2.

16. R. Bell, *A description . . . of the peasantry*, pp 40-41.

17. [Revd George Brittaine], *Irishmen and Irishwomen* (Dublin, 1830), pp 72-73. Richard Lovell Edgeworth expressed in 1811 that some people thought that 'if the poor are taught to read, they may read what is hurtful' (*Appendix to the fourteenth report of the Commissioners of the Board of Education in Ireland*, p. 337). In the same mode, Martin Doyle [pseudonym of Revd William Hickey] reported that 'When the idea of educating the lower classes was first entertained and considered, it was opposed by many, as likely to substitute vain and unsatisfying

knowledge, in the place of sober industry and necessary labour' (*Hints addressed to the small holders and peasantry of Ireland, on subjects connected with health, temperance, morals, &c. &c. &c.* (Dublin, 1833, new ed.), p. 71.

18. Dewar, *Observations*, [part 2], p. 71.

19. *Captain Rock in London* (March 19, 1825), which was the only London weekly that focused on Irish matters; see also Bell, *A description. . . of the peasantry of Ireland*, p. [39].

20. [Miss Chetwode] *Blue-stocking Hall* (London, 1827), i, p. 151, see also pp 152-53.

21. Cited in Ó Ciosáin, *Print and popular culture*, p. 133, and in Thomas Wall, *The sign of Doctor Hay's head* (Dublin, 1958), p. 23; a similar sentiment, citing similar books, is expressed by Bell in his *A description . . . of the peasantry*, p. 40n.

22. Ó Ciosáin, *Print and popular culture*, p. 54; A.G., 'Burton's books' in *The Irish Book Lover*, ii (1911), p. 128.

23. Whitley Stokes, *Projects for re-establishing the internal peace and tranquility of Ireland* (Dublin, 1799), pp 41-42.

24. Cited in Adams, *The printed word*, pp 48-49; Wall, *The sign*, p. 23.

25. [Mary Leadbeater], *The pedlars* (Dublin, 1826), p. 130.

26. W. Carleton, 'The hedge school' in *Traits and stories of the Irish peasantry* (Dublin, 1830), ii, pp 186-187.

27. Dowling, *Hedge schools*, p. 66; Brenan, *Schools*, pp 59-60, 531.

28. *State of Ireland – Minutes of evidence taken before the Select Committee of the House of Lords* ([London], 1824) i, p. 396; ii, p. 325.

29. Cited by 'Biblio', 'Irish chap books' in *The Irish Book Lover*, ii (1911), p. 110. By 1824, 'The supply of such books formed at that time, the principal trade of certain individuals in Dublin: the types from which they were printed were never unset, and edition after edition was produced, according to the demands of the Hawkers and Pedlars, through whose intervention the country was supplied' ([anon.], *Hints on the formation of Lending Libraries in Ireland* (Dublin, 1824), p. 10).

30. I. Heron, *My own memoire on the life of Isaac Heron, a loyalist on pure genuine principles* (Waterford, 1810), i, pp 57-58.

31. *First report of the Commissioners of Irish Education inquiry*, H.C. 1825, xii, Appendix No. 221, pp 553-559.

32. Brenan, *Schools*, p. 49.

33. *State of Ireland – Minutes of evidence*, 1824, vol. 2, p. 325.

Rolf Loeber and Magda Stouthamer-Loeber

34. *The autobiography of William Carleton* (rev. ed. London, 1968), p. 73.

35. J. Glassford, *Notes of three tours in Ireland in 1824 and 1826* (Bristol, 1832), pp 71, 91.

36. Ó Ciosáin, *Print and popular culture*, p. 59; Brenan, *Schools*, pp 185, 224, 226, and passim; D. Kennedy, 'Robert Parke's account of schools in Ballymoney parish [counties Antrim and Derry], 1824' in *Irish Historical Studies*, vi (1948), p. 35.

37. Carleton *Traits and stories* (Dublin, 1843, new ed.), i, p. xvi.

38. Carleton, *Autobiography*, p. 73.

39. Miss Owenson [later Lady Morgan], *Patriotic sketches of Ireland, written in Connaught* (London, 1807), ii, pp 138, 141-142.

40. J.B. Trotter, *Walks through Ireland in. . . 1812, 1814, and 1817* (London, 1819), p. 46.

41. Glassford, *Notes*, p. 128; P. de Brún, 'Some documents concerning Valentia Erasmus Smith School, 1776-95', *Journal of the Kerry Archaeological and Historical Society*, 15-16 (1982-83), p. 79, noted that each of the male pupils in this school had a single book only. Especially from age 13 onward, pupils read fiction.

42. Carleton, *Autobiography*, p. 71.

43. *First report of the Commissioners of Irish Education inquiry* (1825) pp 553-559.

44. J. Woods, *Notes on some of the schools for the labouring classes in Ireland* (Lewes, 1841), p. 31.

45. But see for example, Pollard, *Dublin's trade*, pp 222-223; Ó Ciosáin, *Print and popular culture*, passim.

46. R.B. McDowell, 'The personnel of the Dublin Society of United Irishmen, 1791-4' in *Irish Historical Studies*, ii (1941), p. 29; Robert Munter, *A dictionary of the print trade in Ireland 1550-1775* (New York, 1988), p. 67; Wall, *The sign*, pp 11-12, 39, 90; V. Kinane, 'Some late 18th- and early 19th century Dublin printers' account books: The Graisberry ledgers. 1. Daniel Graisberry's ledger 1777-1785' in Peter Isaac (ed.) *Six centuries of the provincial book trade in Britain* (Winchester, 1990), p. 142.

47. The advertisement is in J.E. Weeks, *A new geography of Ireland* (Dublin, 1779), which is part of a chapman's book, entitled *The geography of youth &c.* (title page missing) (copy in the N.L.I., shelfmark J9107). The dates are based on the publication date on the first title and a manuscript inscription, 1786, by Thomas Glynn, the presumed former owner of the book. The advertisement also mentions several religious books, which because of the

thrust of the present chapter, are excluded from Table 1. The list does not carry prices.

48. Only five out of the fifty-three titles advertised and printed by Cross (see Table 1 microfiche) are known from surviving copies, including one with an early nineteenth century date (see Table 1 microfiche). In addition, he published religious and school books (see ESTC), a reprint of Charlotte McCarthy's *The fair moralist; or, love and virtue. A novel. To which are added Poems on several occasions* (Dublin, 1783), and as co-publisher, [Madame D'Arblay's] *Camilla: or, a picture of youth* (Dublin, 1796, 3v.).

49. Ó Ciosáin, *Print and popular culture*, p. 56.

50. J.W. Phillips, *Printing and bookselling in Dublin, 1670-1800* (Dublin, 1998), p. 73.

51. A constant visitor [?Patrick Kennedy], 'An Irish hedge-school' in *Dublin University Magazine*, lx (1862), pp 601-602; [anon.], 'Irish folk books of the last century' in *Dublin University Magazine*, xlvii (1866), p. 533 (J.J.M., 'Irish chap books,' in *The Irish Book Lover*, i (1910) p. 158, appears largely based on this article); Wakefield, cited by Mr. & Mrs. S.C. Hall, *Ireland, its scenery, character, &c.* (London, n.d., new ed.), ii, p. 363n. (first published, 1843); T.A. Devyr, *The odd book of the nineteenth century* (New York, 1882), pp 36-37 (we acknowledge Kevin Whelan's generosity in showing us this reference); H. Dutton, *Statistical survey of the county of Clare* (Dublin, 1808), pp 236-237.

52. *First report of the Commissioners of Irish Education inquiry* (1825), pp 555-559.

53. J. Ashton (ed.), *Chapbooks of the eighteenth century* (1882, reprinted New York, 1966).

54. V.E. Neuburg, *Popular education in eighteenth century England* (London, 1971), p. 121.

55. Short titles as in Cross' list are used here.

56. Adams, *The printed word*, p. 69, already drew attention to the presence a high number of early eighteenth-century novels among the Belfast chapmen's books.

57. An exception is Richardson's *Pamela*, which was republished in Dublin as *Virtue display'd*, and sold for 3d. (Adams, *The printed word*, p. 66).

58. A detailed list of the schools in which the books were noted can be found on the microfiche.

59. The counts were done conservatively, with references by Carleton not counted, while the 1824 survey of schools in counties. Donegal, Kildare, Galway, and Kerry was given a single count.

60. This excludes books published by the Kildare Place Society in the early nineteenth century, including *Robinson Crusoe* (seventeen schools), *Aesop's fables*, and *Anson's voyages* (four schools). Therefore, it is impossible to ascertain the number of schools in which older editions of these works continued to be used.

61. But less popular was *Jack the batchelor*, described by Dutton as a work on 'a noted smuggler' (Dutton, *Statistical survey of Clare*, p. 236).

62. This is confirmed by two respondents in the survey of schools in the Dioceses of Kildare and Leighlin in 1825 (Brenan, *Schools*, pp 72, 478).

63. Adams, *Printed word*, p. 69.

64. Brenan, *Schools*, p. 383.

65. *Captain Rock in London* (March 19, 1825), p. 18. In addition, *Guy Earl of Warwick* was noted as a hedge school classic.

66. *Wisdoms cabinet open'd, or, the famous history of the seven wise masters of Rome* (London: T. Haley?, [?1680 ed.]), preface; (first noted by Pollard in *Dublin's trade*, pp 220-221).

67. Cited in Ó Ciosáin, *Print and popular culture*, p. 97.

68. David Dickson, 'Paine in Ireland' in David Dickson, Dáire Keogh and Kevin Whelan (eds), *The United Irishmen: republicanism, radicalism and rebellion* (Dublin, 1993), pp 153-150; J. Keane, *Tom Paine, a political life* (London, 1995), pp 324, 333; K. Whelan, 'The republic in the village' in Long (ed.), *Books beyond the Pale*, pp 103-104, 115; M.H. Thuente, *The harp restrung* (Syracuse, 1994), passim; A. Thomson, 'Thomas Paine and the United Irishmen' in *Études Irlandaises*, xvi (1991), pp 109-119; Dáire Keogh, *The French disease* (Dublin, 1993), pp 120, 161.

69. Hislop, Kildare Place Society, p. 215.

70. Whelan, 'The republic in the village', pp 107-108.

71. The exception is [Revd James Porter], *Billy Bluff and the squire; or, a sketch of the times* (Belfast, 1796).

72. Maria Luddy, *Women and philanthropy* (Cambridge, 1995), pp 228-231; D.J. Keenan, *The Catholic church in nineteenth-century Ireland. A sociological study* (Dublin, 1983), pp 126-127.

73. W.K.L. Clarke, *A history of the S.P.C.K.* (London, 1959), p. 220.

74. Cited in Adams, *The printed word*, p. 49.

75. Hislop, Kildare Place Society, p. 232.

76. Adams, *The printed word*, p. 49; Bradshaw, *Catalogue*, i, pp 291-292 gives a listing of 52 titles.

77. C.H. Ford, *Hannah Mor: A critical biography* (New York, 1996), p. 127, and chapter 4. See also, P. Demers, *The world of Hannah More* (Lexington, 1996); Pederson, 'Hannah More meets Simple Simon', pp 84-113.

78. Demers, *The world of Hannah More*, p. 117.

79. Surviving copies show that many of the tracts continued to be reprinted in Dublin until at least the first decade of the nineteenth century (Bradshaw, *Catalogue*, i, pp 299-302).

80. Stokes, *Projects for re-establishing the internal peace*, pp 42-43.

81. *Appendix to the fourteenth report of the Commissioners of the Board of Education in Ireland*, p. 337.

82. Both apparently were compilations (Hislop, Kildare Place Society, pp 210, 333, 336).

83. Hislop, Kildare Place Society, p. 208.

84. [anon.] *Hints on the formation of lending libraries in Ireland* (Dublin, 1824), p. 10.

85. Hislop, Kildare Place Society, pp 208-210.

86. Hislop, Kildare Place Society, pp 221, 228.

87. Hislop, Kildare Place Society, pp 211-212.

88. [Mary Leadbeater], *The pedlars* (Dublin, 1826); [Abigail Roberts], *The entertaining medley. . .* (Dublin, 1818), *The cottage fire-side* (Dublin, 1821), *The history of Tim Higgins, the cottage visitor* (Dublin, 1823), *The history of Richard MacReady, the farmer lad* (Dublin, 1824).

89. Maria Edgeworth wrote in 1804 that her *Popular Tales* were 'not designed for young people – nor for the fashionable *fine* people in society; but for the respectable and useful middling classes of merchants, manufacturers & farmers, for whose entertainment but few books have been professedly written' (cited in W.H. Häusermann (ed.), *The Genevese background* (London, 1952) p. 68.

90. One of the rare publications by Maria Edgeworth issued in Ireland for school children, was her *Dog Trusty, &c.*, which was published at Trim (county Meath) in 1835 for the use of Trim school. In 1818 Maria Edgeworth wrote that she sent Mrs. Marcet 'a little book which my father wrote in his last illness – for my brother's [Lovell's] school [at Edgeworthstown] – This little book is not published' (cited in Häusermann, *The Genevese background*, p. 91).

91. B.C. Slade, *Maria Edgeworth 1767-1849, a bibliographical tribute* (London, 1937), p. 31.

92. 'Edgeworth's Tales' were noted in a Catholic and in a Protestant Dublin school (Brenan, *Schools*, pp 434, 444).

93. Hislop, Kildare Place Society, pp 217, 220, 241-242. For the mention of savings banks in other Kildare Place Society books, see [anon.] *The brothers; or, consequences. A story of what happens every day* (Dublin, 1830); [Thomas Beddoes], *The history of Isaac Jenkins, and Sarah his wife. . .* (Dublin, 1817); [Abigail Roberts], *The cottage fire-side* (Dublin, 1821); her *The history of Tim Higgins, the cottage visitor* (Dublin, 1823); and her *The history of Richard MacReady, the farmer's lad* (Dublin, 1824). In addition, see Mary Leadbeater's, *Cottage dialogues among the Irish peasantry* (Dublin, 1813), which was not published by the Kildare Place Society.

94. Hislop, Kildare Place Society, p. 238.

95. The advice, for example, to women, should at some point be compared to the actual work executed by women in this period (see e.g., M. Cullen, 'Breadwinners and providers: Women in the household economy of labouring families 1835-6' in M. Luddy and C. Murphy (eds), *Women surviving* (Swords, 1989), pp 85-116).

96. Hislop, Kildare Place Society, pp 224-226, 235-238, 240.

97. This notion was already expressed in 1808 by Richard Lovell Edgeworth, who advocated that 'The attention [of young readers] should be turned as much as possible to sober realities' (*Appendix to the third report of the Commissioners of the Board of Education in Ireland*, p. 109).

98. Brenan, *Schools*, passim. Protestant schools in the early nineteenth century continued to hold chapbooks first issued at the end of the eighteenth century, particularly those written by Hannah More.

99. Hislop, Kildare Place Society, pp 247-248; Helen Clayton, *To school without shoes: a brief history of the Sunday School Society for Ireland 1809-1979* (n.p., [1979]), pp 22-23, 27; Castleleyn, *A history of literacy and libraries in Ireland.*

100. Described, for example, in Doyle's *Hints addressed to the small holders . . .*, p. 85.

101. H.D. Inglis, *Ireland in 1834* (London, 1835), i, p. 121. The estate was at Ballykistane, three miles outside Tipperary town. Lord Stanley, later earl of Derby, was the same person as Edward G. Stanley, the chief secretary of Ireland, who established the Irish national system of education in 1831 (Akenson, *The Irish education experiment*, pp 59, 107ff; Hislop, Kildare Place Society, p. 117).

102. Plan of the main house. We are grateful to Mrs. V. Pakenham for drawing our attention to this plan. Lady Wicklow founded a library at Newbridge (also called CastleMcAdam) for girls, and other examples are mentioned by Glassford (Glassford, *Notes*, p. 118, and passim).

103. W. Parnell, *Maurice and Berghetta; or, the priest of Rahery* (Boston, 1820 [first ed., London 1817]), p. xxii.

104. One of the earliest works, probably issued by this society, is [anon.], *John Pascal or the temptation of the poor* (Dublin: Printed by J. & M. Porteus, 1824). Many of the tracts of this society did not have identifiers showing that the tracts were issued by this society. However, several were later published in a collection ([anon.] *Publications of the Religious Tract and Book Society for Ireland* (Dublin and London, 1828), vol. 2.

105. S. Duffy, *Nicholas O'Kearney, the last of the bards of Louth* (Coalisland, 1989), pp 38–42.

106. Not considered here are Irish authors who published in England. An early example in this category is Miss Gunning's (later Elizabeth Plunkett) *The village library; intended for the use of young persons* (London, 1802), which was partly based on Berquin's *Children's friend*.

107. But in fact, it was published as the third volume of Duffy's Library of Ireland. The first *Tales of the Irish people*, later became the nineteenth volume in Duffy's Library of Ireland.

108. William Carleton, *Art Maguire; or, the broken pledge* (Dublin, 1845), pp vii-viii.

109. Mrs. S.C. Hall, *Stories of the Irish peasantry* (London: William & Robert Chambers), 1840, p. [i].

110. S.J. Brown and D. Clarke, *Ireland in fiction* (Cork, 1985), vol. 2, p. 220. Similar, but of a nonfictional type was [Catherine Alexander, Countess of Caledon's] *Friendly advice to Irish mothers on training their children* (Armagh, 1842), which included tips for domestic and farm use, but did not refer to improvements in reading.

111. [Part 1], Dublin, London, 1811; Part 2, London, 1813; another, extended version was published in Dublin in 1818.

112. The second volume of *Cottage dialogues* was considered by the Cheap Book Society in 1815 to be included among the planned publications, but for unknown reasons this did not place (The Church of Ireland College of Education, Dublin, MS. 119, f. 8).

113. Martin Doyle [William Hickey], *Irish cottagers* (Dublin, 1833), preface. When Mary Leadbeater published her two volumes of

Cottage dialogues (1811 and 1813), the London editions were supplied with glossaries for English readers not familiar with Anglo-Hibernian words and expressions. One of the glossaries was prepared by Maria Edgeworth.

114. M. Leadbeater, *Cottage dialogues* (London, 1811), p. iv.

115. Sometimes an original text with an English setting was changed into an Irish setting. For example, [Thomas Beddoes], *The history of Isaac Jenkins, and of the sickness of Sarah, his wife, and their three children* (Madeley, 1792), and [Edward Augustus Kendall], *Keeper's travels in search of his master* (London, 1798) were both adapted in this manner by the Kildare Place Society.

116. Advertised at the back of [Patrick Kavanagh's] *Legends of Mount Leinster* (Dublin, 1855).

117. Martin Doyle [William Hickey], *Common sense for common people* (Dublin, 1835), preface. See also Mrs. S.C. Hall's preface to her *Stories of the Irish peasantry* (Edinburgh, 1840, People's edition), in which she states that she hopes that 'the Cheap Publication now submitted. . . may be placed by the higher class within the reach of the lower.' The subscribers' list for Leadbeater's 1811 Dublin edition of her *Cottage dialogues among the Irish peasantry* showed several subscribers obtaining twenty-one copies (e.g., Maria Edgeworth, her father Richard Lovell Edgeworth), and a few individuals obtaining 100 copies each (Col. Keating (of Temple Carig, Bray), the bishop of Meath and his family, and Charles St. George, Esq.)

118. Brenan, *Schools*, pp 315, 516.

119. Harriet Martineau, *Letters from Ireland* (London, 1852), p. 67.

120. V. Wallace, *Mrs Alexander, a life of the hymn-writer Cecil Francis Alexander 1818-1895* (Dublin, 1995), p. 70.

121. Pederson, 'Hannah More meets Simple Simon', pp 85, 95.

122. D.J. Keenan, *The Catholic church in nineteenth-century Ireland* (Dublin, 1983), pp 129-130, 134.

123. Brenan, *Schools*, p. 128.

124. Brenan, *Schools*, passim. However, the lending libraries set up by the Kildare Place Society also created space for the tracts published by other societies, such as The Bible Society, the Missionary Society, the Sunday School Society, and the Society for the Conversion of the Jews (*Hints on . . . lending libraries*, p. 17).

125. Brenan, *Schools*, p. 262.

126. A. Nicholson, *Ireland's welcome to the stranger* (New York, 1847), pp 304, 313, 318-319, 333-334, 404.

127. Revd J. Furniss, *The book of young persons, 'permissu superiorum'* (Dublin, 1860), p. 25.

128. Brenan, *Schools*, pp 313, 329, 331, 419, 421; Casteleyn, *A history*, pp 38-39.

129. Keenan, *Catholic church*, p. 140.

130. Dutton, *Statistical survey of Clare*, p. 237.

131. Dutton, *Statistical survey of Clare*, p. 237; Bell, *A description*, p. 40; Glassford, *Notes*, pp 71, 91.

132. Brenan, *Schools*, p. 531.

133. The definition of Catholic school is based on the religion of the teacher in the school, or its designation as such in a contemporary record. Some of the undesirable literature could also be found in Protestant schools.

134. Keenan, *Catholic church*, p. 126 states that the Catholic Book Society was founded in 1824.

135. Keenan, *Catholic church*, pp 126, 141.

136. Ó Ciosáin, *Print and popular culture*, pp 57, 144, 149.

137. Keenan, *Catholic church*, p. 141.

138. *Hints on . . . lending libraries*, p. 11.

139. *Twelfth report of the Society for Promoting the Education of the Poor in Ireland . . .* (Dublin, 1824) p. 30; see also an account in *The Dublin and London Magazine* of August 1825, cited in 'Biblio', 'Irish chap books' in *The Irish Book Lover*, ii (1911), p. 110.

140. Cited in Hislop, Kildare Place Society, p. 241.

141. Hall, *Ireland*, ii, pp 363-364.

142. Glassford, *Notes*, p. 61; The Church of Ireland College of Education, Kildare Place Society MS. BS. 29, minutes 29 Nov. 1823.

143. Our notes show four chapbooks published in Belfast between 1826-1830, and another eight in the period 1831-35, compared to less than one in each five-year interval during the period 1800-1825, and two or less in each five year period between 1836 to 1850. The number of chapbooks published in Dublin and Limerick remained small, but never fully disappeared during the heyday of the Kildare Place Society publications in the period 1817-1834.

144. See also Adams, *Printed word*, p. 141.

145. J.J.M., 'Irish chap books,' in *The Irish Book Lover*, i (1910) p. 159. As another example, *Captain Freney* was one of the favourite books read by Hannah Lynch before 1874 ([anon.], *The autobiography of a child* (Edinburgh, 1899), p. 107).

146. A constant visitor [?Patrick Kennedy], 'An Irish hedge-school', pp 601-602; 'Irish folk books of the last century', p. 533; J.J.M., 'Irish chap books,' p. 158; Wakefield, cited by Hall, *Ireland, its scenery, character,* ii, p. 363n; Devyr, *The odd book of the nineteenth century*, pp 36-37.

147. This chapman's book possibly can be identified with the *Hibernian tales* noted by the Commissioners on Education in 1825 (*First report of the Commissioners of Irish Education inquiry,*(1825), Appendix No. 221, p. 555). Adams noted an edition published in Belfast by Joseph Smyth, [?1835] (Adams, *The printed word*, p. 197), whereas we know of an edition published in Dublin by C. M. Warren, [?1835].

148. Hislop, 'Kildare Place Society', pp 246, 249; Bradshaw, *Catalogue*, i, p. 624.

149. Akenson, *The Irish education experiment*, pp 231-232.

150. *Fourteenth report of the Commissioners of National Education in Ireland*, pp 63, 68.

151. [Kildare Place Society] Nine of the titles advertised by Cross in Dublin also appeared in a listing of the contents of the circulating library of John Connor in Cork (late 18th century), including *Gulliver's travels, Modern story teller, Robinson Crusoe, Valentine and Orson, Charles the XIIth, Tales of the fairies, Winter evening tales, Arabian tales*, and *Persian tales* (undated catalogue; We are much indebted to M. Pollard for drawing our attention to this pamphlet).

TABLE 1

BOOKS FOR CHAPMEN ADVERTISED (C.1779-1786)
BY RICHARD CROSS, DUBLIN[1]

---

*Adventures of Lady Lucy
Penelope Aubin, *The life and adventures of Lady Lucy, daughter of
an Irish lord* (London, 1726).

*Anson's Voyages
George, Baron Anson, *A voyage around the world . . . by George
Anson* (London, 1748).

*Arabian tales
Dom Chavis and Jacques Cazotte, *Continuation des mille et une nuits.*
Dom Chavis and Jacques Cazotte, *Arabian tales; or, a continuation
of Arabian nights entertainment* (Edinburgh, 1792), 4v.

Argalus and Parthenia
Francis Quarles, *Argalus and Parthenia* (London, 1629).

*Ascanius
[anon.], *Ascanius; or, the young adventurer . . . [i.e., the Young
Pretender]* (London, 1746).

Ben Johnson's jests
[anon.], *Ben Johnson's jests; or, the wit's pocket companion.*
(London, 1760), 6th ed.

Boyle's Voyages
W.R. Chetwood, *The voyages and adventures of Capt. Robert Boyle*
(London, 1726).

*Captain Freny [sic, Freney]
[James Freney], *The life and adventures of James Freney, commonly
called Captain Freney. From the time of his first entering on the
highway, in Ireland* (Dublin, 1754).

*Charles the XIIth
F.M.A. de Voltaire, *Histoire de Charles XII. Roi de Suède* (Basle,
1731). *The history of Charles XII* (London, 1732).

Chearful companion
[anon.], *The chearful companion. A collection of favourite Scots and
English songs, catches, &c.* (Perth, 1780).

*Cynthia
[anon.], *Cynthia: with the tragical account of the unfortunate loves
of Almerin and Desdemona* (London, 1687).

*Destruction of Troy
*The faythfull and true storye of the destruction of Troye, compyled
by Dares Phrigius* (London, 1553).

*Don Bellianis [sic]
First published in Spain in the 16th century. [J. Shurly], *The honour

Rolf Loeber and Magda Stouthamer-Loeber

of chiualrie . . . in the most famous . . . history of Don Belianis of
Greece (London, 1598).

Don Quevedo's visions

[Don Quevedo], *A particular account of Cardinal Fleury's journey to
the other world* (London, 1743).

*Drake's voyages

R.B. [Nathaniel Crouch], *The English hero: or, Sir Francis Drake
reviv'd* (London, 1695).

English rogues

[Richard Head], *The English rogue described, in the life of Meriton
Latroon, a witty extravagant. Being a compleat history of the
most eminent cheats of both sexes* (London, 1665).

*Esop's fables (sic)

[anon.], *Fables of Aesop and others, newly done into English*
(London, 1484).

*Fair Rosamond and Jane Shore

Originally two different books. [anon.], *Unfortunate concubines: or,
the history of Fair Rosamond, mistress to Henry II, and Jane
Shore, concubine to Edward IV.* [?London, ?date].

*Female policy detected

E. Ward. *Female policy detected; or, the arts of a desinging [sic]
woman laid open* (London, 1716).

*Fortunate and unfortunate lovers

Robert Greene, *The pleasant history of Dorastus and Fawnia*
(London, 1648).

Fortunatus

First printing on the continent, 1509. [anon.], *The right pleasant
and variable tragical history of Fortunatus* (London, 1612).

*Garden of love

[anon.], *The flower of fidelitie. Displaying . . . the various adventures of three foraign princes* (London, 1650).

*Gulliver's travels

Jonathan Swift, *Travels into several remote nations of the world*
(London, 1726), 2v.

*Guy Earl of Warwick

French edition, 1525. *[Guy of Warwick]* (London, after 1494).

*History of the Pirates

[anon.], *The history and lives of all the most notorious pirates*
(Dublin, 1727).

*Irish rogues

John Cosgrave, *A genuine history of the lives and actions of the most
notorious Irish highwaymen, tories and rapparees* (Dublin: 1747),
3rd ed.

170

*Jack the batchelor
[known as] *History of Jack the batchelor* (Dublin, Adv. by Richard Cross between 1779-1786).

*Laugh and be fat
[anon.], *Laugh and be fat; or, an antidote against melancholy* (London, 1733).

*Life of St. Patrick
[anon.], *Life of . . . St. Patrick* (Dublin, Richard Cross, 1782).

*Mary Queen of Scots
P. Le Pesant, *Marie Stuart, reine d'Ecosse*, 1675. [P. Le Pesant], *The life of Mary Stewart, Queen of Scotland and France* [translated from the French] (Edinburgh, 1725).

*Moll Flanders
Daniel Defoe, *The fortunes and misfortunes of the famous Moll Flanders* (London, 1722).

*Modern story-teller
[anon.], *The modern story-teller* (Dublin, 1749).

*Montellion
[anon.], *Lamberto, or a comical history* (London, 1643).

Mother Goose's tales
[anon.], *Mother Goose's melody* (London, [ca. 1760]).

*New fairy tales
[anon.], *A new collection of fairy tales. None of which were ever before printed. Containing many useful lessons, moral sentiments, surprizing incidents and amusing adventures* (London, 1750), 2v.

*Nine worthies
R. B[urton, i.e. Nathaniel Crouch], *History of the nine worthies* (London, 1719).

*Noble slaves
Penelope Aubin, *The noble slaves* (London, 1722).

*Ovid's art of love
Ovid, *Ars amandi: or, Ovid's art of love* (London, 1513).

*Parismus and Parismenus
Emmanuel Forde, *The history of Parismus* ([?London], 1598).

Patrick O'Donnell
[anon.], *The adventures of Patrick O'Donnell. In his travels through England and Ireland, written by himself* (London, 1763).

Persian tales
[anon.], *Persian tales* (London, 1714-15), 3v.

*Pilgrim's progress
John Bunyan, *Pilgrim's progress* (London, 1678).

*Reynard the fox
[anon.], *This is the table of the historye of reynart the foxe* (Westminster, 1481).

Rolf Loeber and Magda Stouthamer-Loeber

*Robinson Crusoe
Daniel Defoe, *The whole life and adventures of Robinson Crusoe* (London, 1719), 3v.
*Seven champions
Richard Johnson, *The most famous historie of the seaven champions of Christendom* (London, 1596/7).
*Seven wise masters
[anon.], *Here begynneth thystorye of ye vii wyse master of Rome* (London, [early 16th c.]).
Solomon's Temple spiritualised
John Bunyan, *Solomon's temple spiritualis'd* (London, 1688).
*Tales of the fairies
[Madame Marie-Catherine d'Aulnoy], *Les contes des fées*. English ed.? *The diverting works . . . IV. Tales of the fairies* (London, 1707).
Triumph of wit
[John Shirley], *The triumph of wit: or the canting dictionary* (Dublin, [1780?]).
Twelve delightful novels
[probably] Mrs. Elizabeth Griffith, *A collection of novels* (London, 1777).
*Valentine and Orson
First published, Lyons, 1489. [anon.], *The history of Valentine and Orson, two sons of the Emperor of Greece* (London, 1503-5).
*Winter evening tales
Nathaniel Crouch, *Winter evening entertainments* (London 1731).
Zulima, or pure love
[E. Le Noble de Tennelière], *Pure love: A novel. Being the history of the Princess Zulima . . . translated from the French* (London: Adv. 1718).

---

[1] The earliest known editions are cited here. A full version of Table 1, detailing later editions of these publications and the evidence for their use in Irish schools in the early nineteenth century is available on the enclosed microfiche. Titles marked here with an asterisk (*) are those for which evidence has been found for their use in Irish schools in the first half of the nineteenth century.

Book learning: the experience of reading in the national school 1831–1900

John Logan

DURING THE NINETEENTH CENTURY the everyday language of a school was a potent expression of the relationship between those who entrusted their children to it and the changing social, religious and political contexts within which it functioned. When a pupil's home language was also that of the school, the likelihood was that the language of instruction was taken for granted and non-contentious. However, as the pace of language change quickened and became a feature of the daily lives of an increasing number of families, the appropriateness of the curriculum and the pedagogy of many schools became problematic. For much of that period, bilingualism was widespread. In some places the ascendancy or the decline of one language or the other was not always clear and the prevailing ambivalence affected the classroom experience of many pupils. From one perspective, a displacement of Irish may not have seemed either necessary or inevitable and for some parents the school may have been regarded as the means of conserving traditional forms of communication and custom. Others looked to the school to facilitate the process of language change and to provide children with the literacy to function within an increasingly Anglophone world.

I

In the earlier decades of the nineteenth century many teachers spoke Irish and some were able to read and write in it. A few offered instruction in Irish – in parts of Munster teaching reading and writing in Irish lingered into the 1830s – but elsewhere the demand for instruction in Irish seems to have been low compared to that for instruction in reading and writing in English.[1] Nonetheless, interests that sought to promote evangelical and utilitarian instruction amongst the poor were not unaware of the extent to which Irish remained the everyday language of many children. Consequently, two societies, the Baptist Society and the Irish Society were established, in 1814 and 1818 respectively, especially for the purpose of teaching Irish-speaking pupils. Other societies, including the Association for Discountenancing Vice, the Kildare Place Society and the London Hibernian Society produced Irish and bilingual texts and recruited Irish speakers as teachers.[2] Among the promoters of charity schooling Irish had influential supporters such as Whitley Stokes, a senior fellow of Trinity College. His interest in Irish had developed within a scholarly context and his belief in its inherent sophistication and his knowledge of its extensive vernacular use prompted him to sponsor Irish translations of Scripture for classroom use. Another advocate, Christopher Anderson, a founder of the Baptist Society, employed the pedagogical arguments that to teach pupils in a language other than their mother tongue was counter-productive and that skills acquired through learning to read Irish might be applied in the reading of English.[3]

The movement to promote schooling through Irish emerged at a time when the political establishment remained generally unsympathetic towards it. In the 1810s and 1820s residual fears of Irish as a symbol of disaffection and rebellion persisted. Some authorities argued that linguistically it was a barbarous dialect. Thus, a social and political consensus amongst the elite supported the view that the promotion of Irish would only serve to 'aggravate social and political divisions'.[4] Perhaps of greater significance than any argument stemming from cultural insularity or political anxiety, was the belief that Irish was in decline because parents did not want their children to use it and that they believed that schooling was an effective means of becoming proficient in it.[5] In such circumstances, the activities of evangelicals who used Irish added to the ambivalence. 'Nobody is taking any interest in the fine subtle Irish language, apart from mean swaddlers who try to lure the Irish to join their new cursed religion,' remarked Amhlaoibh Ó Súilleab-háin, as he observed the work of the Irish Society in south

Kilkenny during the 1820s.[6] Despite the enthusiasm of energetic patrons and teachers, the societies that used Irish in their classrooms lost their early momentum in the face of resistance by Roman Catholic interests and government disapproval of their provocative proselytism. Neither the Kildare Place Society nor the London Hibernian Society was willing to sustain their earlier initiatives of providing Irish texts. Along with most other voluntary societies they continued to organise their schools on the assumption that as soon as was practicable, English should become the language of instruction.[7] Similarly, it was assumed that following their establishment in 1831, the commissioners of national education should devise a curriculum based on the English language.

The language of instruction carried its own powerful message and from the start of schooling, it not only reinforced the words and phrases being learned but it also served as a reminder of its power in places beyond the school. On his first day at the newly opened national school on Cape Clear in 1871, Conchúr Ó Síocháin was reminded that he was on the threshold to a new world:

> The first day I entered the school the master called me up to him and he enquired from me in English what name I had; but I didn't understand him. Then he asked me in Irish:
>
> '*Cad is ainm duit*?' said he. I told him. 'And haven't you any English?' he added.
>
> 'No' said I, 'not a syllable.'
>
> 'Well, little fellow, you'll have to throw away your Irish now and speak English from this out.'[8]

The use of a wholly unfamiliar language added considerably to the difficulties of pupils. It might be lessened however, if teachers, like Ó Síocháin's, were bilingual and prepared to use Irish. In 1837 Jeremiah O'Donovan Rossa observed his own national schoolteacher using Irish to take pupils through their initial uncertain paces:

> I recollect one day that I was in my class and the master teaching us. He had a rod called a pointer, and he was telling a little boy from Maoil what to call the letters. The little boy could not speak any English; he knew nothing but Irish, and

175

the master, putting the tip of the pointer to the letter A on the board would say to him, *'Glao'g A air sin,'* then he'd move the pointer to B and say, *'Glao'g B air sin,'* and so on to the end of the lesson.[9]

Unlike many of his fellow scholars Rossa came from a family where English was spoken and he had some familiarity with it prior to starting at school. Despite that, his early experiences reading *Scripture lessons* were fraught with difficulty:

> I was in my class one day, reading from the little book of *Scripture lessons* and I read aloud that the mother of Jacob and Easu 'bore twines' – 'What's that? What's that?' said the master, smiling, and I again read that that lady of the olden time 'bore twines,' I did not know enough to pronounce the word 'twins', and probably did not know at the time what 'twins' meant. If the schoolmaster was teaching me my natural language – the Irish, and if I had read from the book – *'do bidh cooplee aica'*, I would readily understand that she had a couple of children together at the one lying-in.[10]

Rossa's teacher, like most teachers recruited to the new national schools were local people who shared the language of their pupils. However, if the teacher was from outside, a prospect that become more likely as the system expanded, the possibility of divergence between the everyday language of teacher and pupil increased. A visitor to the new national school at Westport in 1833 found 200 monoglot Irish-speaking pupils under a teacher who had no Irish. To him the gap between his own cultural world and that of his pupils appeared unbridgeable: 'What is the good of all this?' he sheepishly inquired of a visiting official.[11]

The commissioners for national education knew that many pupils were Irish speakers for whom lack of proficiency in English was a major impediment. They may even have been sympathetic towards their plight but few went as far as to re-examine or criticise the principles on which national schooling was based. In general, the commissioners and their inspectors and teachers believed that national schooling provided a stepping stone in the social and material advancement of the pupils and it was assumed that parents too, shared that premise. Consequently, on the few occasions that the commissioners dealt with a request to recognise instruction through Irish, the plea was rejected on the grounds that such a process would not come within their 'plan of education'.[12] During the 1850s, a chief inspector, Patrick Keenan, argued that the use of Irish in the schools attended by Irish-speaking pupils would result in a more effective pedagogy, but if he still held that view at the time he was appointed resident commissioner in 1871 and thus permanent head of the department, he felt unable to act on it.[13] A decade later he was able to argue that knowledge of Irish was not necessary for teachers whose schools were in Irish-speaking districts.[14] By then the promotion of a standard spoken and written English had become deeply embedded in official thinking as a precondition to the forming of a cohesive, national culture. The assumption that underpinned the declaration in one of the lesson books – 'the people of these islands have one and the same language (all at least that are educated), one and the same Queen – the same laws'[15] – may not have been accepted absolutely or enthusiastically by every teacher and pupil but it underpinned official classroom practice until instruction through Irish in Irish-speaking districts was introduced in 1904.[16]

Pupils whose home language was English were not immune to the problems that faced Irish-speaking pupils. They were being schooled at a time when various interests – the publishers of dictionaries, the universities and the public schools, the editors of national newspapers – were forging an agreement on what the characteristics of Standard English might be.[17] The commissioners of national education sought to promote the emerging consensus, notwithstanding the extent to which their language differed from that of their pupils. Thus a typical lesson from the *First book of lessons,* listed 'new' words – bust, gulf, lump, burn, hunt, trust, curd, hurt, turn – and then a sequence of sentences:

> Curd is made of milk. A dog can hunt. Pat has a fine bust. Trust Mark, and he will mend it. Sam must not hurt my horse. A fire will burn. Tell him to turn back. A fork will lift a lump. It is a gulf.[18]

Such texts, without context or narrative, bore little relation to English as pupils spoke it in their everyday lives. It was assumed that when they had learned the alphabet and a selection of one and two-syllable words with ease, that these disembodied lessons would provide a further stage in their schooling. Another lesson book, an anthology of sacred poetry adapted to the 'understanding of children' and published by the commissioners in 1845, must have presented an even greater challenge to the seven and eight-year-olds for whom it was written. Its allusions and metaphors and a vocabulary and syntax that would soon seem archaic, can only have served, at best, as a portent to a culturally remote world:

> Where're I take my walks abroad,
> How many poor I see!
> What shall I render to my God
> For all his gifts to me.[19]

Neither was the language of instruction expected to accommodate itself to regional variation in dialect, idiom or accent: we can now only speculate on what the seven-year-olds who spoke Ulster Scots or the lingering Middle English dialects of Fingal or Bargy and Forth make of this other English. The national school teachers, like their precursors were incorporated in the movement to promote the new metropolitan standard and their accents and forms of communication, no less than those of their pupils, had to be undermined and replaced. [20]

II

Throughout the medieval and the early modern period, reading was taught through spelling.[21] First a pupil was taught a letter by associating its name with its form and its sound and then all the letters in a standard sequence, the alphabet. Combinations of two or three letters, forming words of a single sound or syllable were then learned and the pupil advanced through simple words to reading short phrases. Progress towards the reading of more difficult texts was made through the gradual introduction of longer words and it was assumed that fluency came eventually from sustained practice. It was a pedagogy, which ultimately drew its legitimacy from classical authorities whose stress on imitation as the basis of mental development had rote learning, repetition, drill and copying at its heart.[22] Richard and Maria Edgeworth, experienced observers of teaching, considered the matter unproblematic: the letters of the alphabet, they remarked 'are perhaps in the course of some weeks firmly fixed in the pupil's memory.'[23] Daniel O'Connell boasted how at four he learned his letters from a 'wandering scholar' in an hour and a half and William Carleton remembered that he had learned his letters in a day.[24] Teachers usually directed their efforts towards teaching elementary skills – letters, alphabet, single syllables and monosyllabic words – and reassured themselves that most commonly used words were of one or two syllables. When pupils had learned a store of these it was assumed they had crossed a threshold and had gained access to a wide range of texts, both public and private.

The increase in demand for schooling in the early nineteenth century led to a reappraisal of teaching method. The need to teach a growing number of children while minimising its costs, stimulated renewed interest in the strategies, which might be applied to the teaching of reading. In England, Joseph Lancaster was at the forefront of the movement and he developed and refined the practice of using proficient senior pupils to teach younger pupils. The idea was particularly attractive to the promoters of charity schools and anywhere resources were in short supply. The basis of the method, as developed by Lancaster at the British and Foreign School Society's school at Borough Road in Southwark, was a systematic and accurate classification of pupils 'whose proficiency is on a par' and the matching of each 'classification' to a specific part of the curriculum. He divided the literary curriculum into two sections, the first concerned with the acquisition of skills and the second with the acquisition of knowledge through the use of those skills.[25]

Lancaster's classification of spelling and reading lessons had the traditional alphabetic method as its basis. Pupils started by learning off the alphabet and subsequent classes dealt with a progression through two-letter words or syllables, on to three, four and five letter words and then to words of three or four syllables. The scheme adopted in 1806 by the Lancastrian Schools of the Cork Charitable Society, was typical of that used in such schools:

179

First	learning of letters
Second	learning ab, -eb, etc.
Third	spelling words of one syllable
Fourth	spelling words of two syllables
Fifth	spelling words of three or four syllables
Sixth	spelling words of five and six syllables
Seventh	young readers
Eighth	advanced readers
Ninth	young writers
Tenth	advanced writers.[26]

Lancaster was invited to attend the inaugural meeting of the Kildare Place Society in 1811 and shortly afterwards he secured the appointment of John Veevers, a colleague at Borough Road, as the principal instructor at the Society's training school.[27] Veevers remained with the Society until 1834 and during his time at Kildare Place he established its teacher-training course, wrote several of the Society's text-books and compiled its principal pedagogic treatise, *The schoolmaster's manual*.[28]

The *Manual* was a hybrid formed from traditional practices and the monotorial procedures developed by Lancaster. It proposed a classification of pupils on the basis of proficiency and the traditional subdivisions of alphabet, two letter syllables and words, three and four letter words, disyllables and 'easy' trisyllables and finally, difficult trisyllables and polysyllables.[29] It proposed that pupils should be introduced to the alphabet by a monitor who would guide them through the letters printed on a wall-chart. The monitor would then supervise the tracing of letters with a finger or pointer in a tray of sand.[30] Having learnt the alphabet, pupils progressed to learning monosyllables from a chart or from a primer, saying each letter in turn – for example, 's', 'o' – and then saying the word 'so'. The monitor would then dictate a random selection of words and wait for each pupil to spell them. Polysyllables, regardless of their length, would be taught on the principle that they were merely a sequence of syllables: thus 'present' was taught by learning its components, 'pre' and 'sent'.[31] The *Manual* stipulated that pupils should concentrate on the proper recognition and pronunciation of a word – it was admitted that for most pupils the words in the exercises

180

would be 'for the most part new' – and that an understanding, enabling them 'to read with intelligence' might come when they became more confident. Comprehension, it was suggested, might then be promoted by careful questioning so that the pupil would acquire the habit of scrutinising and reflecting on what was being read.[32]

Lancaster granted the Kildare Place Society the right to adapt his materials and within a month of its foundation the Society had issued a number of large wall-charts containing the alphabet, word lists and simple prose.[33] In 1819 the material was issued in two books. The first, *The Dublin spelling book,* followed the traditional arrangement of a primer with an alphabet, words arranged by degree of difficulty and some simple sentences. Its sequel, *The Dublin reading book,* contained more advanced prose and it was accompanied by *Questions on the Dublin reading book* consisting of ready-made questions and their answers through which the teacher could assess progress. Apart from his influence on Kildare Place Society schools, reformers as diverse as Lord Farnham and Bishop James Doyle, the Christian Brothers and the Presentation Sisters adopted Lancaster's methods. With the affiliation of the diocesan education societies and the Church Education Society to Kildare Place in the 1830s, his pedagogical method spread through the Church of Ireland school network.[34]

Lancaster's most enduring influence, however, may have been in the new national schools. In general, the commissioners of national education adopted the pedagogical practices of the Kildare Place Society and while it would have been politically ill-advised to explicitly acknowledge the source of those ideas, it was clearly underwritten in their recruitment of key staff who had formerly been employed at Kildare Place and through its adoption of *The schoolmaster's manual.*[35] Initially, the commissioners sanctioned the use of textbooks which had been produced by the Kildare Place Society as well as amended versions of those produced by the Catholic Book Society, but these were soon replaced by its own specially commissioned texts. Like the Kildare Place Society, the commissioners believed that the process of learning to read should not be a mere acquisition of a set of skills to be used by the pupils for their own purposes. Their argument, as outlined in their first report

John Logan

to the government, neatly spliced utilitarianism and a political pragmatism sensitive to contemporary social conditions:

> The power of reading is frequently lost to children and even becomes a source of corruption and mischief to them because they have never been directed to the proper use of it: and it is consequently of the highest importance that while they are taught to read, their thoughts and inclinations should have a beneficial direction given to them.[36]

That direction materialised in a set of lesson books whose successive editions formed the basis of national school instruction until the end of the century. Following the pattern of the lesson books and the primers used by the private schoolteachers and the voluntary societies the *First book of lessons* introduced the pupil to the alphabet and to the forms and the sounds of the letters and monosyllables. Not only was this the first step in becoming literate, for many, such as Conchúr Ó Síocháin on his first day at school, it was also the first stage in acquiring a new language:

> He gave me a little book in the English as a gift, a thing he did for every beginner. That was the book that took me a long time until I was able to master it in any way. It must have taken me a month to learn the first page in it, that is the A-B-C, for it was really hard work for me to change my language from the Irish to the English.[37]

The next section introduced the pupil to three, four and five letter syllables and words. In this part of the text, words were linked to form sentences and then arranged into a continuous narrative –Curd is milk. A dog can hunt. – the components of which might not necessarily bear any relation to each other. In the final section the pupil was introduced to longer words and to sentences which formed a short moral tale. Each lesson in this section was preceded with a list of the new words, which would be introduced in the text, and it concluded with an italicised summary of the moral.

The *Second book of lessons* was designed to teach two and three syllable words. These were progressively introduced in a series of scriptural and other stories chosen for their potential to convey 'important religious truths' and 'devout feelings'.[38] It also contained geography lessons, natural history, political economy and grammar. The principle of transmitting 'useful knowledge' was continued as each subsequent book added to the range and complexity of the material. In attempting a thorough reform of elementary instruction the commissioners set out to provide all the books for a full course of instruction. By 1850 they had published ten lesson books, four verse anthologies and special manuals on accountancy, agriculture, Scripture and needlework. In all they had forty-one titles on their list and they issued a supplementary list of thirty-five books not published by them but nonetheless sanctioned for use in their schools.[39]

Throughout the 1830s and 1840s, Robert Sullivan was national education's principal authority on reading. He was one of four foundation school inspectors appointed in 1834 and five years later was appointed professor in the newly opened Central Model Schools at the commissioners' headquarters in Marlborough Street. The syllabus of his course and his published lectures suggest that he expected his students to review a number of continental and American authorities and to become proficient in the system of classification advocated by Lancaster.[40] His overall approach was less pragmatic than that advocated by Lancaster, however, and he brought a reflective and scholarly perspective to reading instruction. Teachers trained by him at the Central Model Schools were expected to be knowledgeable about the derivation of words and the history of the language and were exercised in Saxon, Greek and Latin prefixes and terminations and in classical and literary allusions. He was a staunch, if somewhat isolated representative of the classical and rhetorical tradition in schooling – owing something maybe to his own schooling at Belfast Academical Institution – and clearly he hoped to implant a palpable, if diluted classicism in the national school curriculum. Sullivan believed that both the teacher proprietors and the Lancastrian schools promoted rote memorisation in pupils, and he was determined to transform classroom reading into an 'intelligent' activity. He described his approach as 'explanatory' or 'intellectual', characterised by the teacher leading pupils to inquire into 'and consequently understand' the meaning of words and sentences in each lesson.[41] Pupils should be individually questioned and made explain, he suggested, so that the teacher could be certain that they fully understand what had been read: progression to the next section should not occur until the teacher was satisfied that the previous piece was fully understood. If by such means, understanding was achieved, pupils would then be able to read with 'propriety' and 'expression'.

A similar blend of pragmatism and optimism reappeared in a teachers' manual published in 1856 by Thomas Young, the newly appointed head of the Central Model Schools.[42] He had fully absorbed the case which Sullivan made for the necessity of ensuring that every pupil understood the meaning of each word in a text. This, he suggested could only be established if pupils showed that they could use a particular word in a variety of appropriate contexts. If this were accomplished reading might become a 'vehicle for knowledge' and not what he claimed the teacher proprietors had made it, a 'mechanical repetition'. Young put his advice into a framework, which reflected the inspectors' preoccupation with low standards and their belief that the stipulation of instructional goals for each class of pupil would increase efficiency. Drawing on his own teaching experience, he constructed tables wherein each aspect of instruction was carefully quantified. For example, he suggested that twenty-five and a half hours of instruction spread over thirty-four days should be sufficient for teaching the alphabet.[43]

Seven years later, Young's colleague at the Central Model Schools, P.W. Joyce, published his *Handbook of school management and methods of teaching* and it soon became the most widely used teacher's manual.[44] Writing it, Joyce drew on his own extensive experience as a national schoolteacher, as an inspector and as professor in the Central Model Schools. In particular, he acknowledged the influence of lectures given to pupil teachers by Head Inspector Keenan, during the 1850s.[45] Inevitably, Joyce's method of teaching reading was located firmly within the traditions of Borough Road, Kildare Place and Marlborough Street. Like Lancaster, Veevers, Sullivan and Young before him, he argued that pupils should first learn the shapes, then the names and the power, or sounds of the letters, then the alphabet – broken into 'parcels' or short sequences of letters – followed by monosyllables and short words. Pupils might then progress to longer, more difficult words. Like his precursors, Joyce argued that learning should be reinforced through appropriate exercises. For example, pupils should be made spell out letters and words from a text or from dictation. He decried the tendency of pupils and teachers alike to be satisfied with rote memorisation and he repeated Robert Sullivan's well-worn advocacy of promoting understanding through questioning. For example, having read the phrase, 'that bad man got these gold cups by theft', a pupil might be asked how did the man get the cups, or what is the name given to a man who gets things by theft, or what did the man steal.[46]

Each successive edition of Joyce's *Handbook* followed the plan of the first, repeating the same well-tried advice. From its publication in 1863 it became the essential text for pupil-teachers, a pre-eminence it held until the end of the century. Apart from occasional minor revisions each of its eighteen successive editions followed the plan of the first. For the ordinary teacher its attraction may have lain in its matter-of-fact prose, an empathy with the everyday problems of the national schoolroom and an abundance of practical examples. Its author had learned through experience, he had risen through the ranks of the system and his method seemed to offer a realistic prescription for success.

III

At their foundation the national commissioners adopted Lancaster's curricular classification as an instrument for measuring their achievements. They were as yet without the administrative capacity to make it effective however and consequently the earliest direction to inspectors assessing reading standards was that they should simply note the proportion of pupils that could read fluently.[47] They adopted the practice of the Kildare Place Society and in most instances accepted the statistics compiled by teachers and school managers. The lesson books provided a convenient framework within which pupils might be assessed and the means of regulating progression from class to class. Thus the fifth of the 'Twelve practical rules for the teachers of national schools' obliged teachers to classify pupils by the standard of the book they were in and the inspectors were required to moderate these classifications and attest to their appropriateness.[48] Some teachers and inspectors questioned the appropriateness of the books for the different ability levels and that soon led to the production of sequel texts to provide a more sensitive discrimination.[49] Consequently, by the early 1850s seven lesson books, graded by degree of difficulty, were available as the basis of pupil classification and assessment.

To improve the quality of teaching and assessment the inspectors produced programmes specifying minimum levels of proficiency.[50] For example, the 1855 programme stated that first and second class pupils should be able to spell correctly, understand the meaning of the 'simpler' words in their lesson books, and be able to answer simple questions on the subject matter. It was clear that pupils were not required to understand the meaning of the more difficult words, even though they might be able to read them successfully: the rote memorisation which reformers such as Robert Sullivan and Thomas Young had hoped to displace, remained the essential pedagogic strategy. This continued to concern progressive reformers and demonstrations of comprehension became a feature of school visits and instances of success and failure were cited to support the views of detractors and supporters of the system. When Francis Head visited the Central National Schools in 1851 he was surprised to find most pupils able to spell and offer various correct explanations for the word 'soar' but when Nassau Senior visited in the early 1860s he found that the pupils knew the name and course of the main rivers in Europe but not the meaning of the word 'river'.[51]

There were two contrasting views of what the purposes of national education might be. There were commissioners, inspectors and teachers who argued that the needs of the majority of pupils, rather than those of the small minority who aspired to a higher education, should determine its goals. The needs of most pupils, it was believed, might be met when they acquired an elementary, if uncritical fluency. It was tempting to be satisfied when such pupils showed that they could read a sequence of words and to avoid having to consider whether they could also understand their meaning or use them in a number of contexts. On the other hand there were those who believed that every pupil – regardless of ambition or means –

should leave the national school with more than a superficial knowledge of the simpler books. They argued that if the schools were not reaching such a goal it might be because of the home circumstances of the pupils and the inadequacies of the teachers: the corollary was that as soon as circumstances improved, so too would reading standards. When a head inspector, William McCready, suggested in 1850 that the promotion of higher standards was undermined by poor teaching, he spoke for many of his colleagues and like them he was uncomfortably aware of how few teachers had availed themselves of training.[52] He believed that untrained teachers, like many parents were too easily satisfied when pupils displayed what was referred to as 'book learning' a trait they equated with education. In adulthood O'Donovan Rossa remembered a schooling where his precocious reading of the lesson books was admired by adults who seemed unaware of his confusion or uncertainty. It was a time when his learning, he remembered, 'ran far and away ahead' of his understanding.[53]

On the basis of the assessments carried out in the 1850s and 1860s the reading standard of pupils may be allocated to one or other of three broad categories. Those in the first, consisting of a little over 50 per cent of all those assessed, were able to read 'correctly' either the first or second class book. The second category, on average 20 per cent of the total, consisted of those who read the third or higher book with 'ease and intelligence'. The third category consisted of the 30 per cent or so assessed annually as 'not proficient'. Thus the majority of pupils had, at best, the basic skills of simple word recognition. A small minority would alone acquire higher skills or what the inspectors referred to as intelligence. By the 1850s these contrasting strands of achievement had been given formal recognition in official assessments.

In 1870 a royal commission of inquiry into primary education provided an opportunity for the state to examine the achievements of its national schools. During one of its sittings, its chairman, Earl Powis, asked a head inspector, James O'Connor, if he was satisfied with the extent to which pupils remained at the first book, in some cases for up to two years. O'Connor replied that from his experience of examining children attending workhouse schools, where regular attendance was easily assured, a year at the first book was sufficient, though this might vary with the ability of the pupils. In most schools however, sporadic attendance put a brake on progress: almost half of all pupils were studying the first book and only a quarter were at the third or higher book.[54] Another inspector, Cornelius O'Mahony stated that the reading was 'not good' and generally indistinct.[55] Asked if it could be described as intelligent, he replied that really intelligent reading was very rare and that the inability of many pupils to understand what they read was one of the most prominent faults in the system. He was inclined to blame the impoverished language of the lesson books and in arguments reminiscent of those made by Robert Sullivan in the 1830s and 1840s, he advocated the use of anthologies of classical writers which might 'develop the intellect of the pupils and make them think'.[56] He agreed with the suggestion by a member of the commission that few teachers took the trouble to promote understanding and that their explanation of words was often obscure.[57]

In an attempt to establish the competence which pupils attained before leaving school the commissioners drew an admission from Patrick O'Callaghan, a teacher graded 'first, of the first class', that the majority would hardly be able to read fluently. O'Callaghan agreed with the suggestion that such pupils could hardly read a newspaper and when the commissioners adopted that as a test of reading ability, he had to admit that the majority leaving his school would be unable to do so. He suggested that the ability to write their names or read a simple prayer book might be a more realistic test. He conceded that maybe with a little 'culture' of their own, that three quarters of those who left school might eventually get to the stage where they could read a newspaper, but those who left early did not retain a love of reading and many soon forgot whatever they had learned. When asked to assess the general state of literacy amongst the peasantry he suggested that it was on the increase and that the 'great majority' read in their cabins in the evenings such material as 'pleasing little novels, little histories and lives of the saints' generally obtained from the priest. However, he had to admit that since he was not well acquainted with the peasantry, he could not say if that was actually the case.[58]

Faced with such evidence the commissioners were forced to conclude that the progress of national school pupils was 'very much less than it ought to be'. In the remaining elementary schools – those of the Church Education Society and the teaching religious 'the result is not very different'.[59] Prevailing social attitudes and a deficient pedagogy they believed, had taken their toll. Considering various strategies that might help raise standards, the commissioners argued that teachers might make a greater effort if the grant paid to a school depended on the performance of its pupils. 'Payment by results' had been introduced in England in 1862 and in 1872 the national education commissioners decided to make a substantial part of its grants to schools dependant on the standard reached. To give effect to that, a new syllabus, generally referred to as the 'results programme', was introduced and it formed the basis of instruction, without any substantial modification, until the end of the century.[60]

The new reading syllabus was built on foundations laid over the previous four decades. A Lancastrian prescription of stages and the influence of reformers who hoped to make reading an expressive, sentient activity were both evident. Thus, for example, the main goal prescribed for the third class was that pupils should be able to read their lesson book 'with ease, correctness and intelligence'.[61] Such a goal, its outcome easily observed and measured had strong attractions for an administration promoting efficiency and economy. Less tangible outcomes such as the ability to comprehend and critically evaluate a text were not so easily measured. They were not categorised as essential skills in the official assessments and consequently were accorded less priority by teachers. To promote such higher skills would have resulted in a diversion of resources from the goal of ensuring that all pupils would acquire, at the very least, the ability to read a simple text before leaving the national school.

From 1872 the performance of each pupil was examined annually by an inspector and until the introduction of a revised syllabus in 1900 these assessments, the results of which were published in the commissioners' annual reports, were the chief instrument for allocating a substantial portion of a school's funds. Inevitably the standard of performance set

189

for each stage became the pivot on which the curriculum rotated. Admission to the assessment was allowed only if a pupil satisfied a specified attendance requirement and success was a precondition for progression to the next class. These changes occurred as the number of teachers being trained under the supervision of the commissioners was increasing and the combined effect of these reforms was that the expectations of inspectors, teachers, parents and pupils gradually converged. Not surprisingly, the numbers passing in the annual assessments increased. Throughout the 1870s the average pass rate in reading was 85 per cent and by the 1890s it averaged 95 per cent, never falling below 91 per cent.[62]

In the period between 1870 and 1900 there was a movement from a concentration of pupils in the lower classes – infants, first and second – towards a more even distribution over the full range of standards. Children were spending longer at school and as a result they moved more easily and quickly through each stage of a full course of instruction. In the early 1860s, the lowest standards – books one and two and its sequel – accounted for over 80 per cent of all pupils. In 1872, first and second standard together accounted for 52 per cent of pupils, a decade later they accounted for 37 per cent and in 1892 for 30 per cent. Throughout the 1860s, advanced pupils – those at the fourth book and higher accounted for just under 7 per cent of the total but by the 1890s they accounted for 35 per cent. By then the distribution of the pupil population over each class reflected the fact that a growing number of children were spending a great part of their time between the ages of six and fourteen in school. That trend was given legislative expression in the compulsory school legislation of 1892, but it would take further legislation by each of the two new Irish states in the 1920s and a further thirty years of social change to give the pupil population the symmetrical and even profile which the reformers of the nineteenth century had hoped for.

IV

A reconstruction of the process of reading instruction in the national school and an assessment of its impact solely on the basis of the instructional texts, teachers' manuals and the official assessments would be incomplete and one-sided. The hazy picture that emerges from the official documents may be refined with the personal accounts of pupils. What they reveal is a great cultural and cognitive gap that many pupils crossed only with difficulty. Nonetheless, it would seem that standards in reading, as measured by the inspectors, improved, especially in the last three decades of the nineteenth century. That change occurred within parameters that were determined by the requirements imposed by the commissioners of national education and by the exigencies of the lives of most pupils. By the end of the century the schools had become more efficient at reaching their stated goals and they could rightly draw some satisfaction from that achievement; that those goals remained narrowly utilitarian, culturally exclusive and intellectually limited, is another matter.

Notes

1. Louis Cullen, 'Patrons, teachers and literacy in Irish' in Mary Daly and David Dickson (eds) *The origins of popular literacy in Ireland* (Dublin, 1990), p. 35; Brian Ó Cúiv, 'Irish language and literature 1691–1845' in T.W. Moody and W.E. Vaughan (eds) *A new history of Ireland*, iv (Oxford, 1986), p. 381.

2. Victor Edward Durkacz, *The decline of the Celtic languages* (Edinburgh, 1983), pp 152–155.

3. Christopher Anderson, *A brief sketch of various attempts which have been made to diffuse a knowledge of the Holy Scripture through the medium of the Irish language* (Dublin, 1818).

4. Durkacz, *Decline*, p. 156.

5. Gerard O'Brien, 'The strange death of the Irish language, 1780–1800' in Gerard O'Brien (ed.), *Parliament, politics and people: essays in eighteenth century Irish history* (Dublin, 1989), pp 166–169.

6. Michael McGrath (ed.), *Cinnlae Amhlaoibh Uí Súilleabháin: the diary of Humphrey O'Sullivan*, (4 vols, London, 1928) i, p. 55.

7. Padraig de Brún, 'The Kildare Place Society in Kerry, vi: summary and discussion' in *Journal of the Kerry Archaeological and Historical Society*, xvii (1984), pp 153–206.

8. Conchúr Ó Síocháin, *The man from Cape Clear,* [a translation by Riobárd Breathnach of *Seanchas Chléire*] (Cork, 1975), p. 8.

9. O'Donovan Rossa, *Rossa's recollections 1838 to 1898* (New York, 1898), p. 31.

10. O'Donovan Rossa, *Recollections*, p. 32.

11. *A report of the select committee of the House of Lords appointed to inquire into the progress and operation of the new plan of education in Ireland* H. C. 1837 viii, part i, pp 106–120.

12. Minutes of the commissioners of national education in Ireland, 9 Jan. 1834 and 27 June 1844 (N.L.I.).

13. Commissioners of national education in Ireland [hereafter, National education], *Twenty-second report* [2142–11], H. C.1856, xxvii, pt. ii, pp 72–73; National education, *Twenty-fourth report,* [2456–I], H.C. 1859, vii, p. 135; National education, *Twenty-fifth report,* [2593], H.C., 1860, xxvi, p. 220.

14. National education, *Forty-seventh report*, [C 2925] H.C., 1881, xxiv, p. 12.

15. National education, *Fourth book of lessons for the use of schools* (Dublin, 1853), p. 32.

16. National education, *Seventy-first report*, [Cd 3154], H.C., 1906, xxix, p. 63.

17. E. J. John, *Eloquence and power: the rise of language standards and standard languages* (London, 1987).

18. National education, *First book of lessons for the use of schools* (Dublin, 1836), p. 18.

19. National education, *Sacred poetry adapted to the understanding of children and youth for the use of schools* (Dublin, 1845), p. 7.

20. Robert Sullivan, *The literary class book; or, readings in English literature: to which is prefixed an introductory treatise on the art of reading and the principles of elocution* (Dublin, 1863).

21. Ian Michael, *The teaching of English from the sixteenth century to 1870* (Cambridge, 1987), pp 14–16.

22. Michael, *Teaching*, pp 14–16.

23. Maria and Richard Lovell Edgeworth, *Practical education* (London, 1798), p. 39.

24. Denis Gwynn, *Daniel O'Connell* (Cork and Oxford, 1947), p. 27; David J. O'Donoghue, *The life of William Carleton* (London, 1896), i, p. 11.

25. Joseph Lancaster, *Improvements in education, as it respects the industrial classes of the community: containing a short account of its present state, hints towards its improvement, and a detail of some practical experiments conducive to that end* (London, 1805).

26. Seán Ó Coindealbháin, 'Schools and schooling in Cork city, 1700–1831', *Journal of the Cork Historical and Archaeological Society*, xlviii (1943), p. 46.

27. Susan M. Parkes, *Kildare Place: the history of the Church of Ireland training college* (Dublin, 1984), pp 20–26.

28. Society for the Education of the Poor of Ireland *The schoolmaster's manual* (Dublin, 1825).

29. *Schoolmaster's manual*, p. 29.

30. *Schoolmaster's manual*, p. 38.

31. *Schoolmaster's manual*, p. 39.

32. *Schoolmaster's manual*, p. 44.

33. J.M. Goldstrom, *The social content of education 1808–1870: a study of the working class school reader in England and Wales* (Shannon, 1972), pp 52–61.

34. Parkes, *Kildare Place*, pp 37–39.

35. Eustás Ó Héideáin, *National school inspection in Ireland: the beginnings* (Dublin, 1967), pp 33, 54; Parkes, *Kildare Place,* pp 35–36.

36. National education, *First report,* [70], H.C. 1834, xl, p. 3.

37. Ó Síocháin, *Cape Clear,* p. 9.

38. National education, *Second book of lessons for the use of schools* (Dublin, 1836), p. 1.

39. Goldstrom, *Social content of education,* pp 64–66; D.H. Akenson, *The Irish education experiment: the national system of education in the nineteenth century* (London, 1970), pp 227–250.

40. National education, *Seventh report* [353], H.C. 1842, xxiii, p. 104; Robert Sullivan, *Letters and lectures on popular education in Ireland* (Dublin, 1842).

41. National education, *Seventh report,* [353], H.C. 1842, xxiii, pp 107–108.

42. T.U. Young, *Teacher's manual for infant schools and preparatory classes* (Dublin, 1856) p. 131.

43. Young, *Teacher's manual,* p. 134.

44. Patrick Weston Joyce, *A handbook of school management and methods of school teaching* [first edition] (Dublin, 1863).

45. Joyce, *Handbook,* introduction.

46. Joyce, *Handbook,* [1876 edition], p. 12.

47. National education, *Third report,* [44], H.C. 1836, xxxvi, p. 110.

48. 'Twelve practical rules for the teachers of national schools', in National education, *Twelfth report,* [711] H.C. 1846, xxii, p. 125.

49. National education, *Supplement to the fourth book of lessons* (Dublin, 1846) and, *Sequel to the second book of lessons for the use of schools* (Dublin, 1846).

50. For programmes see, National education, *Twenty-second report,* [2142–11], H.C. 1856, xxvii, pt ii; appendix h.

51. Francis R. Head, *A fortnight in Ireland* (London, 1852), p. 31; Nassau Senior, *Journals, essays and conversations relating to Ireland,* ii (London, 1868), p. 137.

52. National education, *Seventeenth report,* [1405] H.C. 1851, xxiv, pp 102–103.

53. O'Donovan Rossa, *Recollections,* p. 32.

54. *Report of the commissioners appointed to inquire into the nature and extent of the instruction afforded by the several institutions in Ireland for the purpose of elementary or primary*

education; also into the practical working of the system of national education in Ireland, [hereafter *Powis Commission*] [C 6], H.C. 1870, xxviii, pt. i. 28, iii, p. 290.

55. *Powis Commission*, 1870, pt. iii, p. 743,
56. *Powis Commission*, 1870, pt. iii, p. 747.
57. *Powis Commission*, 1870, pt. iii, p. 747.
58. *Powis Commission*, 1870, pt. iii, p. 866.
59. *Powis Commission*, 1870, pt. iii, p. 866.
60. Akenson, *Irish education experiment*, pp 316–319.
61. National education, *Forty-ninth report*, [C 3651] H.C. 1883, xxvi, p. 143.
62. See, National education, *Annual reports*, 1872–1900.

Index

Index